The Herb Kohl Reader

The Herb Kohl Reader

Awakening the Heart of Teaching

Herbert Kohl

With a foreword by William Ayers

THE NEW PRESS

NEW YORK
LONDON

Requests for permission to reproduce selections from this book should be mailed to:
Permissions Department, The New Press, 38 Greene Street, New York, NY 10013.

Published in the United States by The New Press, New York, 2009
Distributed by W. W. Norton & Company, Inc., New York

LIBRARY OF CONGRESS CATALOGING-IN-PUBLICATION DATA
Kohl, Herbert R.
    The Herb Kohl reader : awakening the heart of teaching / Herbert Kohl,
with a foreword by William Ayers.
    p.   cm.
    Includes bibliographical references.
    ISBN: 978-0-1-59558-420-5 (pbk.)
    1. Teaching.   I. Title.
    LB1025.3.K657   2009
    371.102—dc22

                                    2008043939

The New Press was established in 1990 as a not-for-profit alternative to the large,
commercial publishing houses currently dominating the book publishing industry.
The New Press operates in the public interest rather than for private gain,
and is committed to publishing, in innovative ways, works of educational, cultural,
and community value that are often deemed insufficiently profitable.

www.thenewpress.com

Composition by NK Graphics
This book was set in Goudy

Printed in Canada

2   4   6   8   10   9   7   5   3   1

*To Tonia, Erica, and Josh, and all of the students
I have been privileged to teach
and
To Emilia Soledad Kohl Arenas*

CONTENTS

HERB KOHL:
POET LAUREATE OF TEACHING
A Tribute by William Ayers

I first met Herb Kohl in 1967 shortly after the publication of the now-classic *36 Children*, his riveting account of teaching sixth grade in a Harlem public school. I was a new teacher searching for affirmation while struggling to make sense of my own every-day classroom reality—challenges and setbacks, of course, and those tiny hard-won triumphs in acute if poignant contrast with my vast idealism and aspirations. I'd taken off on a summer quest to find every educator and education writer who had inspired me in the previous year—Sylvia Ashton-Warner, Paul Goodman, John Holt, Jerome Bruner, Barbara Biber, Stokely Carmichael, Jonathan Kozol, and Jay Featherstone to start. I was determined—immodestly, I suppose—to meet and talk with each one. Today I have no idea why I thought any of them would agree to set aside time for me, and yet, astonishingly, every one of them welcomed me graciously and with open arms.

I arrived in New York by bus, and my first phone call was to Herb. He invited me over, and when, an hour later, I rang the bell at the unassuming apartment on Eighty-eighth Street, Judy Kohl answered and led me into their tiny kitchen, where the three of us spent the rest of the morning. I mentioned the surprising and overwhelmingly positive reviews of *36 Children*, but Herb was skeptical: "Whenever you're praised for your 'youthful idealism,' look out!" He thought that the praise was patronizing at best and would soon enough be followed with criticism, opposition, "and maybe even a threat." We all laughed. "Anyway, I think they'd be happy if I shut up from now on, so let's see what they're saying in a couple of years."

His insights about this most complex, idiosyncratic, and mysterious craft had an immediate and lasting impact on me, but now, more than forty years and thirty-five books later, it's clear that Herb Kohl's influence has resonated, echoed, and multiplied and that he has directly touched thousands upon thousands of teachers and school people. He has not shut up—not for a minute, in spite of the opposition he anticipated—but has instead produced a steady stream of work that has turned into a torrent as the years have passed.

36 Children is the mother ship, a classic indeed, but no one should stop there—Growing Minds is my favorite book for new teachers, and Golden Boy as Anthony Cool, a photo essay and the first book to try to understand graffiti as more than vandalism, captures the spirit of a spiritless situation and the self-identification of young people who are rendered nameless and faceless and literally cast out. "I Won't Learn from You" does more than understand, explain, and offer concrete strategies to work with resistant students; it also provides a penetrating and sweeping critique of the content and the form of the established educational project in toto, raising the troubling possibility that the rebel kids are right and that our prescription for them (literally what we do to them) is wrong—and that they know it. Making Theater, A Grain of Sand, A Book of Puzzlements, and Mathematical Puzzlements are packed with the kind of workaday advice and practical arts that teachers can use off the shelf or adapt to unique circumstances, much like Kohl's "Good Stuff" column, which appears regularly in the radical teaching journal Rethinking Schools. Painting Chinese is a more reflective piece on how we learn; The University for Our Time, written during the upheavals of 1968, is a more visionary look at what is to be done in higher education; Language and

Education of the Deaf, an important manifesto in the "deaf power" movement and the struggle for dignity, identity, and deaf rights, is more incendiary; *From Archetype to Zeitgeist*, a smart and demystifying answer to the right-wing enthusiasm for all-inclusive lists of important knowledge, is more slyly subversive—all of these are bound together in a single teacher/writer who has managed to keep his vision and his idealism intact, along with his anger, someone still willing to speak the unwelcome truth to power, still trying to comfort the afflicted while afflicting the comfortable, still refusing the detached stance of the scholar or the cool pose of the cynic, insisting in words devout and large that we might still open our eyes and embrace the common good, and that, yes, we still might change the world.

In the past half century Kohl has emerged as a singular figure in education—unique in his reach, his grasp, his authority. Indeed, Herb Kohl is the poet laureate for generations of humanistic teachers.

In part this is because no one has touched every aspect of the enterprise—classroom life, curriculum and teaching, school reform, educational policy—with such luminous force. Like his Harvard classmate Jonathan Kozol, Kohl's writing addresses questions of policy and politics; like his mentors Paulo Freire and Myles Horton, he is fiercely focused on issues of racial and social justice; like fellow teachers Vivian Gussin Paley, George Dennison, and James Herndon, Kohl has a penetrating eye for the layered meanings generated and enacted in everyday classrooms; like his early contemporaries in the Mississippi Freedom Schools, he illuminates the link between individual change and social transformation; and, like his friends Maxine Greene and Jay and Helen Featherstone, he is a philosopher, a storyteller, an artist, an activist.

Herb Kohl's energy and influence stem from his location as a teacher in a classroom—a person on the move and in the mix among schoolchildren—so that his philosophizing and his activism, his stories and his art, emanate from a deep pool of experience in the real world of kids and communities. No other education writer, child advocate, or policy person has logged more time in the grit and grab of this place called school.

His exceptional importance flows finally from his ceaseless advocacy for a particularly precious ideal: the belief that, at its best, education is an enterprise geared toward allowing every human being to reach a fuller measure of his or her humanity. It's the irreducible and incalculable value of every human life linked to the teacherly work of unlocking and releasing the power of each person that has given Kohl's work its fundamental shape and direction.

Like other great educators, Herb Kohl constructed his teaching identity in the cauldron of a classroom; from the very start, his mind was focused, laser-like, on a group of youngsters in Harlem. How did they learn? What were their preferences? If they could choose, what would they do? What strengths and interests did they bring with them into the classroom? How could these be built upon and made into bridges toward deeper and wider ways of knowing? Could conversations about large goals and ethical purposes productively power life in school? More than any textbook or theory, more than adherence to a specific philosophy or ideology, Kohl invented and reinvented himself as a teacher through these kinds of questions, and his students were the essential co-creators.

Herb Kohl's teaching story is an epic, and it begins, as most do, in crisis: How can I possibly succeed, he asked himself, in a crowded and under-resourced classroom, a place with too many kids, too little time, and negligible support? How could he motivate a group of resistant students who seemed to hate the place? How could he be true to his deepest values and his broadest purposes in a place seemingly determined to undermine both? How could he even survive?

Feeling completely inadequate and overwhelmed, guided by nothing more than his own intuition, grounded in an unshakable belief in the incalculable value of every human being, Kohl began to improvise. Since he couldn't get thirty-six children to move in the same direction at the same time, perhaps he could split up the large group, to everyone's advantage. Since he couldn't inspire everyone with a single text, he would bring in lots of books, lots of art supplies and quirky stuff, and let the students choose. Since he didn't like or even recognize himself as a tightly wound taskmaster and petty dictator, he loosened up and slowed down, and he learned how to be with students in a more authentic way, more alive in his own enthusiasms, preferences, and responses. His classroom became a home; his students, family; and the vehicle for his teaching became stories.

And so he began: Write about where you come from. Write about the neighborhood, the street characters, your family, your grandparents, your dreams, your experiences. Who in the world are you? This tentative strategy began to power every aspect of classroom life. Who are you—in the world? What are your chances and your choices? No matter how marginalized, poor, or oppressed his students, Kohl refused a one-sided or patronizing view of their lives. In an unfair and ferocious world, people do get hurt, and they do get hit hard, but pitying the poor is another way of refusing to see these particular human beings in three-dimensional terms. There's always more to know: everyone is a dreamer of dreams, an unruly spark of meaning-making energy on a voyage of discovery and surprise, as well as a conqueror, a creator, an actor, an artist. Everyone in Herb's classrooms, simply by the act of walking through the door, had the right, indeed the responsibility, to be all of these and, most important, to tell his or her own story. The brute facts are never enough—disadvantaged or advantaged, poor or rich, victim or perpetrator—there's always more to say. And who has the right to tell your particular story? A powerful theme in Herb's teaching—really, an ethical pillar—is to trust your own story and never to allow anyone else to tell your story for you.

A large contradiction that productively punctuates much of Kohl's writing is the tension of working in real classrooms in real schools and systems while fighting to hold on to and find ways to enact humane values and the best thinking about learning and teaching. This is a contradiction I've never resolved in my own teaching, but one that I think must be acknowledged and addressed continually as a space of struggle, a place to live, a tension illuminated by Kohl to teach into.

Teachers who easily put the tension to rest will find themselves less productive with students and ultimately dissatisfied with themselves. To say "My job is to get kids ready for the real world, for society as it is" or "My job is to water the little seedlings and watch them grow" is to misunderstand the contradiction and to reduce the complexity. "The real world"? Which one? When I was first teaching, I had an argument with colleagues who thought that since the real world was vicious, tough, unfair, competitive, and mean, we should turn our Head Start center into a boot camp for three-year-olds. How do we keep one foot in the mud and muck of the world as we find it, the world as it is, while the other foot strides hopefully toward a world that is not yet ours?

And on the other side, the watering-the-seeds side, I've known lots of teachers who wanted desperately to be kind and to be liked, and then failed to challenge kids to read. "I love these kids so much," one would say, "and their lives are so hard, I just want to nurture them." Failing to teach them to read is not exactly an act of love.

So the tension, as Kohl would have it, is: teach them to read as an act of love; struggle to nourish and challenge in the same gesture; respect the people who walk through the door, embrace them as fellow human beings, and invite and push them toward deeper and wider ways of knowing. This tension lives on every page of Herb's writing.

All conscientious teachers need to ask themselves what they need to know in order to be successful with this kid and with this one and with this one. Surely knowledge of subject matter, the curriculum, and the disciplines is an important part of the answer, as is, of course, knowledge about the school and its expectations. And don't forget knowledge of yourself. But no less important is knowledge about the child and more: knowledge about the contexts and circumstances of his or her life—family, community, culture, and on and on—knowledge of the society and the world we're initiating youngsters into. This is not only vast, but also dynamic and swirling and expanding and changing.

All children need to develop a sense of the unique capacity of human beings to shape and create reality in concert with conscious purposes and plans. This means that our schools need to be transformed to provide children ongoing opportunities to exercise their resourcefulness, to solve the real problems of their communities. Like all human beings, children and young people need to be of use; they cannot productively be treated as "objects" to be taught "subjects." Their cognitive juices will begin to flow if and when their hearts, heads, and hands are engaged in improving their daily lives and their surroundings. Herb Kohl pioneered in naming and creating the space for that.

Just imagine how much safer and livelier and more peaceful our neighborhoods and communities would become if we reorganized education in a fundamental way. Instead of trying to keep children isolated in classrooms, envision engaging them in community-building activities with the same audacity and vision with which the civil rights movement engaged them in desegregation work forty-five years ago: planting community gardens, recycling waste, creating alternative transportation and work sites, naming and protesting injustices around them, organizing neighborhood arts and health festivals, rehabbing houses, painting public murals. By giving children and young people a reason to learn beyond the individualistic goal of getting a job and making more money, by encouraging them to exercise their minds and their hearts and their soul power, we would tap into the deep well of human values that gives life a richer shape and meaning.

Instead of trying to bully young people to remain in classrooms isolated from the community and structured only to prepare them for a distant, hostile, and quickly disappearing job market, we might recognize that the reason so many young people drop out of schools is because they are voting with their feet against an educational system that sorts, tracks, tests, and rejects or certifies them like products in a factory. They are crying out for an experience that values them as human beings.

Herb Kohl's teaching is values-based; it is generous and deeply grounded in cherishing happiness, respecting reason, and—fundamentally—honoring each human life as sacred and unduplicatable. His clarity about classrooms is not based on being able to answer every dilemma or challenge or conundrum that presents itself, but flows instead from him encouraging us to see classroom life as a work-in-progress—contingent, dynamic, in the making, unfinished, always reaching for something more. The ethical core of his teaching is about creating hope in his students. Because the future is unknown, optimism is simply dreaming, and pessimism merely a dreary turn of mind. Hopefulness, on the other hand, is a political and moral choice based on the fact that history is still in the making, each of us necessarily a work-in-progress, and the future entirely unknown and unknowable. Kohl's writing provides images of possibility and in that way rekindles hope in all of us.

This ethical core is also the political stance of an independent, revolutionary teacher. Herb Kohl is not an ideologue, a dogmatist, or a camp follower; he is, rather, one of those remarkable and rare individuals—eloquent, fantastically courageous, angry, driven by principle—for whom no power is too big to challenge, no injustice too small to fight. He is markedly on the side of profound, fundamental change, the kind of upheaval that would replace greed and repression and hierarchy and surveillance and control with community, peace, simple fairness, and love—all kinds of love for all kinds of people in every situation. Kohl's radical message is simple: choose love.

Herb's characteristic style is informal, his vehicle the simple story well told. His capacity to evoke a scene in his writing with depth and detail, to focus on the local, is matched by his fierce insistence on holding on to the larger concentric circles of context—economic condition, historical flow, cultural surround, political power—in which people necessarily make sense and take action. Even as he describes a particular classroom and a specific interaction, the larger ethical purposes of his teaching are in full view. For Herb, as for many great teachers, story time is sacred because it deals so seamlessly with both the hardest realities and the most far-reaching imagined universes. Storytelling is the chosen tool for ferreting out and constructing the meaning in the rough-and-tumble of random events. Herb Kohl is a master storyteller, a weaver of worlds, a prophet of possibility. He reminds us that we are each other's business, we are each other's hope. Gather around.

ACKNOWLEDGMENTS

First of all, I would like to acknowledge my wife, Judy, who has shared my entire teaching and writing career during our forty-five years of marriage. Then I feel grateful for having Diane Wachtell, Jennifer Rappaport, and Priyanka Jacob of The New Press, who embraced the idea of publishing this reader and provided me with invaluable editing. It has always been a pleasure for me to work with The New Press. In addition I want to thank my agent, Wendy Weil, for her assistance, advice, and counsel.

Finally, I want to acknowledge and express my gratitude toward all the students and colleagues who have taught me over the course of my career. And I thank the community activists and parents who have become friends, mentors, and tutors and who have enriched my work by sharing their knowledge of their own children and their cultures.

Acknowledgment is made to the following sources for previously published material:

"The Tattooed Man: Confessions of a Hopemonger" and "Creative Maladjustment and the Struggle for Public Education" from "*I Won't Learn from You*": *And Other Thoughts on Creative Maladjustment* © 1994 by Herbert Kohl. A section of "Creative Maladjustment and the Struggle for Public Education" appeared in *Dissent*, Spring 1993. Reprinted with the permission of The New Press (www.thenewpress.com).

INTRODUCTION

Over the past forty-five years, I have been teaching and writing. Sometimes the writing has been primary. Other times I taught and found myself too occupied with the work to write at all. I have also tried to balance work with family, and this is reflected in one of the sections of this collection. I've been fortunate enough over the years to write three books with my wife and one with one of my daughters. I've also had the pleasure and the challenge of occasionally having my own children in my public school classes.

However, my family is much larger than the wonderful nuclear family of which I am privileged to be part. It consists of all of my students: the ones for whom I had particular affection, the ones who vexed and challenged me, and even those few I couldn't figure out how to reach or teach. They've ranged in age from five to the mid-twenties, and now many are in their thirties, forties, and fifties.

My teaching was not initially shaped by any particular theory of education but has always been focused on what works with children. For me, theory flows from and is modified by practice. Over the years, through direct work with young people, selective reading, conversations with colleagues, and participation in a variety of school reform efforts, a theory of teaching and learning has begun to emerge. I have sometimes been called a romantic and don't deny that at the center of my work is faith that every student has a core of creativity and decency that can be elicited through education. In addition, I see education as part of the struggle for social justice, and this has pervaded my thinking and practice. I have never separated my commitment to justice from my classroom practice or from my work within the larger educational community. For me, education is a moral practice manifested by the specific content and nature of instruction across subject areas, within the context of a caring learning community.

Central to my growth as an educator has been the conviction that if only the situation, learning climate, materials, and relationships were right, every child could and indeed would learn. Therefore the initial challenge is to discover what is right about students and then be ingenious in discovering what works for them. My philosophy of education, which is still emerging, is based on a strength model of children, not on a deficiency model. It's easy to learn what students can't or won't do from their test results, school records, and initial behavior in the classroom. It's harder to see into the corners of their selves where they are strong and compassionate, and then to break down the barriers to learning that have developed through their previous education or lives outside of the classroom.

The selections in this book illustrate my quest over the past forty-five years to teach children well and to share, through my writing, the experience of teaching well in the context of public education, in schools that are often hostile and uncomfortable places for teachers and students. The book includes selections from the more than thirty-five books I've written, divided into four sections. The first has to do with my development as a teacher. The narratives are quite specific and illustrate life in the classroom and the evolution of effective teaching, beginning with some spectacular failures. The second section is devoted to the practice of teaching. Some of these selections are more strategic and talk about planning, developing curriculum content, and teaching cultural and print literacy. One selection attempts to identify the basic skills essential for the development of creative learning, intellectual sophistication, and democratic citizenship.

The third section is about fatherhood. One of the essential themes in the section is how to develop your own children in the context of a life devoted to social justice. This section also talks about the complex and often difficult balance between raising one's own children and teaching other people's children.

The fourth and final section contains speculations on the sociology of education, learning, and politics. It contains some of my latest thinking about pedagogical issues that are very pressing these days.

My first full-time public school teaching job was in 1962 in a fifth-grade class on the West Side of Manhattan. My students were Puerto Rican, African American, and Haitian and were placed in 5-7—the class at the bottom of the homogenously grouped fifth grade. I was required to teach all subjects, from reading and writing to science, history, and the arts. This gave me the freedom to cross over subject matter, learn many different disciplines, and experiment with ideas over a wide range of subjects, which suited my temperament quite well. As a college students I had majored in philosophy and minored in mathematics; I had taken classes on modern theater, contemporary fiction, astronomy, social sciences, and Italian painting. My mentors in the philosophy department complained about the wide range of classes I was taking and wanted me to take a full, almost exclusive program in philosophy and logic. They said that such classes would prepare me better for a future job in a university philosophy department. But I knew halfway through my time at college that I didn't want to live an academic life. I liked the Bronx, where I came from, and felt more comfortable on the streets than in the academy. I certainly didn't know how I could connect my academic life with my desire to go back home and work within my community at the time, and so I just followed my interests and didn't worry about what my tutors said. This eclecticism has served me well in fifth-grade teaching and in all my teaching and writing. I was and am willing to try just about anything that has a chance of helping people learn. I also love to learn and am constantly in search of new ideas, inventions, techniques, and games.

I've jumped around a lot during my educational career. I'm pretty restless. I like to begin things, come to a level of comfort and mastery with the work, and then turn it over to others and move on to new challenges—always, however, in the field of education.

At the end of my first teaching semester (I began with the fifth grade in January), I was involuntary transferred to a school in Harlem and given a sixth-grade class that had thirty-six children in a classroom with thirty-five seats. The years I spent at P.S. 79 were wonderful. It was there that I began to master my craft and to become close to my students and their families. It was also there that I began to become an educational activist, working with community groups and other teachers to change schools, beginning of course with P.S. 79.

I eventually left P.S. 79 to run a storefront high school. A number of the students at the storefront were former students of mine.

At that time, I also became involved in curriculum reform and helped found the Teachers and Writers Collaborative, which is about to celebrate its fortieth anniversary. The Collaborative brings writers and teachers together to develop writing programs and curriculum and to send writers directly into the classroom. At the same time, I was involved in the Community Control of Schools struggle, working for the I.S. 201 Parent Governing Board.

In 1968 I moved to Berkeley, California, to teach for a semester at the university—a wonderful time for an activist to be in Berkeley. After the semester, a number of teacher friends and I created a small high school, Other Ways, as an alternative to the more formalistic Berkeley High School. We were not a free school but provided our students with small classes, a lot of choice, a role in school governance, and a personalized learning community. We were like a family, which was very important those days when anti-Vietnam protests, racial conflict, the People's Park, and the occupation of Berkeley by the National Guard characterized our daily life. I learned to teach on the run, to set up a school that could be assembled out of the trunks of several cars (which became helpful to other people when I later worked with farmworker communities), and to develop student discipline and self-discipline under pressure. Our school was located in the center of the protest zone off Telegraph Avenue in Berkeley, and we often had to relocate to parks, people's homes, churches, and community centers in order to keep the fabric of our learning community coherent and educationally effective.

The next adventure was running a small teacher education program, the Center for Open Learning and Teaching, with Cynthia Brown, which also involved teaching kindergarten and first grade full time in a Berkeley public school by special arrangement with the principal. My next teaching experiences were at a high school and a one-room schoolhouse in rural Northern California.

Around 1992 I took a break from teaching and worked on school reform with a grant from the Aaron Diamond Fund, and I then went on to work on the development of the New Visions small high schools within the New York City school system. After two and a half years working for George Soros's Open Society Institute as Senior Fellow for Education, I returned to California where, with the help of the dean of education, I was able to create a teacher education program, the Center for Teaching Excellence and Social Justice, at the University of San Francisco. Over the next five years, we credentialed one hundred new teachers, about 75 percent of them people of color. They are some of the most wonderful students I have ever had and, though the program ran out of money two years after I left, the students have a gathering each year at the Coastal Ridge Research and Education Center, which is located at my home in Northern California.

After spending the academic year 2005–2006 as a visiting professor at Swarthmore College, I returned to Northern California and am awaiting my next pedagogical adventure.

Throughout all of this time, I have managed to write more than thirty-five books. True to my eclectic nature, I have written about animal perception (with my wife), math and language puzzles, theater, and poetry. However, the preponderance of my writing has to do with teaching and learning and is rooted in my personal experience as an educator. I never set out to teach in order to write and often don't know what I'll write about until years after the experience takes place. Most of the selections in this reader are drawn from those books on teaching, learning, and educational thinking. It is a special pleasure for me to be able to bring selections from many of these books together and to share them with people concerned about children and learning.

Part I

Becoming a Teacher

The selections in Part I focus on my personal journey and how it led to my becoming a lifelong educator. This part also focuses on the more specific question of how one learns on the job to teach well, and how an understanding of teaching and learning develops through classroom practice. This is not to say that teacher preparation is irrelevant, but very little one does at teachers college is useful in facing one's own classroom of children who are initially strangers.

For that reason, teacher knowledge evolves through teaching and from direct involvement with individual students. Every classroom is a miniature social world set in family, community, cultural, social, and historical contexts. Managing the complex life within the classroom and creating a convivial learning community in which everyone participates willingly is a formidable challenge. It took me from three to five years to feel comfortable with my teaching style, with authority and discipline in the classroom, and with the adaptation and creation of curriculum that is challenging, exciting to students, and comes up to high standards of learning.

In addition to mastering these aspects of teaching, I found myself having to learn about the parents of my students, the community, and the complex social and historical influences on everyday practice. Certainly this is a lot to demand of a young teacher, and the narratives in this part of the reader make it clear what a struggle it is to become a good teacher. But what I hope to convey above and beyond the difficulty of learning to teach well is a sense of the wonderful rewards of facilitating children's growth and earning their respect, admiration, and affection. When I first entered teaching, I felt I was embarking on a privileged and honored vocation. Now, many years later, I feel that there is no more rewarding way I could have spent my life.

The first selection in Part I is from an essay I wrote in order to help myself understand how my passion to become a teacher developed. It also illustrates how my love of storytelling became a central part of my teaching repertoire.

The second selection talks about my early teaching experiences at a school for the emotionally disturbed and as a substitute teacher in the New York City public schools. What I tried to do in telling stories about these experiences is to share aspects of becoming a teacher that I think other people, setting out on teaching careers even now, forty years later, can relate to and learn from.

The third selection is from perhaps my most well known book, *36 Children*. The book is about my first full year of having my own class, teaching thirty-six children in a public school built in 1898 and perhaps not repaired since. In that environment of falling plaster and leaking windows, having only thirty-five desks for my thirty-six students, I worked about twelve hours a day, within the classroom and at my apartment, to be of use to my students. The students did creative and complex work beyond my imagination and also taught me that even in a failing school in a poor and depressed community, great achievement and creativity can emerge. I also learned about the intelligence and resilience of the students and their parents and about the strengths their African American heritage provided them when it was recognized and respected in the classroom. It was during that year that my marriage with education was consummated. During that year, I also met my wife and got married. It was a year of dual blessings.

The final selection, from my career autobiography *The Discipline of Hope*, jumps about thirty years ahead and is an illustration of one of the bolder integrated programs I developed. I hope it shows that I did learn some things over the years. I know I am still learning.

THE TATTOOED MAN:
CONFESSIONS OF A HOPEMONGER

From *"I Won't Learn from You"*:
And Other Thoughts on Creative Maladjustment

It was in November or December of 1949, in the early afternoon, about one-thirty or two, just when the grey Bronx dusk of early winter reminded me that asthma was only a few hours away. My afternoons those days were overpowered by fear of an attack, the same fear that brought on the attacks. Seventh-graders had to go to the library for a lesson on the Dewey decimal system. We all followed along, paying no attention to Mr. Robertson, who was probably drunk as usual. He wasn't in a rush either—going to the library meant one less teaching period for him.

The librarian went on about numbers and indexes, and talked about how wonderful reading was, or something. I was lost studying the nuances of my anxiety, wondering why it was worse this time of year, so bad sometimes that I almost cried on the way home from school. Those days anxiety and asthma settled around me like river fog, and I had no language or concepts to understand them.

Our assignment was to find a book, any book, return to our places at one of the tables, and fill out the Dewey decimal number, title, author, and some other information. Another walk-through assignment. I went to a shelf in the farthest corner of the room and picked a book at random: *The Tattooed Man* by Howard Pease, an intriguing title stolen from my dreams and an author whose name was foreign and mysterious, not Jewish or Irish or Italian, but what? Where do people get such names? Pease and the tattooed man were equally intriguing. I knew tattooed men and masked men and invisible people. I read the subtitle, *A Tale of Strange Adventures Befalling Tod Moran, Mess Boy of the Tramp Steamer "Araby," Upon His First Voyage from San Francisco to Genoa, via the Panama Canal*, thinking of my own fantasies and dreams, my personal twists on the heroes and heroines that I followed on radio and in comic books.

My attention wandered back to the table, to Dewey decimal numbers, only instead of filling out the work sheet I wrote down the book's dedication "For Guard C. Darrah: This memory of rain-swept decks off Panama and the marching roads of France," feeling the rain, thinking how sweet it must be to be wandering, wondering about marching roads and rain-swept decks. I never finished the assignment and to this day have resisted learning how the Dewey decimal system works.

There have only been a few times in my life when I was certain that a book was positioned in a library or bookstore for the sole purpose of my discovering it. This was one. I never begged a librarian to borrow a book before that day, but succeeded in getting *The Tattooed Man* loaned to me for two weeks though students were not allowed to check out books and take them home. That was barely enough time, for I've never been able to read a book that I loved quickly. My style is to linger over the words, question the text, stop reading when my mind is full or when I want time to understand the ideas, guess the writer's next trick, or anticipate the characters' next responses.

That night after homework I picked up the book and joined Tod Moran in San Francisco, where "sea fog hazed like spindrift along the San Francisco waterfront." I couldn't figure out what spindrift was from the context, and only recently looked up its meaning. The word feels right to me when I think of Tod Moran and remember that night when I was drawn into his world and traveled with him to a city smothered in mist, listening with him to "the distant clang of cable cars, the hoar crys of newsboys, the dull rumble of trucks and drays passing in the gloom like ghosts." That sentence stopped me. I read it over, then over again, and spoke it out loud, quietly so my parents and brother couldn't hear. It conjured up a picture in my mind that was more intense than most of my dreams. Howard Pease's words created a world; they were magic and set me on fire with a burning desire to become a writer.

Since that night the necessity of writing has never left me. I still can't explain how or why it happened and often wonder whether the need to write was always in me waiting for some— any—beautiful words to activate it or whether, if my junior high school librarian had not decided to acquire a copy of *The Tattooed Man*, I would still be waiting to be inspired.

I was twelve, San Francisco was a dot on the map of the United States, and drays and cable cars were unreal vehicles contiguous with the horses and submarines of my dream adventures. Only Tod Moran was not like my dream companions. He had a real brother who had mysteriously disappeared at sea. On a ship called the *Araby* he met a tattooed man who knew of his brother. And Tod knew that he, the younger brother, had to find and redeem his older brother. This was not the stuff of comic book dreams. It was reality, the reality of literature, more dimensional, deeper, and more moving than anything I had encountered in comic books.

Tod Moran went to sea and he wasn't even seventeen. That meant only five years for me to wait. When, on page 20, I learned that Tod got a job as mess boy on the *Araby*, I stopped reading for five days and thought about my future, which had suddenly become real to me and not merely composed of heroic fantasies and halfhearted plots to run away from home. I began to think of the actual world as bigger, more variable, and more accessible than I had imagined and realized that I too could change my life and live in different ways and in different places. My imaginings didn't have to be confined to unreal and unrealizable domains.

From the time I was about eight until I was twelve, I often put myself to sleep with guided fantasies of romance and adventure. These fantasies never intruded upon my daytime existence and were called forth by a specific ritual. First tuck under the bedcovers; next turn on my back and look up at the ceiling for the reflection of the Lexington Avenue elevated subway.

On Jerome Avenue the subway was elevated several stories above ground. The apparent contradiction between being elevated and underground was resolved for me every weekend when on my trip to Manhattan I stood at the window of the front car of the train and experienced its plunge underground at the station past Yankee Stadium. At that moment the lights went out, and the dark interior of the train became one with the darkness of the tunnel. I imagined, and I know my friends also imagined, demons and dybbuks and spirits unleashed on the train for that forty-five seconds that the whole world was dark. When I was about thirteen, I thought of writing a science fiction story about a train from the Bronx to Manhattan that became suspended in time the moment it went underground.

The el was part of my thinking as well as part of my nighttime ritual. It was a metaphor of passage, from the Bronx to Manhattan, and from daytime into my nighttime adventures and fantasies. Once I was in the right position to see the el's reflection on my bedroom wall, I had to wait. The third part of my ritual couldn't begin until I heard the train leave the 176th Street station and saw the lights reflected by each of the train windows pass over my bed, sometimes outlined so distinctly that I could make out the silhouettes of the people sitting at each window. After the magic lights had passed, I closed my eyes and called forth my fantasy companion and teacher, the Masked Rider. Sometimes he immediately appeared in dream time and I was already there with him. Other times he was waiting and it seemed as if I walked into the dream and joined him.

I have tried to reconstruct some of the feelings of that experience, and remember that the Masked Rider was faceless and rode a dark horse. He was friendly, very skillful with weapons, but nonviolent, and had many adventures during the three or four years he was willing to come when I summoned him. I was his companion, and on particularly good nights I experienced myself stepping into my dream or fantasy and asking him where we were going that night. Most of our adventures involved a sweet, accepting young woman who could like you without controlling you. I'm not sure that I was aware that my dreams were experiments with love outside the family, but in retrospect they were preparing me for leaving home spiritually as well as physically.

I remember somehow knowing about the Masked Rider's past, though he never explicitly talked about it. He was found as a child wandering across a vast plain wearing a dark mask. No one was bold enough to unmask him and he never showed his face to anyone. He had never even seen his own face. He lived on a dark edge of the world, alone with a bundle of sacred objects, a sword, and a rope. He had stones that resembled faces, a root that was a clenched fist, four beautiful steel knives, a few empty jars, and a vial of black sand. The most sacred object was a small clay head worn featureless by time, a faceless relic the Masked Rider found when he was a child. He sometimes rode a black, featureless horse. At those times they were one, horse-and-rider, all in black.

During the day I listened to *Captain Midnight* on the radio. I also listened to *The Shadow*, *The Lone Ranger*, and *The Thin Man*. The Masked Rider was my personal reconstruction of the freedom and power these programs represented for me. My encounters with the Masked Rider were not like other dreams over which I had no control. I was both in a fantasy world and semi-awake outside of that world, aware of what was going on. I could at times experience the adventures we had together and at other times witness my own adventures. I could even give advice to the me in the dream, and somehow in dream logic it made sense for me to exist on both planes simultaneously, within and outside the fantasy. My double and I lived through all of those adventures together.

During our adventures the Masked Rider rescued the young, nurtured them for their own sake, and left them to grow strong. And he showed me how to be caring and tough at the same time.

There are times when I've wondered whether the dream of being a teacher of young children, which I've nurtured since I was twelve or thirteen, isn't intimately connected with my admiration for the Masked Rider and my desire to be as nurturing to others as he was to me.

I never told anyone about the Masked Rider, for two reasons. First, I was afraid he would disappear; and second, I was afraid people would think I was crazy.

With both *The Tattooed Man* and the Masked Rider, I was learning to move through and beyond the world as I knew it and imagine other, more congenial and exciting possibilities. Over the years, I've also encouraged my students to learn how to dream beyond the world they lived in and imagine ways in which life can be made fuller and more compassionate. The ability to see the world as other than it is plays a major role in sustaining hope. It keeps part of one's mind free of the burden of everyday misery and can become a corner of sanity as one struggles to undo the horrors of an unkind and mad world.

Nurturing children's abilities to imagine ways in which the world might be different is a gift we owe all children. This can be done in many ways. Telling children stories, for example, allows them to enter worlds where the constraints of ordinary life are transcended. The phrase "enter into" is not merely a metaphor: children step into good stories, just as I stepped into the world of the Masked Rider, and listen as if in a trance. Phrases like "Once upon a time" or "Long ago in a land far away" are ritualistic ways of informing children that reality is being suspended and fantasy taking over. When I've taught kindergarten, story time was sacred. If someone came in and interrupted an absorbing story, the children would look up as if awakened from a dream and would often chase intruders away. It seemed as if a violation of their inner space had occurred, some involuntary awakening from another world.

Those times I've taught high school, poetry has been my vehicle for honoring the imagination. The legitimate breaking of the bonds of factuality offered by poetry has helped me overcome adolescent cynicism about the power of fairy tales and myths.

I remember making up stories and telling them to my three children when they were young. The stories I had heard from my grandparents at their ages didn't seem right for my children. The stories I wanted to tell involved the children themselves or at least surrogate characters who represented them. The stories revolved around four characters. Three—Mimi, Tutu, and Jha—were modeled on the children: Mimi on Erica, who was six at the time; Tutu on Tonia, who was seven; and Jha on Joshua, who was four. The fourth character was called Overall. He lived underground in a worldwide network of sewers that went under oceans, deserts, and mountains as well as cities. He appeared as steam and spoke with a Yiddish accent. He was, for me, a representation of all the humor, bitterness, rage, gentleness, roughness, and intelligence of the Yiddish world of my grandparents and of the Bronx I knew as a child. He may also have been an embodiment of the asthmatic fog that was both suffocating and nurturing during my Bronx childhood.

Overall was my way of trying to share with my children, in a story setting, the flavor and spirit of a part of their inheritance they could never directly experience. Overall had one peculiar power that figured in all of the stories I made up over the three or four years that the stories continued: whenever and wherever there was real trouble for the three young adventurers, a manhole cover appeared on the ground and Overall steamed up through the holes in the cover, coming to the rescue.

Overall also presented each of the children with a present: detached eyeballs that they could carry around and use to see things they wished to see. They could look into the eyeballs and see distant places, could plant the eyeballs in places where they wanted to spy on what was going on, and could even see into the past and sometimes the future. In the case of the future, however, the eyeballs became teary and the images were cloudy and indefinite so that future vision was unreliable.

The eyeballs were only part of the powers I, as storyteller, granted Mimi, Tutu, and Jha. Erica is a Capricorn, so she, Mimi, got the power to climb the steepest hills and to butt through the hardest materials, and the ability to solve riddles. Tonia is a Cancer, so Tutu had the power of moving sideways as quickly as forward or backward, of grabbing on to things and not letting go until she got what she wanted, and of having immense patience and the ability to think through complex problems and come up with interesting solutions. Joshua is a Scorpio, so Jha had the power of sudden stinging attack, the ability to make caves and tunnels underground, and a sharp intellect that let him understand other people's thoughts and feelings.

Each story began as a simple voyage on a ship in mid-ocean or in the middle of a forest or the depths of a city like New York. I would set the scene and then ask the children where they wanted to go. They helped me spin out the story and teased out of me all kinds of enemies and friends, characters to people the story world. I always kept Overall for particularly difficult times and always gave him a story or two to tell, one that was directly set in the Bronx where I grew up and obliquely related to the situation. They had to be patient, to learn his ways of teaching by storytelling. As the tales grew in complexity and the children demanded I remember details and take up a telling at exactly the point it was dropped, I realized the importance of our half hour or hour together. I could introduce them to what I remembered and loved about my growing up through the character of Overall. They could frame adventures out of their fears and anxieties. We could embark on adventures and voyages together, and our imaginations played with the possible. As long as none of the characters was killed, we could go on indefinitely imagining worlds and testing powers. I was drawn into the tales even on days when I felt no stories in me. The children provided the energy for the telling and remembered all of the little details that made the world come alive. At times when my imagination failed, they also took up the telling and contributed to the making of that alternate world.

Even now, more than thirty-five years later, with the details of all of the stories forgotten, Overall is alive for all of the children, as are Mimi, Tutu, and Jha. The circle within which the tales were created was magical in a way. The children could experiment with being strong; I could memorialize my grandparents and pass on something of their world. In addition, the four of us could enter a world of the possible and keep alive the idea that the world did not have to be the way it was and that we could exercise powers that could lead to its transformation.

I also try to tell empowering stories when I teach, and I encourage students to create their own tales and imaginings. In periods of stress, when people don't take the time to tell or listen to stories, they sacrifice their imaginations and allow hope to slip away. I've never had any problem trading formal learning for storytelling in my classes, and I believe the students have been richer for it. After all, seeding hope is at the center of the art and craft of teaching.

Creating hope in oneself as a teacher and nourishing or rekindling it in one's students is the central issue educators face today. After forty-five years of teaching, trying to reform public schools, and continuing to work in a framework of hope, I have had to examine the sources of my own hope and my struggles with the temptation to despair and quit. They go back to the Bronx, to the Masked Rider and the Tattooed Man. They also go back to adults who passed through my life those days in the way poems do now—as sources of images that tutor my sensibility and tease my usual ways of looking at the world into new images of the possible.

I remember an old man who walked through our neighborhood two or three times a week crying, "I buy old clothes." I must have been seven or eight at the time. He had a sack of rags tied into a bundle strapped to his back, and I remember thinking he was a hunchback with magical powers. Over the years I've built up memories of him and stories about his life, though I have no way of knowing how much my image resembles the man himself or his life. For me he has a high-pitched voice, a long thin nose, and very dirty though sensitive hands.

He wasn't the only peddler in the neighborhood, but other than the scissors- and knife-sharpening man who carried his grinder on his back, he was the only one on foot. There was an ice man with a tired horse that the old people used to joke about, and an Italian fruit and vegetable man with a horse-drawn wagon that smelled of apples, peaches, onions, and fresh soil. There was also the egg and butter man who was modern and carried his produce from upstate to the Bronx in the back of his station wagon.

The "I buy old clothes" man was my favorite. I liked to follow him close enough to talk with him if I dared. Other kids followed him at a distance and made fun of him. They were afraid to get too close since he was our bogey man, the person who, the grown-ups told us, always knew what you were doing and had curses that could cause harm at unexpected moments. The people in my parents' generation both demonized him and were ashamed of him. He was one of us—a Jew—but too Old World, too poor, too unashamed of his peddling. He was not a good model, in our parents' minds, for we were to be a generation headed out of the ghetto to college and the professions.

I was scared of him too, but also loved him because the scorn, disdain, mockery, and foolishness he encountered didn't seem to bother him at all. He had secrets that I wanted to know and, scared as I was, I was determined to talk to him. I don't know if I ever did, but at some point during my adolescence I constructed a short exchange we might have had, one which has stuck in my memory. I told him I knew what he was buying, but that I wondered if he was also selling something, and his response was, "Hope, I'm selling hope."

He was a hopemonger. I have never forgotten that—hope can be sold, it can be taught or at least spread, it can survive in the strangest and most unlikely places. It is a force that does not disappear. I keep that idea as a counter to the cynicism of reality-mongers, who try to sell the idea that compassion is a form of weakness and hope and justice are illusions. It is a guiding principle of my teaching and writing, one that provides the moral grounds of the struggles I have been involved in over the past fifty years.

The image of myself as an "I buy old clothes" teacher, a monger of hope, still delights me. One of my fantasies during the 1970s was to send hobo reading teachers across the country to help solve the problem of illiteracy and make themselves available to help eliminate poverty. These teachers would set themselves up on the streets, in parks, on basketball courts, in marketplaces, in front of schools, and offer reading lessons and writing services while they mongered hope.

Thinking about education and learning outside of the context of formal institutions and the way they define people is central to the ability to see the strengths in people and look beyond their failures and despair. This is particularly true when trying to understand what children might become if the world were a more decent place. Looking at a child, understanding something of who she or he is or might become, is not a simple neutral act or a matter of finding the right objective test or experimental situation. Central to what you see in someone is what you are looking for. If you want to find a child's weaknesses, failures, personal problems, or inadequacies, you'll discover them. If you look at a child through the filter of her or his environment or economic status, and make judgments through the filters of your own cultural, gender, and racial biases, you'll find the characteristics you expect. You'll also find yourself well placed to reproduce failure and to develop resistance in some children, a false sense of superiority in others. On the other hand, if you look for strengths and filter the world through the prism of hope, you will see and encourage the unexpected flowering of child life in the most unlikely places.

BEGINNING TO TEACH

From Growing Minds:
On Becoming a Teacher

Growth

Ever since I was a child, the details of growth have fascinated me. I remember wondering how babies learned to walk and talk, how grownups learned to dance, read, and drive cars and trucks, but mostly about how buildings grew on empty lots. My father, grandfather, and uncles were all in the construction business and often they took me to their jobs and let me wander around. I saw structures rise, saw the guts of buildings assembled and then concealed. My relatives always had many jobs going simultaneously, each in a different state of development. On one the site was being cleared, on another the basic structure was being created. Some jobs were almost done and plasterers, lathe workers, and cabinetmakers were putting in the details and painters finishing the surfaces.

In time, the work my relatives did became a central metaphor for my perception of growth in people. I didn't want to work with bricks and steel and wood, but with children. Yet as a teacher I've always thought of myself as part of the construction business. All of us are in different stages of completion or renovation, and none of us is ever without the need for some kind of building. A teacher has to become a construction expert, someone who knows how to help draw together skills and resources to create a harmonious functioning whole, or who knows how to renovate a structure that is dysfunctional or damaged.

Growing Minds is factually accurate, except that names and individual traits have been changed where necessary.

My father's expertise was renovation. One Sunday he and my grandfather took me to a job they were thinking of bidding on. The job was to put in stores on the first two floors of an old twenty-story apartment building and to convert the next five floors to offices. My grandfather had the blueprints of the building, which he read without effort even though he never learned to read English. I watched both of them carefully because they were doing things that seemed very strange to me. My grandfather would go to a certain place at the front of the building and bang a long nail through the brickwork. My father tapped on the wall in several places. Then they took a ladder out of the truck and climbed up the face of the building about a story and did the same things. I could feel that they were becoming very tense but couldn't figure out what was happening until my grandfather said, "Those son-of-a-bitches dropped half the beams. This thing shouldn't be standing up anymore."

My father explained to me that some builders eliminated a beam here, a girder there, to make more profit. He added that you could never trust plans to reveal the actual structure of a building. You had to probe the building itself, let it reveal itself. If you bid a job simply on the basis of the blueprints, you'd likely end up cheated and put your workers in danger.

In looking at young people growing, I've learned to apply the same ideas. A child is not an abstraction that can be fitted neatly into some scheme or theory, for growth never quite fits the laws of development psychologists invent. You have to discover who a child is by tapping and probing gently before a plan for construction or reconstruction can be developed. And you have to love to see a beautiful structure emerge, to have pride, as my father and grandfather did, in doing a good job.

Of course, people are not buildings and that's what makes observing their growth so interesting. Buildings do not build themselves, but people do. Understanding the complex relationships between self-growth and nurturing growth is essential to becoming a good teacher. Further, the love of nurturing and observing growth in others is essential to sustaining a life of teaching. This implies that no matter what you teach or how you present yourself to your students, you have to be on the learners' side and to believe that they can and will grow during the time you are together. I am not sure of how that belief develops, yet it is characteristic of every fine teacher I've known.

During my first few years of teaching I tenaciously held to the belief that if only I tried hard enough, every one of my students would read, write, calculate, and, even better, find some aspect of knowledge to master in depth. Some students, however, challenged that belief (or, more accurately, article of faith) to the extreme—indeed, the harder I tried to get them to learn, the more resistant they became. James Donald, for example, seemed to resent any implication that he was teachable. He was sixteen, two years older than any other student in my sixth-grade class and more than four years older than most of them. He spent the entire day sitting rigidly at his desk, fists and jaws clenched. He never looked at me, refused to respond to questions, refused to laugh at what other students found funny. He didn't play tricks and wasn't defiant. He just sat in his remoteness, driving me to try the craziest tactics to get him to try to read or write. Grades didn't mean anything to him, even praise didn't seem to touch him. He was doing his time, and despite my greatest efforts he didn't pick up a book or pencil or crack a smile throughout the whole year. The only thing he did with pleasure was play an aggressive, not graceful, but extremely focused and effective game of basketball.

This happened during my third year of teaching. I didn't have children of my own yet and still could give twelve hours a day to my students. Every day after school I ran a basketball league. James was one of the stars even though he didn't talk, not even on the court. He took on the biggest, toughest players and intimidated them all. He played smart basketball, anticipated other people's moves, passed so accurately he always had as many assists as points even though he was high scorer in most games. He was all intelligence on the court. Yet I couldn't do anything with him in the classroom. It would have been easy to quit on James, but I found myself reaching for new methods, techniques, ideas. Even though I found nothing that worked with him, I felt I was learning ways to reach other resistant, educationally damaged youngsters.

I met James about four years after he left my class. He had just finished his junior year at a high school in the Bronx and was all-city honorable mention in basketball. James was friendly for the first time since I'd known him, though his fists and jaws were no more relaxed than they were in the sixth grade. He told me he had loved to watch me try to teach him, that it was a battle of wills and he had been determined to win. But he also told me that he had listened even though he never responded to me and that he had taught himself to read and write well enough to stay in high school and play ball. He also thanked me for not throwing him out of the class.

Students like James have continued to confirm my perhaps irrational belief that all youngsters can learn despite any handicaps and that good teaching consists to a large degree in being obsessed with helping others grow.

Altruism: The Calling to Teach

I believe the impulse to teach is fundamentally altruistic and represents a desire to share what you value and to empower others. Of course, all teachers are not altruistic. Some people teach in order to dominate others or to support work they'd rather do or simply to earn a living. But I am not talking about the job of teaching so much as the calling to teach. Most teachers I know, even the most demoralized ones, who drag themselves to oppressive and mean schools where their work is not respected and their presence not welcome, have felt that calling at some time in their lives.

Between the ages of ten and twelve, many children have running-away-from-home fantasies. This was certainly true for me and for my friends growing up in the Bronx in the late 1940s. Bobby dreamed of going down to the seamen's hall and shipping out to Hong Kong on a tramp steamer. Ronnie wanted to hitch-hike to Chicago and become a boxer. Marilyn swore she would join the Haganah and be a freedom fighter in Israel. My fantasy was so bizarre that I was afraid to tell it to my friends. I wanted to run off to a small rural town in the Midwest and become an elementary school teacher.

No one in the family ever suggested I become a teacher and none of my relatives were teachers. I had two teachers, however, who were as sensitive to the growth of their students as my father and grandfather were to the quality of the structures they built, and who inspired me to want to teach. Mrs. Cooper was my kindergarten teacher. I don't remember anything about her class, but I do remember vividly meeting her on the street throughout my elementary and junior high school days and chatting with her about all my classmates and their brothers and sisters. She never forgot the name or face of any student she taught during her forty years at P.S. 82 and used to say she was more interested in how her former pupils grew after they left her than how well they did in her class. She was the repository of the neighborhood's memory and helped arrange class reunions, connect people with jobs, and provide information about marriages and births and deaths. She had only good to say about her former pupils. No matter how they turned out, they were still kindergarten children to her, beginning to learn their way in a difficult world. Considering the number of people who asked for her advice or who shared information with her, she seemed to me more active as a teacher after her retirement than even during her days in kindergarten.

Mrs. Cooper was respected by everybody in the neighborhood and welcome in every home. She was a model of kindness and generosity in the midst of a harsh, sometimes violent environment, and I remember wanting to command similar respect when I grew up. She made teaching seem like the most honored work one could do.

The other teacher who influenced me was Mrs. Lennon. She revealed to our fifth-grade class that the world was much larger than and different from the Bronx. Of course, we had all been told or read that the world had many peoples and cultures, and also that the arts were important. But Mrs. Lennon showed us. She described her travels and told us about the people she met and talked to. I think my romantic notion of the Midwest as a place of freedom and beauty came from her description of several small towns at the foothills of the Rockies where she had vacationed and made a number of friends.

Every day in class we listened to classical music and looked at classical or modern paintings. She read from novels to open the day and usually closed the day with a poem. I didn't understand or like most of what she presented to us, but I didn't resist it since I could see that she put her whole being into her presentations. She hummed with the music, would tell us to listen to the violins or trumpets, would repeat a line or two of poetry several times, almost singing it. And she told us not to bother trying to like or understand what she exposed us to, just to open ourselves up and listen and look. She explained that she was just planting seeds and that it would take time for them to grow in us. I had never known anyone so serious about art, literature, and music or so curious about the way people lived. Somehow these seeds she planted, some of which sprouted within me, as well as her obvious love of the thirty-nine eleven-year-olds she shared her experiences with, led me to believe that a teacher's life was exciting. You could travel and learn, you could start in the Bronx and maybe even become a teacher in the Midwest, showing what you know about New York and at the same time learning about the country and the mountains. You could help other people learn things about the world that they never imagined existed and share your enthusiasms.

Inspired by her, I decided to try teaching and recruited my younger brother and his friends as students. At eleven, my image of what teachers did was fairly simple. A teacher told students things they didn't know and showed them how to do things they couldn't do. In addition, a teacher had to make sure the students learned what they were told and that they didn't fool around too much.

I decided to teach Ted and four of his friends how to play checkers. I knew how to play checkers and they didn't, and I felt confident that I could control five seven-year-olds. Thus I met all my criteria for qualifying as a teacher and saw no reason why I shouldn't succeed.

My first and last session with Ted and his friends was a disaster. I set up the checkerboard and explained how the pieces are placed and how they move. Ted and Jay listened carefully and moved the pieces diagonally, just as I'd shown them. Jumping was next. Jay seemed to get the idea, but Ted jumped three spaces, jumped his own pieces, jumped from black to red, jumped everywhere but where he was supposed to. I was beginning to lose my patience when I noticed Tommy and Paul. They were supposed to be waiting patiently at the other board. Instead they were building towers out of checkers and throwing marbles at them. The checkers were all over the room. I don't know why it took me so long to discover that. By the time I got them to pick up the checkers and set their board up, Ted and Jay were building towers. I remember getting angry at my brother, calming down, and then getting really angry at him the next day when he told me that he and his friends had known how to play checkers all along and that they had decided to take lessons from me in order to annoy me by pretending not to learn. It was the first but certainly not the last time in my teaching career when the students were in control.

The Persistence of My Fantasy

My fantasy about being an elementary school teacher maintained its strength throughout college, though I never told anybody about it until the week before my graduation from Harvard. My tutor asked me what I wanted to do after graduation and in a moment of intimacy I shared my dream with him. He laughed and expressed a viewpoint I was to hear many times after that: "People don't go to Harvard to become elementary school teachers."

After graduation I spent a year on a scholarship at Oxford and then returned to New York, where I studied philosophy at Columbia University. Elementary school teaching was still on my mind, but graduate school was comfortable and I put off making a decision about teaching until I passed my comprehensive exams for a Ph.D. in philosophy and was a year or two away from settling down as an assistant professor at some university. The thought of sitting in classes and seminar rooms and talking about sense data and other philosophical esoterica for the rest of my life was grim. I wanted to be among children, to meet all kinds of people, to live in a world more like the Bronx than Harvard.

At the age of twenty-four I took the step I'd always wanted to take. I didn't go to that small town in the Midwest, but first to a school for severely disturbed children and then to a ghetto community in New York. Now, after forty-five years of teaching, I live in a small rural town in Northern California and still work with elementary and junior high school youngsters.

What was it that made teaching children more romantic to me than medicine, business, mathematics, or other careers I've flirted with? And why is it that teaching young children is as interesting and challenging now in Point Arena, California, as it was in Harlem and Berkeley and the other places in which I've taught? The only answer I find even partially satisfactory is that the romance of teaching is related less to individual students than to the phenomena of growth itself. It is wonderful to witness young people discovering that they can have power and to be able to help them acquire the skills and sensitivity they need to achieve the goals they come to set for themselves.

Wanting to teach is like wanting to have children or to write or paint or dance or invent or think through a mathematical problem that only a few have been able to solve. It has an element of mystery, involving as it does the yearly encounter with new people, the fear that you will be inadequate to meet their needs, as well as the rewards of seeing them become stronger because of your work. And as is true of the other creative challenges, the desire to teach and the ability to teach well are not the same thing. With the rarest of exceptions, one has to learn how to become a good teacher just as one has to learn how to become a scientist or an artist.

After withdrawing from graduate school at Columbia, I went to the New York City Board of Education to apply for a teacher's license. In 1960 there were hundreds of teaching jobs available in the city schools, and I assumed my education alone qualified me for one of them. The first secretary to the assistant superintendent in charge of licensing and credentials gave me several forms to fill out. She looked over my forms and told me to wait. An hour later, another secretary took the forms and told me she'd be right with me. After another hour, she returned and referred me to a third secretary, who handed me a sheet of paper informing me that I had no education courses and therefore didn't qualify for any teaching job in the system. I began to explain to her that I had taught math during summer school at Harvard, had experience working with youngsters, and knew a lot about literature and science. She paid no attention and simply referred me back to the first secretary, who told me that the best thing was to enroll at Teachers College, Columbia, or at the ed school at NYU. I pleaded to talk to someone higher up and was politely informed that everyone was busy and that there was nothing for me to talk about anyway, that qualifications were qualifications. Trying to get someone to listen to you at 110 Livingston Street was like trying to kick down the Empire State Building.

There was no way I would return to college at that point in my life. A friend of mine told me that private schools didn't have the same requirements as public schools, and so I got a private school directory and went from school to school asking if a job was available. I began alphabetically and got down to the *L*'s before hearing of a teaching job that was open and didn't require a credential. I heard of it through the League School, which served severely disturbed children. The secretary there, who was the opposite of the public school gatekeepers I'd encountered, told me of an opening at the Reece School for the Severely Disturbed.

I went immediately and was hired after a half-hour interview with Mrs. Reece. It was Thursday and I was to begin on Monday. I asked if there was any preparation to make. Mrs. Reece assured me that I'd learn on the job.

My First Job

I was a teacher at last. Even though the salary was three hundred dollars a month and I didn't have the slightest idea of what or how well I'd do with my students, I remember walking, practically skipping, down Lexington Avenue from Ninety-fourth Street, where the school was, to my apartment on Eighty-fourth, feeling giddy with excitement. Being paid to teach—doing what I'd dreamed of doing and being paid too—how wonderful could the world be?

Elation gave way to anxiety Sunday night, and by Monday morning I had visions of being rejected by a class of twenty-five bizarre children. What was a severely disturbed child and what did he or she do in school? What could be done for them? Did they grow like normal children? Would my job merely be custodial or would there be excitement to it? I walked slowly up Lexington Avenue to school Monday morning wondering if I really wanted to teach that much.

The school was located in a three-story brownstone and the classroom I was assigned to work in was on the top floor. I was introduced to Sarah, the other third-floor teacher, who was my supervisor. The class we were to share was unlike anything I'd ever experienced during my own schooling. There were only five ten- and eleven-year-old boys in the class and I was expected to work with only two of them and help out with a third. Sarah had an organization chart that showed me how every minute of the day was to be spent and gave me copies of the workbooks my students were using at the moment. From that first day throughout my stay at the Reece School I was a "by-the-book" teacher and followed the school's routine and its curriculum. It was a secure if not particularly creative way for me to begin my career, especially as my students' behavior required constant monitoring and they needed regular, predictable tasks to perform.

John and Fred were the boys assigned to me, and Harry, the most remote and the saddest child in the class, was with me part time. Sarah worked with him the rest of the day, as well as with Roger and the several Tommy Rinaldos we had to contend with. Tommy was a concentrated energy force who lived many lives on many planets, and his condition often determined how our day went. There were times when he was charming and other times when he became so wild and obsessed with images and phantoms that he had to be held down. He might become the Tommy Rinaldo Broadcasting Company and predict doom for the world as he tore through the school destroying everything in sight and crying at the same time. Or he would hold conversations with the generals in his imaginary army, Sisbeer and Cubrio. He was also the boss of the Rinaldo Construction Company, saw cities built and wrecked while describing the actions in minute detail to the rest of us. And there were moments when he would embrace Sarah or me and beg us to have his men go away, or would fall asleep exhausted after living through the battles raging inside himself. I admired the beauty and the power of his language and the force of his fantasies and was touched by his occasional gentleness and weakness. After one of his rampages he would fall limp and sleep for hours. I remember him waking up once and telling me that it was time to declare a National Leave Rinaldo Alone Week.

Even though Tommy wasn't officially my student, I dreamed of helping him become a poet or a builder, or just reducing his pain into livable and sharable form. I talked to him, at times held him while he broadcast declarations of war and proclamations of peace, and tried to get inside his world or to interest him in mine. But by the time I left the Reece School, I had given up on him.

He seemed to me to be surrounded by doors that had no keys, by one-way windows, by empty space. Somehow he had decided not to grow but to rage on until he collapsed.

Thinking about my three students, John, Fred, and Harry, and about Tommy, reminds me of a quote I found in a collection of letters from the English poet Sir John Suckling: "And Jack, if you would make a visit to Bedlam, you shall find that there are rarely two there mad for the same thing." No two of my students were mad for the same thing. Each of them was terrified of the world and had built up a system of protection that though bizarre and sad kept him from falling to pieces completely.

Recently I came upon a report I wrote in 1961 that gives a specific sense of how my first teaching days went. Here are a few excerpts:

The day begins ritualistically. Each student gets settled in his own way, then sits at his own table and gets ready to work. At exactly 9:00 (it would upset Harry if we began a minute before or after 9) we begin academics.

Fred puts his arithmetic book on the table and awaits his assignment. He immediately gets to work when told to, but cannot start without instructions. John has a more difficult time getting settled and so I speak to him, teach him whatever is new, or set him at work on familiar material. After about 15 or 20 minutes he is settled enough for me to shift my attention to Fred and teach him new work, or what is more usual, help him with problems that require understanding as well as mechanical calculation.

About 9:45 Fred finishes his arithmetic and begins spelling. He can understand directions by himself if he has come across similar ones before, but has to be eased through anything new or different. While Fred is doing spelling, John spends time practicing script writing, which he is still in the process of acquiring. Academics lasts until 10:15 or 10:25 depending upon Fred and John's ability to concentrate and work profitably. Fred is on Book 5 in spelling and is beginning to encounter dif-

ficulty; John has some troubles in Book 3, due more to attention difficulties than to a lack of understanding.

The rest of the day went on in much the same way. There was
nothing particularly interesting about the educational content of
the material I was required to teach. The students, however, had
such individual styles and needs that I was obliged to learn quite
quickly how to change the curriculum so that it would be useful
to them. John worked best with material that was visually interesting; Harry needed to learn in even more structured and organized ways than the texts we had; and Fred needed funny writing
that dealt with feelings. After a few months, I found myself re-
working the basic curriculum into three different curriculums, a
tendency I've never lost.

My initial anxiety over teaching disturbed children disappeared with prolonged contact with the students. They eventually
emerged as eleven-year-old children, somewhat different from
most eleven-year-old children, with greater pain, disorientation,
and confusion, but nevertheless distinct and interesting people.

Teachers College and Student Teaching

After six months at the Reece School, I began to think about
public school teaching again and about working with so-called
normal children. The slow rate of change of my students depressed me. I'd see a tiny positive difference negated by a change
in the weather or in the emotional constellation of the class. I
saw the children's fear of change overwhelm their desire to grow.
I also knew I was beginning to do kind and decent work. But it
wasn't enough, was too slow, too removed from the world of
lively, articulate children I wanted to work with. I kept thinking
of the secretary at the New York City Board of Education and resigned myself to going to Teachers College, Columbia, and taking courses, any courses, that would get me a regular elementary
school credential and a job in the public schools.

Every beginning teacher has to face similar questions: What kind of child do you want to spend five hours a day with? How many children do you like to work with at one time? What age do you enjoy being with? The central question teachers have to answer for themselves is: What kind of growth do you want to nurture?

My wife is an excellent teacher of severely disturbed children, takes pleasure in observing small increments of growth, and has the patience to see them disappear and reappear. She likes to work with small groups. I'm different. I like large groups and enjoy noise and defiance, and dramatic change. Teaching friends of mine all have their preferences: Some like to work with adolescents, some with very young children. Some change every three years in order to experience growth on different age levels. Others are subject obsessed and enjoy stimulating scientific, mathematical, literary, or historical understanding. What we all realize, however, is that our most effective teaching arises from being in a situation where the growth we nurture is something we find beautiful to witness.

My time at Teachers College dragged. I spent the summer of 1961 taking classes on the teaching of arithmetic and reading, on curriculum development (which taught us how to make our own Ditto masters), on educational counseling (which told us to be nice to children), and on children's literature (which exposed us to books that, it seemed to me then, were written to avoid exposing children to poetry and fiction that dealt with life in complex and controversial ways). My professors gave the impression that they knew how to mold one into a good teacher. All you had to do was be nice, be organized, fit into the system as it was, follow the methods you learned at Teachers College, and you'd have a long and happy career.

The content of what was being taught to us was vacuous, the skills and techniques could have been mastered by a high school sophomore and the psychology found in any Miss Lonelyhearts column. The reality of life in the classroom, the complexity and variability of children, the effect of the school and community on the teacher, the role of culture in learning—these were never dealt with and I cannot recollect anything specific about those classes other than that they were boring. The classes I hoped to learn the most from, those about the education of disturbed children, were the worst. They talked about categories of disturbance, about interventions and therapeutic strategies, and said nothing pertinent or helpful about John, Fred, or Harry.

If it wasn't for the nurturance, good sense, and eventual protection of my supervisor Dorothy McGeoch, I never would have survived Teachers College and gotten a teaching credential. Throughout my experience I have always been lucky to find one or two teachers who helped me to grow the way I came to help my students. Without those teachers and colleagues, none of us sustain a life of teaching. It makes good sense when going to a new school to take time to look for such a colleague, to find someone whom you want to learn from and share what you know with.

I had two student teacher placements instead of the more usual one. My first placement was at P.S. 140, right opposite Peter Cooper Village, a middle-class development on Manhattan's East Side. I was assigned to a well-ordered, smoothly functioning, traditional sixth-grade classroom. The day opened with reading the headlines and one article from the front page of the New York Times and went step by step through group reading, individualized reading, spelling, math, social studies, art—what seemed to me an endless series of disconnected lessons that students had to go through. Here were normal children doing just what my students at the Reece School were doing. At Reece it was clear that the structure and the workbooks existed as much to control behavior as to teach anything. It hadn't occurred to me until I had spent six weeks at P.S. 140 that the same thing was being done to normal students. Every day was the same, every lesson the same, every question like every other. I didn't hear student voices except on the playground and in the lunchroom. The teacher, Mrs. Jay, only spoke to the students about formal matters (absence notes, parents' permission forms, etc.) or when she gave orders or asked questions about a lesson. I wanted to object to what I saw, to try to have conversations with my students and find out what interested them. They looked so lively and alert on the playground. Fortunately Dorothy McGeoch convinced me to keep quiet and do what I was told. She reminded me that my goal in student teaching was to pass the course, not reform the school. I could try that, she said wryly, when I got my credential and was doing real work.

I almost survived 140. However, I made a number of inadvertent mistakes that led to the involuntary termination of my student teaching two weeks before it was to have ended. The first mistake was to treat the principal informally. I had always been able to relate to my professors and colleagues at the Reece School on a first-name basis and didn't realize that formal address was required in exchanges between student teachers and staff and administration.

Another mistake was fraternizing with students. I said hello to every youngster I passed on the street, in the yard, or in the hall. After a while some children began asking me questions about myself or telling me the neighborhood or school gossip. I didn't realize it made the other teachers as well as the administrators around the school angry to see me chatting with the students, and it wasn't until I left the school that another student teacher told me that the principal had held me up as an example of how a teacher should not behave. He informed the other teachers at the school that eating lunch with the students and playing with them on breaks instead of having coffee in the teachers' room was unprofessional behavior that contributed to the breakdown of discipline and respect and could not be allowed in an orderly school.

Mrs. Jay, my supervising teacher, didn't like to have me in the room. I was too arrogant toward her, an attitude that I now see as foolish and one that may well have kept me from learning from her. She contrived to have me work with a small number of her "slower and difficult" students in a small conference room down the hall. I was given four students—Stanley Gold, the biggest and oldest boy in the school, who it turned out was half Jewish and half Puerto Rican; Betty Williams, who was African American;

Robert Moy, who was Chinese and had recently arrived in the country; and Ana Suarez, who was Puerto Rican. With one exception, they were the only minority children in the class of thirty-five.

When I first heard of the arrangement, it felt like being demoted to the Reece School—one teacher and four deviant youngsters. However, it proved to be a gift. I couldn't have learned more about children, culture, and learning in such a short time than I did from working with those four lively, intelligent, defiant, and thoroughly delightful youngsters.

As soon as we left the classroom the four came alive, chatted about what was going on, asked me about myself, particularly why I wanted to be a teacher. Once I sat down to read with them, some unexpected things began to happen. Betty didn't know the alphabet, or even how to hold a pencil. I asked her how long she'd been in school, since everything about formal learning seemed so foreign to her. She told me that this was her first year, that she had come from a small farm community in the South where the children didn't go to school much. When Betty first came to school in September, there was a suggestion she be put in the first grade, but that was abandoned because she was so tall. She spent her time in the sixth grade in the back of the room, flipping through picture books.

Betty was my first teaching success. I taught her how to hold a pencil, read stories to her and had her copy them, gave her flash cards using words she wanted to know, and watched her learn to read. She wasn't dumb or a failure—just a child who hadn't learned to read and was learning at twelve, not a bad age to begin formal reading instruction.

Working with Betty showed me the futility of trying to teach reading solely through phonics. Betty grew up in the Deep South, and she and I simply didn't pronounce *a, e, i, o* and *u* in the same way. In fact, between my Bronx accent and her Southern accent, there were few words that sounded identical to us. The meaning of sentences and the content of stories, however, made it easy to overcome these differences. Betty and I spoke about books and understood each other perfectly. The more we talked about books, the more interested she became in reading well. Our lessons were planned around questions she raised about reading. I began to realize that she was my best source of information about teaching her to read. As long as she could specify what caused her reading problems, I could help her. If endings like *-ion* or *-ally* were a problem, I could simply tell her how they were used and pronounced. If combinations like *-oa* or *-ae-* or *-ea-* created confusion, it was easy to undo them as long as she could point to them. Through teaching Betty and the other three youngsters that were assigned to me, I learned how to use students' knowledge of their own learning problems as a major source for designing educational programs.

Betty's mother met me one day after school. She told me that Betty was very happy about learning to read and she wondered if I could give her materials so Betty could practice more at home. In her eyes I was a real teacher, though I knew I was only improvising. Nevertheless, I bought six inexpensive simple reading books at a remainder bookstore, six pencils and a pencil sharpener, a notebook and a pack of three-by-five index cards, and packaged them in a plastic box with Betty's name stenciled on it. That was her personalized reading kit and from what I heard several years later from another student, she had used it and taught herself to read.

Robert Moy, another one of my four, also fascinated me. I tried to administer a Gates Reading Test to find out his level and gave up one-fourth of the way through. He couldn't read any English, could hardly pronounce the sounds of the language. There was a math section on the test and I tried that since there was no reason to assume he couldn't do math because he couldn't read English. He scored 100 percent or the equivalent of twelfth-grade level in math. A few days later I gave him an eighth-grade math test and he scored in the ninety-ninth percentile, yet in class he was in a fourth-grade workbook because he couldn't read the verbalized math problems. I remember feeling at the time that the main difference between the Reece School and P.S. 140 was that in 140 the adults were doing crazy things to sane children instead of the other way around.

I noticed some Chinese writing on Robert's book and asked him if he wrote Chinese. Yes, he knew over a thousand characters and would be delighted to teach them to me. I shared my discovery about Robert's writing ability with my supervising teacher and she made a note of it, to use, as she told me, during the China unit she was planning for the second half of the school year. She didn't say anything to Robert. I watched as he systematically went about learning bits and pieces of English. He may not have been well schooled at 140, but somewhere he had been educated well. He just needed to be pointed in the right direction and given a few basic instructions in order to learn to read skillfully.

The students I got closest to in that class were Ana Suarez and Stanley Gold. Neither had a reading or a math problem. Older than the other students, they were leaders in the small ghetto a few blocks from the school and had no relationship with most of the students in P.S. 140, which was at that time over 80 percent white. The teachers, they claimed, didn't like them and so they "refused to do any work, period," as Stanley said.

I brought Ana romances and gothics, which she loved. After learning that Stanley's father was a woodcarver and Stanley a talented artist, I got him some art instruction books. That was my first reading class—Betty copying Dr. Seuss, Robert teaching me Chinese, Ana reading romances and talking endlessly about the story, while Stanley drew and read about art.

My relationship with Stanley Gold led directly to my being removed from 140. Stanley and I prepared an art project to present to Mrs. Jay's class during the morning I would be expected to run the whole class by myself. Mrs. Jay would evaluate my student teaching on the basis of the math, language, and art lessons presented then. I decided to put math and art together and do a lesson on how cathedrals stand up. I was intoxicated with the cathedrals I'd seen in France, and Stanley had shown me pictures of carved models of churches his father had made. For the lesson, Stanley was going to draw on the chalkboard a schematic of a cathedral with flying buttresses and then do a scale drawing of Chartres that compared it in size with the school and the Empire State Building. The math component of the lesson was an introduction to scale and relative proportion. The whole thing was to take up the first hour of class time. The lesson couldn't have worked, but I didn't know it. The class wasn't prepared for an open-ended discussion about anything, much less about flying buttresses; the math was too sophisticated; I had no experience working with a whole class and no sense of how to maintain control. To make matters worse, that day Mrs. Jay was absent and a sub appeared at the door at eight-forty. Stanley and I had been in the room since eight o'clock, he drawing on the board and I setting up the materials for my other lessons. The sub looked at Mrs. Jay's lesson book and let me take over.

The class came in and settled down. I began talking about the plans for the morning and then asked if anyone knew what a cathedral was. Six hands went up, three people shouted, someone made a strange noise. If Mrs. Jay was there, none of that would have happened, and it might have been possible for me to rescue part of the lesson because of the control her presence exerted. But with a sub in the room, I got more loudness than openness. After fifteen minutes the sub walked to the front of the room, banged a ruler on the desk, and in an experienced voice informed the class that she not only knew how to maintain order but demanded it instantly. She got her silence and then turned to Stanley, then to the buttressed church on the board, and commanded, "Erase that." He refused, she commanded again, and Stanley turned to me and asked if I was going to make him erase it. I saw our whole relationship dissolving, felt the possibility of his withdrawing from me as he did from all his other teachers, and I turned to the sub, saying something like "It stays." She then commanded me to erase the board. I refused and she stormed out of the room.

Somehow I fumbled through what was left of my lesson plans

until recess. After my class left the room, the principal came in and told me to take the rest of the day off.

When I returned the next day, there was a note taped to my locker in the student teacher's lounge, informing me to go to the principal's office. The locker was emptied of all my books and materials, which the principal later presented to me in a neatly sealed box while instructing me that I was never to return to P.S. 140 again, for any reason. I had violated the sacred law of the teaching profession: Never under any circumstances support a student against another teacher in the presence of students. I was not even allowed to say good-bye to the class.

Halfway out of the building, I started crying quietly. It felt as if I was being sent away from home, from what I loved more than anything else. The place, the children, the energy, the best and the worst of that school, all of a sudden were precious, and now I would never get my credential and be part of it.

Dorothy McGeoch rescued me. She somehow managed to bury the principal's report and get me assigned to Walden School, a small progressive private school on Central Park West. However, every moment I could manage was spent with Stanley or the Suarez family and their friends in the neighborhood of P.S. 140.

The Public Schools at Last

When I finally obtained my credential and got hired at P.S. 145 in February 1962, it seemed a long journey had ended. My calling to teach had been confirmed and I was ready to practice my craft behind the doors of my own classroom.

I had begun to get an idea of how I would like to see a classroom function. Conversation would be essential, for students must have a chance to talk about what they were studying and about their lives as well. The teacher would be part of the conversation, more informed about issues of content but also a listener and a learner. The students shouldn't all have to do the same thing at the same moment and shouldn't always have to be watched. Life in the classroom should be more like life at home or in a restaurant, a playground, or any place where activity occurred without constant surveillance. This implied that I would allow the students to be independent so that they would not feel at war with me and the school.

Small-group learning, individual projects, class discussions and events, and fun were some of the ingredients I wanted to develop in my work. I also wished to incorporate interesting content, compelling reading and drama, exciting math and science ideas and experiments, historical explorations and re-creations, even philosophy. I also wanted to mix the subjects together—to study light, for example, from a perspective that was artistic, scientific, and literary.

To teach this way, some classroom reorganization, in terms of space, time, and behavior, would be necessary, but the specifics of how to create an open classroom were very vague to me. I had never seen or read about a working model of that kind of learning, a situation I now find ironical, given that my M.A. in education is from Teachers College, where such models were created and refined from the 1920s to the 1950s. I sometimes wonder how much finer a teacher I might have been if my degree was taken in '32 instead of '62.

I began my career in P.S. 145 with a sense of how I'd like to encourage the growth of my students but with no sense of the specifics of organization, management, discipline, pacing, and transformation of interesting content into a challenging curriculum. My strengths were energy, enthusiasm, knowledge in many different areas, a love of books and learning, a delight in being in the presence of children, an almost fanatic determination not to fail as a teacher, and a faith in my fifth-grade students' ability to learn no matter how limited they seemed when I first encountered them. My class had managed to wear out half a dozen teachers by the time I took over in February. A third of the students spoke only Spanish, the class itself was a dumping ground for problem students, and there were no books in the room. No matter—I was full of confidence, even of a sense of destiny.

My first week of teaching left me in despair, almost wishing I'd finished my doctorate in philosophy and could teach Wittgenstein to a group of docile graduate students. The first mistake I made was to introduce myself to the class as Herb instead of Mr. Kohl. I had done so at Walden and it seemed like a good idea. But twenty blocks away at P.S. 145, the only adults you called by their first names were those you didn't respect and were trying to bait. In one short week I went from informal Herb, with an open collar and sweater, to Mr. Kohl, with a suit and tie, a very controlled manner, and an unnatural stern look. My students had quickly taught me that I had to establish my authority before I could teach them anything.

In fact, after several weeks I found myself doing everything I had sworn never to do in the classroom. The day began with students copying something I'd written on the chalkboard. After that they'd fill in purple Ditto forms with simple math examples, then read out loud, then go to recess and repeat the process. In my heart I wanted to talk to my students, to share what I knew with them and find out who they were and what they knew. Yet all I was doing was filling up time and trying to get through the day without a scene.

Yet there were scenes—fights, thefts, furniture overturned or thrown around, papers torn up, pencils broken. Occasionally there were moments when one student or another did start a conversation with me or follow a suggestion I had made or, most wonderful, look happy and relaxed in the room. I took to studying faces and gestures in ways I'd never done before. Every moment of silence in the room was a time for me to observe, to guess (usually wildly and incorrectly) about who these children were who were forced to be with me five hours a day.

After a while little things happened that made our lives together better. Vincent made a joke about my hair and I laughed. Gloria said that teachers don't laugh, so I couldn't be a real teacher. Another time, Carlos told me that the reason Victor was so shy in class was that he had just come from Puerto Rico and couldn't speak any English. I asked Carlos to be my interpreter and set aside twenty minutes a day for my students to teach me Spanish, even though my principal told me that speaking Spanish in class was against Board of Education rules. Little by little I felt that I was becoming myself in the classroom and abandoning my stance as the Teacher.

One girl's mother had a back injury and was in traction in the hospital. She was from Puerto Rico and couldn't eat the institutional American-style food served to her in the ward. Her family was worried about her health. She was weak and hungry and her back wasn't getting any better. One lunchtime, her daughter Rafaela, who was one of the few quiet children in my classroom, asked me if I would do her a favor. She wanted me to sneak *pasteles* and other tasty Puerto Rican food to her mother at the hospital. It would fit in my briefcase, she said, and no one would question a teacher.

Why did she ask me? I wondered if she picked up something that first inept day when I introduced myself as Herb. More likely, she was desperate and I was the only one left to turn to. Whatever the reason, the day I visited the hospital I had the best-smelling briefcase you can imagine and Consuelo, Rafaela's mother, had a wonderful dinner.

Everyone in the class knew I'd broken the hospital rules, did something they thought was dangerous, and didn't ask for any money or other return. They began to open up because of that and other gestures that led them, as they later told me, to like being in class. They'd appreciated my making pencils available for children who couldn't afford them, allowing them to pass notes if it didn't interfere with anything, giving them time to talk before work began, providing colored paper for them to cover their books with, letting them take home books and games I brought to school, and trusting them to be able to run the film-strip viewer by themselves.

One of my ways of relating to them got me in trouble again. I had maintained my habit of saying hello to every student I met and of stopping to chat with students before and after school. One day the principal called me into his office and delivered the familiar reprimand that I was getting too close to students, and that it was undermining their respect for me. My experience, I said, was that the opposite was true, that those small gestures of friendship and concern were the basis for genuine respect. An older teacher who had overheard our conversation told me at lunch that I'd never last at that school.

It was true that one could hardly tell from my students' unruly behavior during class that we were beginning to know and care about each other. But before and after class were different. Students came early and stayed after school to talk with me, the same students, often, who acted the most defiantly and crazily during the school day.

The two notable ones were James T. and Felipe, whom the rest of the class called the Dynamic Duo, after Batman and Robin. There were days when I felt that I was in a match against the Duo, with the rest of the class as audience and judge. I didn't want to win it, but I couldn't lose, either, if I was to be of any use to the whole class. How was I to end this confrontation without victors or vanquished, without loss of face on anyone's part? I was encountering the central problem of discipline in the classroom.

James T. and Felipe were veterans of school wars and knew dozens of strategies that effectively demoralized their teachers. I knew that the problems they created had to be solved within the classroom, not by the principal's office. Fortunately the two boys were as interesting as any children I've known, and when I got home after school and thought about the day, I would have to laugh at how smart they were about taking control of the class away from me. Unlike the children at the Reece School, they knew what they were doing, and could talk their way out of the havoc they created. When it suited them, they could also be serious, intelligent, and sensitive. But for a while, having fun at my expense was their main game.

One Monday, for example, I was preaching to the class about how important it was to study animal life. I had bought a fifty-gallon aquarium over the weekend and brought it to class. My idea was to have goldfish, guppies, and algae eaters to study, as well as water plants and perhaps some snails. James T. and Felipe listened attentively for a change. When the bell rang for lunch, the Dynamic Duo gathered a few other boys and two girls, Gloria and Haydee, who always ran with their gang. They were talking excitedly about fish and aquariums. I couldn't make out what they were saying, for it was a mixture of English, Spanish, and Haitian French. At lunchtime the whole bunch asked to borrow the class wastebaskets and then took off. I knew something was up because they had left their lunches behind in the classroom.

I found out what the gang had in mind when I returned from lunch and almost slipped on the water that was flooding out of our aquarium. A stream was heading under the door and probably down the hall toward the principal's office. The aquarium was overflowing, the four faucets of our two blocked-up sinks were on full force, and in the aquarium and the two sinks were dozens of overgrown goldfish, actually carp, that the gang had caught in the wastebaskets on their fast trip to a nearby pond in Central Park.

The smallest fish was six inches, the largest could have been close to two feet. The fish were too big for the sinks or the aquarium; several were flapping around on the floor, gasping for air. James T. and Felipe turned to me, beaming, and said, "See, Mr. Kohl, you don't need to buy no fish. We took care of it."

At that point, Gloria, Haydee, Josi, and John came into the class with a garbage can filled with yet more carp. They told me they had dumped the can's contents in front of some rich apartment house because they had people there who always cleaned up the garbage. I didn't know whether to blow up or laugh, to resign my job or congratulate the class for stocking the aquarium, and try to cover for them and myself. I simply did not know what to do. Felipe rescued me. He told me not to worry, that all the dead and big fish would be taken home and eaten. James T. added that it would be a whole system, just like I was talking about in the morning. Nothing would be wasted.

I managed to get through the afternoon, but have no idea how. We ended up with an aquarium that contained three greedy seven- or eight-inch-long carp that ate bits and scraps of everything including the few guppies and goldfish I foolishly tried to introduce.

In a way the aquarium was like our class. Several large fish overwhelming all the others and a teacher who, though bigger than the students, was always on the verge of being eaten up by the class.

James T. and Felipe were the kind of children who some cynical educators would classify as hyperactive, educationally handicapped, retarded, disturbed, learning disabled, and so forth. They were all of these in class, and in their lives none of these. They hated school, had experienced five and a half years of bad teaching, and acted out their hostility to stay sane in an insane situation. I watched them grow, from tossing books around the classroom to sneaking looks at them and by June asking me for help in reading after school. They changed slowly, yet compared to the children at the Reece School, they seemed to be leaping forward.

James T. turned out to be a very skilled artist. He told me that when he saw colors he could taste them in his mouth, and I once caught him dipping his fingers in our tempera paints and licking them. I surprised him one day by giving him a box of pastels. I made up some story that the school was providing special art material to students of talent to help decorate the halls. James T. made several beautiful pastel drawings. A particular favorite of mine (which I still have) is a drawing of Moby Dick on black construction paper. The black underlies the pastel white whale, deep blue water, and pale blue sky, giving the whole an appropriately ominous feeling.

I mounted a number of James T.'s pastels on poster board and hung them in the hall. This got me in trouble several weeks later when the district art supervisor came into my class and in front of the students told me to take down James T.'s posters. I remembered what had happened to me with the sub in 140 and decided to stall. I muttered something that could have been taken for assent, but explained that we were about to take an important phonics test. By this time I'd learned that phonics always takes preference over any other matter.

The supervisor didn't give up easily on the pastels and was waiting in my classroom when I returned from dismissing the class. The assistant principal accompanied her. Lois was a very sympathetic woman who protected her teachers. I could see James T. and Felipe hiding behind the swinging doors down the hall. The supervisor advised me that pastels were a sixth-grade medium and that since I was teaching fifth grade, my students couldn't use pastels. She showed me a passage in the school district's art curriculum manual that confirmed her contention and insisted again that the offending art be removed. She also wanted to confiscate the pastels in my room. I politely objected, pointing out that the 5-1 class, of so-called gifted students (my class was 5-7, the bottom of our grade), used pastels. My motivation was to show my students and particularly James T. that he could do work that was as good as or better than that of some of the students in 5-1. She said that the only reason 5-1 was allowed to use pastels was that they all read and did math on a sixth-grade or better level. By now I was getting angry and was about to argue that art and reading skills had no direct relationship, that the development of any skill could lead to confidence in other areas, that there was no set sequence of the use of art materials, that . . . Lois put her hand on my shoulder and shrugged. Her eyes told me what I quickly realized. We were in an educational madhouse and my students and I would be the losers if I protested any further. James T.'s work came down. The supervisor even demanded that I turn over the pastels, but since they were not the brand bought by the school I was able to keep them.

James T. and Felipe burst into the room when my visitors had left. They wanted to know why I had given in and accused me of not caring about them. James T. picked up the box of pastels and carefully selected one of his favorite colors, a deep red, and broke it. Before he could destroy the set, I grabbed it and told him it was mine, not the school's, and he couldn't treat my property that way. I also told him that the drawings had to come down or I'd be fired; it was as simple as that. I wanted to stay with the class, not be fired, and would hang them up in the classroom if it was okay with the assistant principal. He could also keep the pastels and use them in class; they were a gift. He said he'd think about it and the two of them left.

The next morning James T. and Felipe were waiting for me at the classroom door. James T. had drawn an elaborate sheriff's badge, which Felipe presented to me. It said: "Honorary Student."

Felipe could make leaps like that. His mind and his temperament were poetic. I liked to play language games with the class when they were under control. There was one particular exercise where students had to do variations on the metaphor "He had a heart of gold" by using the form:

_____ had a _____ of _____
[name]   [body part]   [animal/
                                                             vegetable/
                                                             mineral]

Typical responses were:

She had a heart of stone.
He had a head of rocks.
He had a fist of steel.

Felipe's responses were:

James T. has a finger of yellow blood.
Gloria has a half face of gold and another half face of angry.

James T. loved yellow and occasionally used his finger to apply yellow tints to some of his work. Gloria was well known for being two-faced—sweet, kind, fickle, and dangerous.

James T. and Felipe weren't the only children who taught me how to teach them and gave me hints about what interested ten- and eleven-year-olds. One day Lilian, one of the few quiet children, was looking through my salesman's case that I kept full of learning materials. Carrying the case to school had become a habit after a few weeks at 145, when I realized how much children love to discover new things without having to be told they must learn about them. The case usually contained books, magazines, games, magnets, magnifying glasses, free samples, newspapers— anything I thought might interest the class. The children were allowed to look through it and borrow something after they had handed their finished work in to me and waited while I graded it. That day Lilian came upon a blueprint of one of my father's old jobs, which I had asked for. She spread the blueprint on the floor and began puzzling out what was on it. Carlos Gomez, whose father was the janitor of a large apartment house, immediately recognized it as the floor plan of a building. His father had taught him a bit about blueprint reading and he attracted a crowd of about a dozen admiring classmates as he revealed the mysteries of architectural drawing to Lilian.

Carlos was usually quiet and studious. He always finished his work quickly, always asked for more, never wanted to pause and chat. This was the liveliest I'd seen him, and watching the scene in the back of the room caused me to wonder what was locked up in all the children, what they knew and could contribute. How to find out? How to do so when so much of my energy went into controlling them and filling in forms and doing workbooks just to get through the day in moderate peace?

I taped the blueprint to the blackboard and explained that my father was a builder. Vincent asked if he would come to visit the class. Gloria wanted to know if he was better looking than I was. It was almost three o'clock and so instead of explaining at length, I described the function of a blueprint and assigned the students the task of drawing a blueprint of their apartments for homework. It was the most successful assignment I'd given so far.

When the students brought their assignments in the next day, it was clear that something special had happened. Just about everyone had drawn a coherent representation of where they lived. A number of students had got help from brothers and sisters. Some used top-down perspective, others mixed different perspectives; different labeling systems were invented. We spent the entire morning looking over the drawings and talking about them. Many of the children knew each other's apartments and picked up on a missing window or misplaced chair or table. We concluded the discussion by drawing floor plans of the classroom.

The morning was one of the few I experienced at 145 that gave me a glimpse of what a good classroom could be like. If I had been more experienced, it would have been possible to follow up and develop a more extended curriculum revolving around building construction, model making, scale drawing, and symbol systems in general. But the burden of daily routine, the fear that reading, writing, and arithmetic wouldn't be adequately mastered if I followed the students' interests and planned around them, and the simple fact that learning to teach was exhausting work that left little time to research and plan, sent me back to my usual routine the next day.

But by June the first two hours of the morning were won. We talked and read together. I took my Spanish lesson. We discussed history, science, and art. No one acted too disruptively. The last hour of the morning was a strain on all of us. It was my most rigid time of day, and whenever possible I extended recess and left for lunch early.

The students won the afternoon. By one o'clock I was too exhausted to entertain, discipline, or teach the class. But eventually this time became fun for all of us. They could paint, draw, sculpt, do science experiments, read or do math, get individual help from me, listen to music, and occasionally dance. The only conditions were that they couldn't fight (they did occasionally) and they had to put everything away and clean up before three (they didn't occasionally). Contrary to my fears when I agreed to let the students have the afternoon to themselves, they didn't all paint the whole time, or sit filing their nails, or argue. Some students chose to do math, others science or reading, as well as art. The art itself became increasingly interesting and I began to bring in books on techniques and set them problems. The students used me too— asked for help, for resources and ideas. I still felt guilty about these "loose" afternoons, but they provided an important stage in learning how to maintain control without being coercive and how to teach skills in a creative and informal context.

June was the best teaching time I'd ever had and I was already looking forward to September. In one of the final faculty meetings, the principal gave a talk about how he wanted an open exchange between himself and the staff and asked if anyone had any comments on the school's reading program. There was silence in the room. One teacher yawned, the others kept their eyes away from the principal and their hands down. But I raised my hand and went on about how there was no coherent reading program at the school and offered ideas I'd heard or read about that could help our students. The principal smiled and thanked me for my input, but his eyes made it clear that I should have kept my mouth shut. The woman sitting next to me, an older teacher who had been very helpful to me in my first two months, whispered, "You won't be here next year."

She was right, of course. I was involuntarily transferred out of P.S. 145 with the feeling that I was being thrown out of a garden I'd worked on just as the blooming season was beginning and before the ripening of the fruits.

My alarm clock rang at seven-thirty, but I was up and dressed at seven. It was only a fifteen-minute bus ride from my apartment on 90th Street and Madison Avenue to the school on 119th Street and Madison.

There had been an orientation session the day before. I remembered the principal's words. "In times like these, this is the most exciting place to be, in the midst of ferment and creative activity. Never has teaching offered such opportunities . . . we are together here in a difficult situation. They are not the easiest children, yet the rewards are so great—a smile, loving concern, what an inspiration, a felicitous experience."

I remembered my barren classroom, no books, a battered piano, broken windows and desks, falling plaster, and an oppressive darkness.

I was handed a roll book with thirty-six names and thirty-six cumulative record cards, years of judgments already passed upon the children, their official personalities. I read through the names, twenty girls and sixteen boys, the 6-1 class, though I was supposed to be teaching the fifth grade and had planned for it all summer. Then I locked the record cards away in the closet. The children would tell me who they were. Each child, each new school year, is potentially many things, only one of which the cumulative record card documents. It is amazing how "emotional" problems can disappear, how the dullest child can be transformed into the keenest and the brightest into the most ordinary when the prefabricated judgments of other teachers are forgotten.

The children entered at nine and filled up the seats. They were silent and stared at me. It was a shock to see thirty-six African

American faces before me. No preparation helped. It is one thing to be liberal and talk, another to face something and learn that you're afraid.

The children sat quietly, expectant. *Everything must go well; we must like each other.*

Hands went up as I called the roll. Anxious faces, hostile, indifferent, weary of the ritual, confident of its outcome.

The smartest class in the sixth grade, yet no books.

"Write about yourselves, tell me who you are." (I hadn't said who I was, too nervous.)

Slowly they set to work, the first directions followed—and if they had refused?

Then arithmetic, the children working silently, a sullen, impenetrable front. *To talk to them, to open them up this first day.*

"What would you like to learn this year? My name is Mr. Kohl."

Silence, the children looked up at me with expressionless faces, thirty-six of them crowded at thirty-five broken desks. *This is the smartest class?*

Explain: they're old enough to choose, enough time to learn what they'd like as well as what they have to.

Silence, a restless movement rippled through the class. *Don't they understand? There must be something that interests them, that they care to know more about.*

A hand shot up in the corner of the room.

"I want to learn more about volcanoes. What are volcanoes?"

The class seemed interested. I sketched a volcano on the blackboard, made a few comments, and promised to return.

"Anything else? Anyone else interested in something?"

Silence, then the same hand.

"Why do volcanoes form?"

And during the answer:

"Why don't we have a volcano here?"

A contest. The class savored it, I accepted. Question, response, question. I walked toward my inquisitor, studying his mischievous eyes, possessed and possessing smile. I moved to congratulate him, my hand went happily toward his shoulder. I dared because I was afraid.

His hands shot up to protect his dark face, eyes contracted in fear, body coiled ready to bolt for the door and out, down the stairs into the streets.

"But why should I hit you?"

They're afraid too!

Hands relaxed, he looked torn and puzzled. I changed the subject quickly and moved on to social studies—How We Became Modern America.

"Who remembers what America was like in 1800?"

A few children laughed; the rest barely looked at me.

"Can anyone tell me what was going on about 1800? Remember, you studied it last year. Why don't we start more specifically? What do you think you'd see if you walked down Madison Avenue in those days?"

A lovely hand, almost too thin to be seen, tentatively rose.

"Cars?"

"Do you think there were cars in 1800? Remember that was over a hundred and fifty years ago. Think of what you learned last year and try again. Do you think there were cars then?"

"Yes . . . no . . . I don't know."

She withdrew, and the class became restless as my anger rose.

At last another hand.

"Grass and trees?"

The class broke up as I tried to contain my frustration.

"I don't know what you're laughing about—it's the right answer. In those days Harlem was farmland with fields and trees and a few houses. There weren't any roads or houses like the ones outside, or street lights or electricity. There probably wasn't even a Madison Avenue."

The class was outraged. It was inconceivable to them that there was a time their Harlem didn't exist.

"Stop this noise and let's think. Do you believe that Harlem was here a thousand years ago?"

A pause, several uncertain Noes.

"It's possible that the land was green then. Why couldn't Harlem also have been green a hundred and fifty or two hundred years ago?"

No response. The weight of Harlem and my whiteness and strangeness hung in the air as I droned on, lost in my righteous monologue. The uproar turned into sullen silence. A slow nervous drumming began at several desks; the atmosphere closed as intelligent faces lost their animation. Yet I didn't understand my mistake, the children's rejection of me and my ideas. Nothing worked, I tried to joke, command, play—the children remained joyless until the bell, then quietly left for lunch.

There was an hour to summon energy and prepare for the afternoon, yet it seemed futile. What good are plans, clever new methods and materials, when the children didn't—wouldn't—care or listen? Perhaps the best solution was to prepare for hostility and silence, become the cynical teacher, untaught by his pupils, ungiving himself, yet protected.

At one o'clock, my tentative cynicism assumed, I found myself once again unprepared for the children who returned and noisily and boisterously avoided me. Running, playing, fighting—they were alive as they tore about the room. I was relieved, yet how to establish order? I fell back on teacherly words.

"You've had enough time to run around. Everybody please go to your seats. We have work to begin."

No response. The boy who had been so scared during the morning was flying across the back of the room pursued by a demonic-looking child wearing black glasses. Girls stood gossiping in little groups, a tall boy fantasized before four admiring listeners, while a few children wandered in and out of the room. I still knew no one's name.

"Sit down, we've got to work. At three o'clock you can talk all you want to."

One timid girl listened. I prepared to use one of the teacher's most fearsome weapons and last resources. Quickly white paper was on my desk, the blackboard erased, and numbers from 1 to 10 and 11 to 20 appeared neatly in two columns.

"We're now going to have an *important* spelling test. Please, young lady"—I selected one of the gossipers—"what's your name? Neomia, pass out the paper. When you get your paper, fold it in half, put your heading on it, and number carefully from one to ten and eleven to twenty, exactly as you see it on the blackboard."

Reluctantly the girls responded, then a few boys, until after the fourth, weariest, repetition of the directions the class was seated and ready to begin—I thought.

Rip, a crumpled paper flew onto the floor. Quickly I replaced it; things had to get moving.

Rip, another paper, rip. I got the rhythm and began quickly, silently replacing crumpled papers.

"The first word is *anchor*. The ship dropped an *anchor*. Anchor."

"A what?"

"Where?"

"Number two is *final*. *Final* means last, *final*. Number three is *decision*. He couldn't make a *decision* quickly enough."

"What *decision*?"

"What was number two?"

"*Final.*"

I was trapped.

"Then what was number one?"

"*Anchor.*"

"I missed a word."

"Number four is *reason*. What is the *reason* for all this noise?"

"Because it's the first day of school."

"Yeah, this is too hard for the first day."

"We'll go on without any comments whatever. The next word is——"

"What number is it?"

"——*direction*. What *direction* are we going? *Direction.*"

"What's four?"

The test seemed endless, but it did end at two o'clock. What next? Once more I needed to regain my strength and composure, and it was still the first day.

"Mr. Kohl, can we please talk to each other about the summer? We won't play around. Please, it's only the first day."

"I'll tell you what, you can talk, but on the condition that everyone, I mean *every single person in the room*, keeps quiet for one whole minute."

Teacher still had to show he was strong. To prove what? The children succeeded in remaining silent on the third attempt; they proved they could listen. Triumphant, I tried more.

"Now let's try for thirty seconds to think of one color."

"You said we could talk!"

"My head hurts, I don't want to think anymore."

"It's not fair!"

It wasn't. A solid mass of resistance coagulated, frustrating my need to command. The children would not be moved.

"You're right, I'm sorry. Take ten minutes to talk and then we'll get back to work."

For ten minutes the children talked quietly; there was time to prepare for the last half hour. I looked over my lesson plans: Reading, 9 to 10; Social Studies, 10 to 10:45, etc., etc. How absurd academic time was in the face of the real day. *Where to look?*

"You like it here, Mr. Kohl."

I looked up into a lovely sad face.

"What do you mean?"

"I mean do you like it here, Mr. Kohl, what are you teaching us for?"

What?

"Well, I . . . not now. Maybe you can see me at three and we can talk. The class has to get back to work. All right, everybody back to your seats, get ready to work."

She had her answer and sat down and waited with the rest of the class. They were satisfied with the bargain. Only it was I who failed then; exhausted, demoralized, I only wanted three o'clock to arrive.

"It's almost three o'clock and we don't have much time left."

I dragged the words out, listening only for the bell.

"This is only the first day, and of course we haven't got much done. I expect more from you during the year . . ."

The class sensed the maneuver and fell nervous again.

"Take out your notebooks and open to a clean page. Each day except Friday you'll get homework."

My words weighed heavy and false; it wasn't my voice but some common tyrant or moralizer, a tired old man speaking.

"There are many things I'm not strict about but homework is the one thing I insist upon. In my class *everybody always* does homework. I will check your work every morning. Now copy the assignment I'm putting on the blackboard, and then when you're finished, please line up in the back of the room."

What assignment? What lie now? I turned to the blackboard, groping for something to draw the children closer to me, for something to let them know I cared. *I did care!*

"Draw a picture of your home, the room you live in. Put in all the furniture, the TV, the windows and doors. You don't have to do it in any special way but keep in mind that the main purpose of the picture should be to show someone what your house looks like."

The children laughed, pointed, then a hand rose, a hand I couldn't attach to a body or face. They all looked alike. I felt sad, lonely.

"Do you have to show your house?"

Two boys snickered. *Are there children ashamed to describe their homes?—have I misunderstood again?* The voice in me answered again.

"Yes."

"I mean . . . what if you can't draw, can you let someone help you?"

"Yes, if you can explain the drawing yourself."

"What if your brother can't draw?"

"Then write a description of your apartment. Remember, *everybody always* does homework in my classes."

The class copied the assignment and lined up, first collecting everything they'd brought with them. The room was as empty as it was at eight o'clock. Tired, weary of discipline, authority, school itself, I rushed the class down the stairs and into the street in some unacknowledged state of disorder.

The bedlam on 119th Street, the stooped and fatigued teachers smiling at each other and pretending *they* had had no trouble with their kids relieved my isolation. I smiled too, assumed the comfortable pose of casual success, and looked down into a mischievous face, the possessed eyes of the child who had thought I would hit him, Alvin, who kindly and thoughtfully said: "Mr. Kohl, how come you let us out so early today? We just had lunch . . ."

Crushed, I walked dumbly away, managed to reach the bus stop and make my way home. As my weariness dissolved, I only remembered of that first day Alvin and the little girl who asked if I liked being "there."

The books arrived the next morning before class. There were twenty-five arithmetic books from one publisher and twelve from another, but in the entire school there was no complete set of sixth-grade arithmetic books. A few minutes spent checking the first day's arithmetic assignment showed me that it wouldn't have mattered if a full set had existed, since half the class had barely mastered multiplication, and only one child, Grace, who had turned in a perfect paper, was actually ready for sixth-grade arithmetic. It was as though, encouraged to believe that the children couldn't to arithmetic by judging from the school's poor results in teaching it, the administration decided not to waste money on arithmetic books, thereby creating a vicious circle that made it even more impossible for the children to learn.

The situation was almost as dismal in reading—the top class of the sixth grade had more than half its members reading on fourth-grade level and only five or six children actually able to read through a sixth-grade book. There were two full sets of sixth-grade readers available, however, and after the arithmetic situation I was grateful for anything. Yet accepting these readers put me as a teacher in an awkward position. The books were flat and uninteresting. They only presented what was pleasant in life, and even then limited the pleasant to what was publicly accepted as such. The people in the stories were all middle-class and their simplicity, goodness, and self-confidence were unreal. I couldn't believe in this foolish ideal and knew that anyone who had ever bothered to observe human life couldn't believe it. Yet I had to teach it, and through it make reading important and necessary. Remembering the children, their anxiety and hostility, the alternate indifference, suspicion, and curiosity they approached me with, knowing how essential it is to be honest with children, I felt betrayed by the books into hypocrisy. No hypocrite can win the respect of children, and without respect one cannot teach.

One of the readers was a companion to the social studies unit on the growth of the United States and was full of stories about family fun in a Model T Ford, the first wireless radio in town, and the joys of wealth and progress. The closest the book touched upon human emotion or the real life of real children was in a story which children accepted a new invention before their parents did, even though the adults laughed at the children. Naturally, everything turned out happily.

The other reader was a miscellany of adventure stories (no human violence or antagonists allowed, just treasure hunts, animal battles, close escapes), healthy poems (no love except for mother, father, and nature), and a few harmless myths (no Oedipus, Electra, or Prometheus). I also managed to get twenty dictionaries in such bad condition that the probability of finding any word still intact was close to zero.

The social studies texts (I could choose from four or five) praised industrial America in terms that ranged from the enthusiastic to the exorbitant. Yet the growth of modern industrial society is fascinating, and it was certainly possible to supplement the text with some truth. I decided to work with what was given me and attempt to teach the sixth-grade curriculum as written in the New York City syllabus, ignoring as long as possible the contradictions inherent in such a task.

The class confronted me, surrounded by my motley library, at nine that second morning and groaned.

"Those phoney books?"

"We read them already, Mr. Kohl."

"It's a cheap, dirty, bean school."

My resolve weakened, and I responded out of despair.

"Let me put it straight to you. These are the only books here. I have no more choice than you do and I don't like it any better. Let's get through them and maybe by then I'll figure out how to get better ones."

The class understood and accepted the terms. As soon as the books were distributed the first oral reading lesson began. Some children volunteered eagerly, but most of the class tried not to be seen. The children who read called out the words, but the story was lost. I made the lesson as easy as possible by helping children who stumbled, encouraging irrelevant discussion, and not letting any child humiliate himself. It was bad enough that more than half the class had to be forced to use books they couldn't read.

The lesson ended, and a light-skinned boy raised his hand.

"Mr. Kohl, remember that ten minutes you gave us yesterday? Couldn't we talk again now? We're tired after all this reading."

I wasn't sure how to take Robert's request. My initial feeling was that he was taking advantage of me and trying to waste time. I felt, along with the official dogma, that no moment in school should be wasted—it must all be preplanned and structured. Yet why shouldn't it be "wasted"? Hadn't most of the class wasted years in school, not merely moments?

I remembered my own oppressive school days in New York City, moving from one subject to another without a break, or at most, with a kind teacher letting us stand and stretch in unison; I remember Reading moving into Social Studies into Arithmetic. How hateful it seemed then. Is it a waste to pause, talk, or think between subjects? As a teacher I, too, needed a break.

"You're right, Robert, I'm tired, too. Everybody can take ten minutes to do what you want, and then we'll move on to social studies."

The class looked fearful and amazed—freedom in school, do what you want? For a few minutes they sat quietly and then slowly began to talk. Two children walked to the piano and asked me if they could try. I said of course, and three more children joined them. It seemed so easy; the children relaxed. I watched closely and suspiciously, realizing that the tightness with time that exists in the elementary school has nothing to do with the quantity that must be learned or the children's needs. It represents the teacher's fear of loss of control and is nothing but a weapon used to weaken the solidarity and opposition of the children that too many teachers unconsciously dread.

After the ten minutes I tried to bring the children back to work. They resisted, tested my determination. I am convinced that a failure of will at that moment would have been disastrous. It was necessary to compel the children to return to work, not due to my "authority" or "control" but because they were expected to honor the bargain. They listened, and at that moment I learned something of the toughness, consistency, and ability to demand and give respect that enables children to listen to adults without feeling abused or brutalized and, therefore, becoming defiant.

I tried How We Became Modern America again. It was hopeless. The children acted as if they didn't know the difference between rivers, islands, oceans, and lakes; between countries, cities, and continents; between ten years and two centuries. Either their schooling had been hopeless or there was a deeper reason I did not yet understand underlying the children's real or feigned ignorance. One thing was clear, however, they did not want to hear about the world and, more specifically, modern America from me. The atmosphere was dull as I performed to an absent audience.

"The steam engine was one of the most important . . . Alvin, what was I talking about?"

"Huh?"

He looked dull, his face heavy with resignation, eyes vacant, nowhere . . .

The morning ended on that dead note, and the afternoon began with an explosion. Alvin, Maurice, and Michael came dashing in, chased by a boy from another class who stuck his head and fist in the room, rolled his eyes, and muttered, "Just you wait, Chipmunk."

As soon as he disappeared the three boys broke up.

"Boy, is he dumb. You sure psyched him."

"Wait till tomorrow in the park."

The other children returned and I went up to the three boys and said as openly as I could, "What's up?"

They moved away. Alvin muttered something incomprehensible and looked at the floor. As soon as they reached the corner of the room the laughter began again. Maurice grabbed Michael's glasses and passed them to Alvin. Michael grabbed Alvin's pencil and ran to the back of the room as one of the girls said to me:

"Mr. Kohl, they're bad. You ought to hit them."

Refusing that way out I watched chaos descend once more. Only this time, being more familiar with the faces and feeling more comfortable in the room, I discerned some method in the disorder. Stepping back momentarily from myself, forgetting my position and therefore my need to establish order, I observed the children and let them show me something of themselves. There were two clusters of boys and three of girls. There were also loners watching shyly or hovering eagerly about the peripheries of the groups. One boy sat quietly drawing, oblivious to the world. As children entered the room they would go straight to one group or another, hover, or walk over to the boy who was drawing and watch silently. Of the two boys' groups, one was whispering conspiratorially while the other, composed of Alvin, Maurice, Michael, and two others, was involved in some wild improbable mockery of tag. Alvin would tag himself and run. If no one was watching him he'd stop, run up to one of the others, tag himself again, and the chase was on—for a second. The pursuer would invariably lose interest, tag himself, and the roles would be switched until they all could collide laughing, slapping palms, and chattering. The other group paid no attention—they were talking of serious matters. They looked bigger, older, and tougher.

There wasn't time to observe the girls. The tag game seemed on the verge of violence and, frightened, I stepped back into the teacherly role, relaxed and strengthened with my new knowledge of the class, and asked in a strong quiet voice for the homework. I felt close to the children—observing them, my fear and self-consciousness were forgotten for a moment. It was the right thing. The girls went to their desks directly while the boys stopped awkwardly and made embarrassed retreats to their seats.

I am convinced that the teacher must be an observer of his class as well as a member of it. He must look at the children, discover how they relate to each other and the room around them. There must be enough free time and activity for the teacher to discover the children's human preferences. Observing children at play and mischief is an invaluable source of knowledge about them—about leaders and groups, fear, courage, warmth, isolation. Teachers consider the children's gym or free play time their free time, too, and usually turn their backs on the children when they have most to learn from them.

I went through a year of teacher training at Teachers College, Columbia, received a degree, and heard no mention of how to observe children, nor even a suggestion that it was of value. Without learning to observe children and thereby knowing something of the people one is living with five hours a day, the teacher resorts to routine and structure for protection. The class is assigned seats, the time is planned down to the minute, subject follows subject—all to the exclusion of human variation and invention.

I witnessed the same ignorance of the children in a private school I once visited, only it was disguised by a progressive egalitarian philosophy. The teachers and students were on a first-name basis; together they chose the curriculum and decided upon the schedule. Yet many of the teachers knew no more of their classes than the most rigid public-school teachers. They knew only of their pupils and their mutual relationships in contexts where the teacher was a factor. It was clear to me, watching the children when the teacher left the room, that the children's preferences "for the teachers" were not the same as their human preferences (which most likely changed every week). That is not an academic point, for observation can open the teacher to his pupils' changing needs, and can often allow him to understand and utilize internal dynamic adjustments that the children make in relation to each other, rather than impose authority from without.

After the first few days of the year, my students are free to move wherever they want in the room, my role being arbiter when someone wants to move into a seat whose occupant does not want to vacate or when health demands special consideration. I have never bothered to count the number of continual, self-selected seat changes in my classes, yet can say that they never disrupted the fundamental fabric of the class. Rather, they provided internal adjustments and compensations that avoided many possible disruptions. Children fear chaos and animosity. Often they find ways of adjusting to difficult and sensitive situations (when free to) before their teachers are aware they exist.

Only fourteen of the thirty-six children brought in homework that second afternoon, and twelve of them were girls. One of the boys, I noticed, was the quiet artist. Here was a critical moment that plunged me back into the role of participant and destroyed my objective calm. What was the best reaction to the children's lack of response, especially after I'd been so pompous and adamant about homework the first day? How many of the twenty-two missing homeworks were the result of defiance (perhaps merited), of inability, of shame at what the result might reveal? Was there a simple formula: *Good = do homework* and another *Bad = not do homework?* Or would these formulas themselves negate the honesty and sincerity that could lead the children to find a meaningful life in school? At that moment in the classroom I had no criteria by which to decide and no time to think out my response. It would have been most just to react in thirty-six different ways to the thirty-six different children, but there was no way for me to be most just at that moment. I had to react intuitively and immediately, as anyone in a classroom must. There is never time to plot every tactic. A child's responses are unpredictable, those of groups of children even more so, unless through being brutalized and bullied they are made predictable. When a teacher claims he knows exactly what will happen in his class, exactly how the children will behave and function, he is either lying or brutal.

That means that the teacher must make mistakes. Intuitive, immediate responses can be right and magical, can express understanding that the teacher doesn't know he has, and lead to reorganizations of the teacher's relationship with his class. But they can also be peevish and petty, or merely stupid and cruel. Consistency of the teacher's response is frequently desirable, and the word "consistency" is a favorite of professors at teacher training institutions. Consistency can sometimes prevent discovery and honesty. More, consistency of response is a function of the consistency of a human personality, and that is, at best, an unachievable ideal.

I've said many stupid, unkind things in my classroom, and insulted children when they threatened me too much. On the other hand, I've also said some deeply affecting things, moved children to tears by unexpected kindnesses, and made them happy with praise that flowed unashamedly. I've wanted to be consistent and have become more consistent. That seems the most that is possible, a slow movement toward consistency tempered by honesty. The teacher has to live with his own mistakes, as his pupils have to suffer them. Therefore, the teacher must learn to perceive them as mistakes and find direct or indirect ways to acknowledge his awareness of them and of his fallibility to his pupils.

The ideal of the teacher as a flawless moral exemplar is a devilish trap for the teacher as well as a burden for the child. I once had a pupil, Narciso, who was overburdened by the perfection of adults, and especially, of teachers. His father demanded he believe

in this perfection as he demanded Narciso believe in and acquiesce to absolute authority. It was impossible to approach the boy
for his fear and deference. I had terrified him. He wouldn't work or
disobey. He existed frozen in silence. One day he happened to pass
by a bar where some other teachers and I were sitting having
beers. He was crushed; *teachers don't do that*. He believed so much
in what his father and some teachers wanted him to believe that
his world collapsed. He stayed away from school for a while, then
returned. He smiled and I returned the smile. After a while he was
at ease in class and could be himself, delightful and defiant, sometimes brilliant, often lazy, an individual reacting in his unique way
to what happened in the classroom.

It is only in the world of Dick and Jane, Tom and Sally, that the
always right and righteous people exist. In a way, most textbooks,
and certainly the ones I had to use in the sixth grade, protect the
pure image of the teacher by showing the child that somewhere in
the ideal world that inspires books all people are as "good" as the
teacher is supposed to be! It is not insignificant that it is teachers
and not students who select school readers, nor that, according to
a friend of mine who edits school texts, the books were written for
the teachers and not for children for this very reason.

Of course the teacher is a moral exemplar—an example of all
the confusion, hypocrisy, and indecision, of all the mistakes, as
well as the triumphs, of moral man. The children see all this, whatever they pretend to see. Therefore, to be more than an example,
to be an educator—someone capable of helping lead the child
through the labyrinth of life—the teacher must be honest to the
children about his mistakes and weaknesses; he must be able to say
that he is wrong or sorry, that he hadn't anticipated the results
of his remarks and that he regretted them, or hadn't understood
what a child meant. It is the teacher's struggle to be moral that ex-
cites his pupils; it is honesty, not rightness, that moves children.

I didn't know all of this when I decided that second day to forget the twenty-two undone homeworks and remark that the first
homework wasn't that important. I was just feeling my way.

I accepted the twelve homeworks that were completed without ceremony or praise. At that moment it seemed as wrong to overpraise the children who did the work as to degrade those who didn't, since I didn't understand why they did it. They may have done it because they yielded to my intimidation. I let the issue pass, and having the attention of the class, moved on to arithmetic, art, a homework assignment . . . everything was fine until it was time to leave. Half the class lined up, ready and anxious to leave. The other half contrived disorder and puzzled me by their halfhearted fights. Another game of tag-myself erupted. The children who wanted to leave turned on the others, the atmosphere was restless. I wanted to leave too, turned angry, and threatened.

"I'm going to keep you here until you're in line and quiet."

Three voices answered, "Good," threats were passed, and losing my resolve, I ignored the disorder and led the children down into the chaotic street.

I tried for the next six weeks to use the books assigned and teach the official curriculum. It was hopeless. The class went through the readers perfunctorily, refused to hear about modern America, and were relieved to do arithmetic—mechanical, uncharged—as long as nothing new was introduced. For most of the day the atmosphere in the room was stifling. The children were bored and restless, and I felt burdened by the inappropriateness of what I tried to teach. It was so dull that I thought as little as the children and began to despair. Listening to myself on the growth of urban society, realizing that no one else was listening, that though words were pronounced the book was going unread, I found myself vaguely wondering about the children.

But there were moments. The ten-minute breaks between lessons grew until, in my eyes, the lessons were secondary. Everything important happening in the classroom happened between lessons.

First, it was the piano, Leverne wanting to play, picking up a few tunes, teaching them to other children, to Charisse and Desiree, to Grace, Pamela, and Maurice. Then it was the six of them asking me to teach them to read music and their learning how in one afternoon.

There was Robert Jackson. I took time to look at his art, observe him working. He was good, accurate; he thought in terms of form and composition. Seeing I was interested, other children told me of Robert's reputation, and the neighborhood legend about him—when he was four, his mother gave him a pencil as a pacifier, and he began to draw. They told of the money he made drawing, of his ability to draw "anything."

I watched the girls gossiping, talking about records, parties, boys. After a few days, talk of the summer was exhausted. The children began wandering about the room looking for things to do. They seemed relaxed and eager to work then, though bored and restless during lessons. Unwilling to lose this will and energy I brought checkers and chess to school as well as magazines and books. I developed the habit of taking five minutes in the morning to describe what I had brought in. I sketched the history of chess and told the class about the wise man who asked a king, as reward for a favor, for the number of grains of wheat that resulted from placing one on the first square of a checkerboard and then progressively doubling the amount until the whole board was occupied. I commented that the king went broke, and that afternoon, to my surprise, three children told me I was right and showed me how far they'd gotten trying to figure out how much wheat the king owed the wise man.

The checkers provided quite a lesson for me. Only four of the boys in the class knew how to play. Two of them grabbed one set while another set was grabbed by Sam, a tall, respected boy who nevertheless could not play checkers. He sat down with one boy who could play and managed a game with the help of the fourth boy who could play. Within a few days all of the boys knew how to play. The boys also learned that the laws of physical dominance in the class didn't coincide with the laws of checker dominance, and learned to accept this. Over a period of a few weeks the rights of winners and losers were established and respected.

During the first few days there were fights, the board was frequently knocked to the floor, and the game was called "cheap" and "phoney." But nothing very serious or extended could develop in a ten- or fifteen-minute period, and whenever things seemed a bit tight I quickly ended the break and the class returned to "work." After a week six or seven boys retained their interest in checkers while three began to explore chess. They grabbed the game, asked me to show them how to set up the men and make the moves, and then they took over. Within a week, two more boys had joined them in developing an idiosyncratic version of chess (when they forgot the moves they were too proud to ask me) which satisfied them very well.

Leverne stuck to the piano and Robert drew while several other boys kept searching the room for something to do. One of them, Ralph, showed me a copy of the *New York Enquirer* one day and asked me what I thought about it. I facetiously remarked that he could probably do better and stick closer to the truth. Two days later he asked me what I'd meant, and struggling to remember what I'd said, I came up with the idea that he report what went on in his neighborhood. He looked at me strangely and asked me if I meant it. I said, "Sure," and he sat down and wrote, though it took him nearly a month to show me what he was doing. The girls were more interested in magazines that I had brought in, and some of them asked me for books.

In retrospect the first few weeks seemed hopeful. I had begun to know the children even though it was in ten-minute snatches; and they had begun to be comfortable with each other and to concentrate on things and move about the class with curiosity instead of hostility. At the time, however, I felt depressed and lonely. The ten-minute periods of some relationship, the occasional sparks of creativity I caught in the children's conversations or in the way they solved problems in their games or social relations, only frustrated me the more. I felt remote, was afraid of wasting the children's time, not confident in my exploration of time in the classroom. Worse, discipline problems developed as the pressure of uninteresting and alien work began to mount over the weeks. Alvin could no longer sit still, he had to be chased; John frequently refused to work altogether; Dennis paused, abstracted, in the middle of something, unable to continue; and Ralph, the boy who wrote in his free time, would walk out of the room, cursing, if I looked harshly toward him. Margie and Carol did their work quickly, then chattered away, oblivious to my commands, demands, pleas . . .

And there was a second line of disorder. Maurice and Michael were ready to follow Alvin; Thomas S., Samuel, and Dennis were ready to follow John. Carol and Margie had their followers too, and Charisse, a charming, brilliant girl, was always on the verge of making an enemy or starting a fight. There were perhaps twelve children who didn't have to be, or couldn't be, defiant.

Each day there were incidents, and ultimately I accepted them as inevitable and impersonal. Alvin's malaise or John's refusal to work were natural responses to an unpleasant environment; not merely in my class but a cumulative school environment which meant nothing more to most of the children than white-adult ignorance and authority.

There are no simple solutions to such discipline problems, and sometimes it is necessary to learn to be patient and indulgent with a child who won't behave or refuses to work. A teacher must believe that such problems exist in his classroom because he hasn't found the right words or the right thing to teach, and not that they lie in the heart of the child. Not every child can be reached, and there are some children uninterested in learning anything; but they are very few, and even with them one doesn't know.

I volunteered to take care of science supplies for the school, mentioning casually that I noticed that there were some in the closet. The principal gave me the closet key with a smile that said, "Anytime you want to do more work, come to me. Who knows what you could find hidden in the other closets. . . ." Then he asked, truly puzzled, "Do you think those children will get any-thing out of it?"

We had the equipment, and that was the important thing at the moment. The boys went through many experiments, put to-gether elaborate combinations of bells, buzzers, and lights, and contrived a burglar-alarm system for the classroom. They made a fire extinguisher and invisible ink. After a week they were joined by several girls who took over the equipment as the boys broke away to help Robert with the Parthenon. The groups formed and re-formed as projects developed and were abandoned. It was good to see the children, once so wild over a simple game of chess, move freely about the room, exploring socially and intellectually. Still there were moments of doubt and anxiety; it was difficult to see where this classroom of mine was going.

As usual the children led me. I have found one of the most valuable qualities a teacher can have is the ability to perceive and build upon the needs his pupils struggle to articulate through their every reaction. For this he needs antennae and must constantly work upon attuning himself to the ambience of the classroom. To the mastery of observation of children must be added the more difficult skill of observing his own effect upon the class, something only partially done at best. But if the easy guides of a standard cur-riculum and authoritarian stance are to be discarded any clues arising from actual experience in the classroom are welcome.

I had brought many things from home for the children; now they brought things for me to learn from. Sam brought in a Moms Mabley record and from the other children's reaction it was obvi-ous that she was "in." I had never heard of her and asked the class who she was. They all volunteered information: that she was an-cient, funny, and nice, that she liked young boys and kids, that people lined up on 125th Street whenever she was at the Apollo Theater, that she sounded on people in the audience.

Sam shyly suggested that we listen to the record instead of doing reading, and I reluctantly agreed. It was still difficult for me to dis-card my schedule with confidence. There was another problem—I explained to the class that there was no phonograph in the room or, as far as I knew, in the school.

Thomas S. and Dennis jumped up, asked me to write a note saying I wanted to borrow a record player, and disappeared with the note, only to reappear in five minutes with a machine. They knew the exact distribution of all the hidden and hoarded supplies in the school, and I learned to trust their knowledge over official statements of what was available.

We listened to Moms, the class explaining the jokes, translating some of her dialect for me. It pleased them to be listened to. After that we kept a phonograph in the room, and the children brought in the latest records. We listened to them together at the end of the morning or the afternoon. I transcribed the words and every once in a while put them on the blackboard and discussed what the songs were all about. One particularly interesting song was "Do You Love Me?" by Barry Gordy, Jr.

I asked the kids if it really was that important to be able to dance. They replied in veiled terms that I couldn't understand. I pushed them. Why couldn't I understand? Dancing is a simple social phenomenon, it has to do with parties and popularity, not the soul. . . .

That hit something direct. One of the boys said, just loud enough for me to hear, that dancing *was* a soul thing. Others took up the argument, it was a way of being together, of expressing yourself when you were alone, of feeling strong when everything was wrong, of feeling alive in a dead world.

"Besides, Mr. Kohl, they don't only mean dancing. That's a way of saying you can't do nothing, that you're weak. Dancing is kind of, you know, like a symbol."

Alvin explained it to me. It was only a step from there to letting the kids actually dance in class. I started on Friday afternoons, and later let the kids dance when the afternoon work was done. At first only the girls were interested. Half of them would dance (it was The Wobble at that time), while the others would read or talk, or even begin their homework. The boys would hover about the dancers, joking, moving ever so slightly with the music, pushing Michael and Maurice into the Wobble line, urging them to continue the satire of the girls' movements that they were performing in a corner. Once in a while everyone danced—I even tried to overcome my leaden-footed self-consciousness and take a few steps, but my soul wasn't free enough.

Music became an integral part of the classroom. The children brought in their records; I responded with my own. One morning I put twenty-five records ranging from blues and Fats Waller through Thelonious Monk and Coltrane to Mozart and Beethoven on top of the phonograph. During the morning breaks the kids explored freely, and when the music began to interest some individuals enough, I brought in biographies of the composers, pictures of the musicians. We talked in small groups during social studies of chain gangs, field music, modern jazz, rock and roll, child prodigies, anything that came up. A dialogue between the children and myself was developing.

It deepened quickly. Alvin and Ralph decided to wait for me at eight o'clock and spend an hour in the classroom before the class arrived. They were soon joined by Maurice, Michael, Reginald, Pamela, and Brenda W. At one time or another during the year every child went through a phase of coming early. The only limitations I had to impose on this were forced upon me by other teachers who didn't want to be bothered by children so early in the morning and complained to the administration.

I would arrive at the school at eight. Several of the children would be waiting and we would walk the five flights up to the room. One of the boys would take my briefcase, another the keys. Once in the room the children went their own ways. Maurice and Michael went to the phonograph, Alvin to his latest project with Robert Jackson. The girls would play jacks or wash the boards. Grace explored the books on my desk. Every once in a while one of the children would come up to my desk and ask a question or tell me something. The room warmed up to the children, got ready for the day. At first the questions were simple, irrelevant.

"Mr. Kohl, what's today's date?"

"Where is Charles this morning?"

Then there was some testing.

"Mr. Kohl, when are you going to be absent?"

"Will you come back here next year?"

By the end of October a few children were coming to my desk in the morning and saying things that nothing in my life prepared me to understand or respond to.

"Mr. Kohl, the junkies had a fight last night. They cut this girl up bad."

"Mr. Kohl, I couldn't sleep last night, they was shouting and screaming until four o'clock."

"I don't go down to the streets to play, it's not safe."

"Mr. Kohl, those cops are no good. They beat up on this kid for nothing last night."

I listened, hurt, bruised by the harshness of the children's world. There was no response, no indignation or anger of mine, commensurate to what the children felt. Besides, it was relief they wanted, pronouncement of the truth, acceptance of it in a classroom which had become important to them. I could do nothing about the facts, therefore my words were useless. But through listening, the facts remained open and therefore placed school in the context of the children's real world.

At eight o'clock on October 22, Alvin pushed Ralph up to my desk. Ralph handed me "The Rob-Killing of Liebowitz," and retreated.

Last night on 17 St. Liebowitz collected the rent. They told him not to come himself but he came for many years. The junkies got him last night. He wouldn't give them the money so they shot him and took it. They was cops and people runny all over roofs and the streets.

There were people from the news and an ambulance took Liebowitz.

I read Ralph's article to the class and asked them if it were true. There was an awkward silence, then Neomia said with bitterness:
"If you don't believe it you can look in the *Daily News*."
"Mr. Kohl, you don't know what it's like around here."
The others agreed, but when I pressed the class to tell me, silence returned. The more I tried to get the class to talk the dumber the children acted, until they finally denied that there was any truth in Robert's article whatever. The topic was too charged for public discussion; it somehow had to be made private, between each individual child and myself. After all, not everybody saw the same things, and worse perhaps, if things were so bad it would be natural for some of the children to be afraid. So I asked the class to write, as homework in the privacy of their apartments, and tell me what their block was like, what they felt about it. The papers were not to be marked or shown to anybody else in the class. If anybody objected, he didn't have to do the assignment. This was probably the first time in their school lives that the children wrote to communicate, and the first sense they had of the possibilities of their own writing.

The next evening I read the responses.

Neomia   WHAT A BLOCK!
My block is the most terrible block I've ever seen. There are at lease 25 or 30 narcartic people in my block. The cops come around there and tries to act bad but I bet inside of them they are as scared as can be. They even had in the papers that this block is the worst block, not in Manhattan but in New York City. In the summer they don't do nothing except shooting, stabbing and fighting. They hang all over the stoops and when you say excuse me to them they hear you but they just don't feel like moving. Some times they make me so mad that I feel like slaping them and stuffing and bag of garbage down their throats. Theres only one policeman who can handle these people and we all call him "Sunny." When he come around in his cop car the people run around the corners, and he wont let

anyone sit on the stoops. If you don't believe this story come around some time and you'll find out.

Marie

My block is the worse block you ever saw people getting killed or stabbed men and women in building's taking dope. And when the police come around the block the block be so clean that nobody will get hurt. There's especially one police you even beat woman you can't even stand on your own stoop he'll chase you off. And sometimes the patrol wagon comes around and pick up al the dope addicts and one day they picked up this man and when his wife saw him and when she went to tell the police that that's her husband they just left so she went to the police station and they let him go. You can never trust anyone around my block you even get robbed when the children in my building ask me to come down stairs I say no because you don't know what would happen. Only sometimes I come down stairs not all the time.

Sonia   THE STORY ABOUT MY BLOCK

My block is dirty and it smell terrible.

The children picks fights. And it hardly have room to play, its not a very long thing to write about, but if you were living there you won't want to stay there no longer, it have doopedics and gabbage pan is spill on the side walk and food is on the ground not everyday but sometimes children make fire in the backyard. on the stoop is dirty. I go out to play that the End about My block.

Ralph   MY NEIGHBORHOOD

I live on 117 street, between Madison and 5th avenue. All the bums live around here. But the truth is they don't live here they just hang around the street. All the kids call it "Junky's Paradise." Because there is no cops to stop them. I wish that the cops would come around and put all the bums out of the block and put them in jail all their life. I would really like it very much if they would improve my neighborhood. I don't even go outside to play because of them. I just play at the center or someplace else.

Gail   MY BLOCK

My block is sometimes noisy and sometimes quiet when its noisy children and grownups are out side listening to the boys playing the steel drums or there's a boy who got hit by a car or something. When the block is quiet, there is a storm, raining or snowing and people don't come out side. Farther down the block near Park Avenue, some of the houses are not kept clean.

There's a lot right next to a building and there's a lot of trash, you can see rats running back and forth. The Sanitation Department cleans it every week, but it just gets dirty again because people throw garbage out the windows. From Madison Ave. to about the middle of the block the houses are kept clean. The back yards are keep swept and the stoops are clean. I like my building and block.

Charles

My block is a dirty crumby block.

The day after we talked about them. I had asked for the truth, and it presented its ugly head in the classroom, yet I didn't know what to do about it. That was all I could say to the children—that I was moved, angry, yet as powerless to change things as they were. I remembered How We Became Modern America, the books I couldn't use, and felt dumb, expressionless—how else can one put up with such lies of progress, prosperity, and cheerful co-operation when we do face problems? The next day the children wrote of how they would change things if they could.

Neomia

If I could change my block I would stand on Madison Ave and throw nothing but Teargas in it. I would have all the people I liked to get out of the block and then I would become very tall and have big hands and with my big hands I would take all of the narcartic people and pick them up with my hand and throw them in the nearest river and Oceans. I would go to some of those old smart alic cops and throw them in the Oceans and Rivers too. I would let the people I like move into the projects so they could tell their friends that they live in a decent block. If I could do this you would never see 117 st again.

Kathleen   MY BLOCK

If I could change my block I would have new house but in it I would have all the bums take out of it. There would be garden where I live. There would be some white people live there we would have all colors not just Negro. There would be 7 room apt. There be low rent for the poor family. The poor family would have the same thing as the average or rich family have. There would be club for the boys and girls. There would be place where the Old could come. Where the young can share there problem.

Thomas C.

Well I would like to change my block into a play street, first I'd take all the junkies out the block and take the parking cars out the block and make whaw that everyman put their cars in a garage at nights. Because too many children get hit by cars and make all the buildings neat and clean with stream and hot and cold water.

Anastasia

The very first thing that I would like to do to change my block if I could, put up a no litering sign to keep away stange people who hang aroung the steps. Nexs I would have less garbage containers on the sidewalks, expecially those that are uncovered because they are unsightly and unhealthy, and last but at least. I would make a carfew at least 5 p.m. for ander age children to be up the corners, sidewalks, and if they are not, hold their parents severly responsible for any harm that befails them.

Charles

If I could do anything to chang my block tear down the buildings on both sides. And have a school on one side and a center on the other. Inside the center there would be a swimming pool inside and also a gym. And outside a softball field and also four baskball courts.

Sonia
if I could of change my block I would make it cleaner no gabbage pans open and falling down and not so many fights and don't let it have dead animals in the street.

How we became modern America, how we became modern man—that was our problem, my problem to teach, but where to start, at what moment in history does one say, "Ah, here's where it all began"? How could the children get some saving perspective on the mad chaotic world they existed in, some sense of the universality of struggle, the possibility of revolution and change, and the strength to persist? That, if anything, was my challenge as a teacher—it was spelled out before me unambiguously. Could I find anything in human history and the human soul that would strengthen the children and save them from despair?

I had reached this point by the end of October, a few days before Halloween.

Halloween in Harlem is frightening and exciting. I remained at school until four o'clock that afternoon cleaning the classroom and thinking. Things seemed painfully slow, the children distant. Darkness seemed to be setting in everywhere; maybe it was the coming of winter, I don't know, but I was on the verge of tears. Another beautiful morning, then a chaotic hostile afternoon. My energy disappeared and at that moment it didn't seem possible to continue all the way to June. The silence of the room comforted me, however. I walked about picking up papers, looking at the desk tops and scratches: "Alvin is a chipmunk," "Michael's mother's best friend is a roach," "Margie likes Carol"—it was good to discover such underground vitality in the class. The children's confounding contradictory presence was still there. I found myself smiling, thinking of the next day, of my fiftieth new beginning of the year. Things didn't seem so bad. I wanted to be home planning and preparing for the next day, so I packed my books and left.

The street was something else. Painted creatures streaking up and down, stockings full of flour crashing on heads, chests, missiles descending from rooftops, wild laughter, children fighting, tumbling over a world they owned for half a day.

I remembered my own sedate Halloweens—planned trick-or-treating and plastic masks. Suddenly Sylvia ran up, threatened me with a stocking. I fumbled for a quarter which she threw to some little children. They dove for it as she bumped me and ran off. Someone else chalked my coat—it was Michael, or maybe Maurice—I moved as quickly as possible to the bus stop, changed my mind and took a cab home. My heart was pounding; the wildness frightened me. But by the time the cab reached 90th Street I was jealous. No mask or ritual occasion had ever set me free.

After dinner I had to be on the streets again. It was five flights down. I reached the landing of the second floor lost in a fantasy of Harlem Halloweens. There were people talking on the ground floor, a couple saying good night to someone who had moved in, a female face. I realized how lonely I was; wanted to wait until the couple had left and then trick-or-treat myself.

They left, the door was closed and I stared at it, paused, then decided that if a light was still on after I had a beer I would knock. I returned after six beers and it was on. To be true to the children and myself, I knocked. That was how I met Judy, my wife.

We talked well into the night, two months of days with 6-1 poured out of me, the anguish and the hope, my own uncertainty and my confidence. All of the contradictions that lived in my classroom were articulated for the first time. I showed her the children's writing, the ridiculous textbooks I had to use. Then, after it had all tumbled out, I could look at her and try to discover who she was.

We talked of college, Harvard and Chatham, of how distant it seemed. We had both been to Europe; she had just returned though I had been back for several years. I remembered that once an academic career in philosophy seemed all that was open to me; remembered dreading spending my life at a university, reading, pretending to be interested in what I was doing. Judy talked of herself. I don't remember exactly what she said—at that moment in my life I felt the strength to fall in love, and though it happened more slowly than that, a life for the two of us began that Halloween. I was momentarily freed of my obsession with school, and when, after we parted that night, I thought about the children, it was with a freshness I hadn't known for weeks. Things began to fit together; it gradually became clear what had to be taught to the children.

There was no other place to start than at the beginning, before so-called civilized man had already built decay into his "eternal" works. We had to begin with man just emerging as Homo sapiens, and with the growth of civilization in its birthplaces—Africa and Asia. Since I had to teach the children I had to learn myself. My education, like most in the West, went no further back than Greece. Egypt, Mesopotamia, India, China—thousands of years earlier, yet no less sophisticated or, it may turn out, significant to the history of modern man—were ignored. History for years has been arbitrarily limited in schools in the United States to European and post-Columbian American history. This gives one a false perspective on the development of man, one precariously close to a white perspective.

That year I did a lot of probing and research, tracing Greek myths to earlier African and Asiatic sources, discovering the wonders of Sumer and Akkad, of the early Indian kingdoms and the Egyptian dynasties. As this whole new world opened for me I shared it with the children in class. Other teachers thought there was something ludicrous in researching to teach at an elementary level. They advised me to find a text and keep one lesson ahead.

The one-lesson-ahead morality is what makes so many elementary school classes dull and uninspiring. The teacher doesn't understand much of what he is teaching, and worse, doesn't care that he doesn't understand. How can the children be expected to be alert, curious, and excited when the teacher is so often bored?

The need for elementary teachers who are serious-thinking adults, who explore and learn while they teach, who know that to teach young children mathematics, history, or literature isn't to empty these subjects of content or complexity but to reduce and present them in forms which are accurate, honest, and open to development and discovery, and therefore require subtle understanding and careful work, cannot be exaggerated.

As I learned early history, there was a text for the class that did make my work easier. Through some ironic chance, P.S. 103, with no complete set of arithmetic books and barely enough American history books, did have one set of forty-five new social studies books that started with the "cave man" and went through to modern man. Copies of the book were spread throughout the fifth and sixth grades, three or four per room, as part of the miscellaneous collection of obsolete or irrelevant textbooks that passed for class libraries. Once again, making judicious use of Thomas and Dennis, I managed to piece together the full set of books for my class.

As a framework around which to build a history of man's social and cultural life the book wasn't bad, yet it was so vast and ambitious—the entire history of mankind in two hundred illustrated pages. I had to select and elaborate, create a focus and perspective for the class. I also had to let them know it was *my* focus and that there were any number of other ways to look at the same events and facts. One could look at "progress," at artistic creativity, invention, power . . . I wanted to look at the internal and external conditions of human existence that gave rise to human inequalities, at the attempts that have been made to rectify them and the degree to which certain inequalities may be inevitable. I wanted the children to see themselves in the perspective of history, to know the changes of fortune, of the balance of wealth and power, that have constituted history, and of the equally real change of the oppressed into the oppressor. I wanted them to be able to persist, revolt, and change things in our society and yet not lose their souls in the process.

It was the most romantic and idealistic thing I ever attempted and the one I believed in the most. I am not so idealistic or romantic now. My recollections of 6-1 are tinged with bitterness and too clear knowledge of the present and what I failed to give the children, what I couldn't give them. Yet the effort was worth it. Robert Jackson and Alvin remember what we learned, however remote it is from their present lives; other kids remember too, Michael and Ralph, Dennis, Pamela and Grace, the ones I've spoken to recently. They remember, but that year is remote. In the excitement of living through that year I forgot what a short time a year is in a lifetime of trouble.

That's now another story. Forty-five years ago I worried about the textbook. It presented history as an increasingly successful and thoroughly inevitable movement toward the present and expressed a hopelessly dated and unrealistic faith in "history's" capacity to solve human problems satisfactorily. Events and cultures were "important" only as they related to the successes of mid-twentieth century America (meaning the United States of America and blithely omitting Canada and Latin America). In the book there was no sense of uncertainty or indecision, of the complexity of understanding historical events and the shifting perspective of the present. Its every page seemed to say, We are over the hump, things are fine, we are rational. There was no humility or depth in its pages—it presented Greece without slaves or passion, all Apollo, no Dionysus; Rome without debauch or greed; industrial and urban society without exploitation or slums. The children were firmly expected to learn that the way the book presented history was *the* way it had happened. There was but one way the past could be viewed and that was as a moralistic justification of our present life. In a world of rapidly changing perspectives this is a hopeless and dangerous way to teach history.

For my class it was even more perilous, for if to the United States' two hundred years was added the rest of the history of mankind to justify the misery and oppression the children experienced, the inevitability of their situation and the hypocrisy of "history" would only be more fully confirmed. I had to create out of the material in the book a vision of history totally at variance with the book's orientation. It was essential for the children to learn of change and of the needs of the powerful to believe the present eternal. They had to see that one man's "barbarian" was another's "civilized" ideal, one nation's hero another's villain. They had to learn how uneasy and difficult any marriage of history and morals has to be.

There is no point in continuing to document each child's problems and pains. Enough has already been said. The thirty-six children are suffering from the diseases of our society. They are no special cases; there are too many hundreds of thousands like them, lost in indifferent, inferior schools, put on the streets or in prep schools with condescension or cynicism. When I think of my work as a teacher one of the children's favorite myths, that of Sisyphus, continually comes to mind: the man condemned to roll a rock up a mountain only to see it fall back to the bottom, to return to the bottom himself and take up his unending task. With hope and without cynicism, I try to make myself available to my pupils. I believe neither that they will succeed nor that they will fail. I know they will fight, falter, and rise again and again, and that if I have the strength I will be there to rejoice and cry with them, and to add my little weight to easing the burden of being alive in the United States today.

FRESH WATERS ARE EVER FLOWING

From *The Discipline of Hope: Learning from a Lifetime of Teaching*

You cannot step twice into the same river; for fresh waters are ever flowing in on you.

—Heraclitus

Alder Creek

Alder Creek, where the North American continental tectonic plate rubs against the Pacific plate, and the San Andreas fault runs out to the Pacific Ocean, is about five miles north of my home in Point Arena, California. I love to take daily walks along the creek and out to the sea with my golden retriever, Mazi; together we have seen three years of the creek's transformations. Walking along the fault feels dangerous, as if we are daring the earth to split again. At the same time stepping on ground where tectonic plates meet infuses a simple daily experience with a sense of the planet as a whole. Though the creek is not spectacular and there are many more dramatic beaches in our area, a daily visit to Alder Creek has become part of my life, much as writing and teaching have.

Taking daily walks, stealing an hour from work to stretch and simply breathe without an agenda or purpose, is a recent phenomenon in my life. For the first fifteen years I lived in Point Arena I probably walked by the ocean or went to a beach less than once a month, and then only when Judy or my children dragged me or when some guests just had to be taken to see the ocean. I realize now that I had imposed certain limits on my own freedom because of my obsession with getting work done, being "relevant," and "making a difference." It took an encounter with potentially life-threatening high blood pressure to make me realize that everyday speed was a threat to lifelong effectiveness, and that the energy and intensity I wanted to bring to every moment would be better gathered up and parceled out sensitively over time. Walking every day, listening to the ocean, watching the changes the creek lived through in its yearly cycles were not a waste of time that could be better spent writing, teaching, or agitating for change. Rather, this was proportioning time, time to meditate—to ruminate, as one of my high school philosophical heroes, Spinoza, put it, *sub specie aeternitatis*, "under the aspect of eternity," as if one could step out of time and observe all of history, fixed and ended once and for all. From this metaphysical distance everything one does or dreams of doing is final: important on a moral scale and insignificant on the level of ego.

What I love most about Alder Creek is the way it changes *and* remains the same, much the way writing and teaching for me over thirty-five years are always different and the same. As I became a regular at the creek, the words of Heraclitus, another philosopher whose ideas have fascinated me for years, took on an inner life and at times echoed in my head like a trite melody or phrase that's impossible to get out of the mind:

> You cannot step twice into the same river; for fresh waters are ever flowing in on you.
> We step and do not step into the same river; we are and are not.

During the course of a year the mouth of Alder Creek changes from a small, almost stagnant lake that reaches toward but never spills into the Pacific Ocean to a roaring stream that sweeps silt and uprooted trees, sometimes even second-growth redwoods, into the sea, which in turn tosses driftwood and logs back onto the shore or shoots them—and occasionally the bodies of dead birds, seals, or even a dolphin—up the creek during high tide. In the midst of summer there are lovely warm swimming holes nestled in caves created by cracks in the rocks along the north bank of a gently flowing stream. During a winter storm descending from Alaska there is no discernible creek; the ocean rushes over the beach, obliterating it and tossing all the driftwood onto what used to be its far bank. So I walk and do not walk along the same creek over the course of a year.

I first visited Alder Creek about nineteen years ago, during summer. About half a mile upstream, some of the local high school students had made a delightful short film about summer love and one of the actors took me to visit their shooting locale. At that spot the stream flowed gently through some alders and around a gravel bar with a touch of grass growing over it. For years that was my fixed image of the creek. Compared to my present dynamic sense of the creek as the total of all of its cycles, moods, and variations over the course of time, this image is merely a snapshot, one momentary step into an ever-changing environment. And I know that even my daily experiences with the creek are inadequate to grasp the fullness of its being. The tectonic plates move apart three inches a year; the earthquake fault responds to underground pressure; the frequency and intensity of storms hitting the shore vary from year to year; and the silt coming down the creek, which affects its banks and the life it supports, changes according to various conditions upstream ranging from logging and land development to annual rainfall and gravel mining.

The reason I have been so drawn to Alder Creek and obsessed with its changes these days is that now, at sixty, I've been thinking a lot about the paradoxes of identity and change in my own life and work. Like the creek, I've experienced small and easily understood changes, more subtle long-range changes in patterns and strategies, and wild storms that produced major diversions or disruptions. Beyond my own personal changes I've been thinking about the changing faces of the students I work with and the continual shifts in their environment. Most recently I've also been thinking about the dangerous ways in which schooling seeks to suppress organic change and force growth into artificial channels that not only control learning but actually shrivel the imagination and impoverish life.

For many educators, planning for a school year consists of setting a time schedule, fixing on the course sequence, deciding beforehand what to evaluate, and determining the norms of acceptable performance. If you took a cross section of any day of the school year you would find the same structure and the same kinds of activities, especially on a secondary school level. The content might differ according to some present sequence of learning, but the rhythms of the day and the life surrounding learning would be the same. It would be as if the U.S. Army Corps of Engineers, coming in to normalize Alder Creek, enclosed it in a large tunnel, turned its bed into a concrete chute, and set up computer-controlled water flow. The result would be the spiritual and physical death of the creek. A similar dissolution of imagination and spirit takes place in the channeled and constricted learning environments characteristic of most schools.

In the spring of 1986, when my son Josh was a junior in high school, he and a number of his friends certainly felt that way about their own schooling, and they let the staff know it. As troublemakers, they were peculiar. They had no problem with the formal demands of schooling; with a minimum effort—in some cases, *no* visible effort—they did as well as they cared to do in the boring and undemanding environment of Point Arena High School. This gave them the freedom to think about what was wrong with schools without having to agonize over whether they were stupid.

Josh and his friends Abel, Oona, and Sean first focused their critique of the school on "Senior Slave Day." One day toward the end of each school year, the seniors would hold a mock slave auction to raise money for their class trip. Each senior was auctioned off to an underclass person and made to do silly things. Most students and the entire faculty thought it was a harmless, fun event.

"Senior Slave Day" was not unique to Point Arena High. The writer Alice Walker lives in a neighboring school district whose high school did the same thing; she wrote a powerful and angry letter to the local newspaper saying that the event was an insult to African American people and an example of the subtle ways in which school rituals make light of racism and therefore reinforce it. The local school board and principal defended the students, and the event continued for several years, creating rancor and divisiveness in the community.

Josh and his friends took Alice Walker's letter to their principal and student council. The issue created serious debate among the students, a rare and refreshing event. During the event about a dozen students held a protest with the explicit support of Judy, me, and a small number of other parents. Two friends of Josh's who were seniors refused to participate in the auction. For that, the principal told them they had to pay extra to go on the class trip—they hadn't raised their share of slave money. Reuben and Bryce decided to stay home instead of pay up and to this day feel that they did the right thing.

The next year the name but not the structure of the event was changed. It became Senior Service Day and the "services" of the seniors were auctioned off. Josh and his friends became even angrier at the school.

Josh, Abel, Oona, and a friend of theirs, Ian, who had graduated from Point Arena several years before, had a reggae band, which practiced several nights a week in our living room. Both Judy and I loved their music and the energy they put into creating a wonderful sound, so for the most part having the practice in our house was a privilege. During one band break, Oona jokingly complained to me about having to take civics, sociology, and economics during senior year. She said that economics was nothing more than learning how to borrow money, use credit cards, and write checks. Josh added that sociology at Point Arena meant safe-sex and drug and alcohol education. Either Ian or Abel added that civics was all about obeying the law and conforming. Oona, who was a brilliant straight-A student, added that she would love to have a challenging and interesting course for a change, and Abel suggested that I teach sociology, civics, and economics the next year.

It was an intriguing idea. My plan for that year was to write in the mornings and figure out a way to work with young people in the afternoons. I knew I was not welcome at the high school, having been part of a group of parents and educators who had tried and failed to reform it, and I did not feel like teaching in a hostile environment. If I could teach at home, have a class of reasonable size, control the curriculum, and structure the time so that my mornings were free to write, maybe it would work out.

Several things made it possible for the class to go ahead. Judy and I live on eleven acres, which we share with a small education and development center we created, the Coastal Ridge Research and Education Center. In addition to our house and Judy's studio, we have three cottages. One is a residence for visiting educators, a second my office and study. The third and biggest building is a library and seminar room, ideal for a class of about a dozen people.

Consequently I had fully insured, comfortable facilities in which to hold the class. I had the appropriate teaching credentials, so there was no problem with state and local education codes. In addition, it was possible to schedule the classes for a double period at the end of the afternoon so the students wouldn't have to run back and forth from school to our place, about three miles outside of town. Civics was a year-long class, and economics and sociology each lasted a semester so the double period in the afternoon would suffice.

The major problems were the curriculum and the approval of the principal. To my surprise, he was open to the idea of my taking eight students for special sections of sociology, civics, and economics. I'm not sure why, though I believe a number of factors played a role. An advantage of a small-town school (there were only 128 students, with about thirty-two in Josh's whole senior class) is that there's no school bureaucracy to worry about. The principal and I could talk things through, and as long as he had the approval of the school board he was free to make decisions about adding classes. That left the curriculum. There were course descriptions for all three classes, and I had to find a way to cover the material they outlined. The principal and I agreed to give the class an advanced-studies designation; I agreed to cover the course descriptions—and add more complex material as well, if he would let me do it my way. In addition, we agreed that I would write out class descriptions showing how my sections would cover the required material, as well as an additional description of how my sections would differ from the usual classes.

I had no problem with these requirements. My goal for the class was not to reform the high school so much as to experiment with different ways of teaching mandated curriculum. I looked at the official class outlines and at the list of educational materials usually used to teach them. Each class had a commercial textbook. The class outline was no more than a summary of the text's chapter outline. It was not clear what came first, the text or the outline of the class. In fact, according to students who had taken the course before, anyone who'd read the text and the teacher's manual and passed the classes with a B or better could probably have taught the classes. It was strictly by-the-book teaching, with an occasional optional research paper for people who wanted to get extra credit or make up for missed homework or failed exams.

I didn't want to use a textbook. Instead, I wanted to use original sources, to put the students in touch with the thinking and writing of people who had shaped sociology, made and interpreted the Constitution, and reflected upon economics. In addition I wanted to set the three classes in the context of the world, not just the United States.

Many critics of educational reform worry about the erosion of standards that they claim accompanies progressive curriculum re-

form in general and integrated, theme-based teaching in particular. But doing things differently does not mean doing them less
well or making fewer demands upon the students. High standards
don't trouble me. What does is how the adoption of specific standards becomes an excuse to regulate the form and structure of education as well. However, there are many routes to the same goal;
some are linear and fit into a textbook, step-by-step curriculum.
Others take meandering paths, pausing for conversation and the
exploration of topics and themes that are not in the curriculum
per se but that illuminate the ideas being taught. Creative teaching and learning need the freedom to find a route to the standards
that suits the students' and teachers' knowledge, experience, and
interests. I knew I wasn't going to use the textbooks but rather
find a way to actively engage my students in a project that could
lead to a working internalized understanding of civics, sociology,
and economics.

In Point Arena, with Josh and his friends, I took the "Aims
and Objectives" straight from the standard curriculum and
worked them into a creative curriculum that, to return to my
Alder Creek metaphor, became part of teaching within a moving
stream.

The final approval for the classes came in June, so I had the summer to finalize my list of students and plan the class. Josh, Oona,
and Abel decided to join; since he was interested in teaching, I
hired Ian to be my teaching assistant–apprentice teacher. Thus we
involved the whole reggae band in the class.

Ilana, the school valedictorian, who was a good friend of Josh
and Oona, also signed up, as did our next-door neighbor Amanda
and her friend Sage. Another friend of theirs, Melissa, indicated
interest and joined us for a while but dropped out. There was Dominique, an exchange student from Belgium who insisted on
coming to class despite considerable opposition from her host
family, which was extremely conservative and had been overtly
hostile to my educational work in the past. Also with us was
Sean, a friend of Josh's who had the reputation of being ex-

tremely smart and relentlessly resistant to authority. From third grade through sixth, Oona, Ilana, Josh, Amanda, and Sean had all come to a summer camp Judy and I ran and had been in plays I directed. Sage and Dominique were new to me as students, though I knew Sage's mom from the days when Sage and Josh were on the T-ball team I coached.

Some friends in New York didn't believe me when I said I'd volunteered to teach a public high school class for nothing and even paid for a teaching assistant out of my own pocket. In addition, they worried about what this implied for the union. That wasn't a problem: as when I'd taught at Hillside Elementary, I didn't take any teacher's job or prevent any new teacher's hiring, and the regular classes were still offered. Basically, I absented eight students from the high school for two periods five days a week for one school year in order to set up a laboratory of learning. My goal was to explore, in a somewhat ideal setting, how learning could take place; later I'd try to apply what I'd learned to more usual public school settings.

In addition to being small and off campus, this class differed in another way from most urban public high school classes, even those in small, experimental high schools. If you have children of your own in a small town like Point Arena, it is almost impossible not to know everybody else's children too. Teaching Josh and his friends was very different from teaching in other circumstances, because with the exceptions of Dominique and Sage, I had watched all the children grow up and had worked with them in one way or another for about ten years. I could talk to them over the summer and find out about their current concerns and interests. And I could inform them, as my own process of planning the class developed, of what to expect from me.

What came across in my summer discussions with the kids was that they were bored in school and looking for an intellectual challenge. The problem was not to keep them from playing around but to fulfill their expectations of being exposed to new and exciting ideas. One of the main demands on educators' ingenuity is how to be serious and challenging with adolescents without boring them or creating discipline problems that interfere with learning.

I didn't want to waste my students' time with textbooks that they could easily read themselves if they chose to. On the contrary, I wanted to create a class during which they would be drawn into an understanding of citizenship and get a feel for how money and work were intertwined and how resources were shared or hoarded throughout the world. I also wanted to help them understand culture and class and to work toward some useful definition of the health of society that could be used to weigh the quality of one's life. Most of all, I wanted them to feel that the class was a voyage, an exploration of fundamental human issues that connected them with the intellectual traditions and academic knowledge involved in building a democratic society. I wanted them to become engagé—that is, passionately concerned with understanding and shaping the world they lived in.

In structuring the class, I had to overcome the separation of content and process. What we studied and how we were to study it were not two separate or separable aspects of learning. By 1986 I had developed an integrated planning process; for once, I would be able to implement and test it in a learning environment I was free to modify however I wanted.

I started by clearing the planning wall in my study. That wall, which is about five feet long by nine feet high, starts out as a blank slate and over the course of my thinking through the structure of a book or an educational project gradually fills up with notes, ideas, and suggestions. At the beginning of a project the wall is very loosely organized. Anything relevant that occurs to me is noted on the wall. I don't try to impose a premature structure on the material I'm gathering. The idea is to achieve a sufficient density of possibilities before beginning to group the material under categories, which emerge from the material itself rather than from some preconceived structure.

As an example of how these categories develop, one of the first things I began thinking about and making notes on was the strengths the students brought to the class. First, there was the reggae band, whose members were beginning to realize that it had to be run as a small business as well as an artistic group. Clearly they had a personal interest in understanding the economics of small business. A note to this effect went up on the wall: "Bands as small businesses." And another raised the question: "How could the band develop a spreadsheet?"

Sean, who was a surfer and a skater, could make and repair surfboards and skateboards; he was skilled with epoxy and wood. That led to several notes on making things out of wood, on epoxy modeling, and on the public order and safety issues relating to surfing and skating.

Oona was an excellent writer; her interests led me to think about desktop publishing and, once again, home business and small businesses.

Before the band became his passion, Josh had been a model builder; he had spent several years obsessed with making a perpetual motion machine. Again I noted model building, and began to think about the kinds of models students could build for a class on sociology, civics, and economics. The analogy of physical models with economic models was obvious, so a note stating that went up on the wall. Then it occurred to me that architectural models, and perhaps a model of a society, could also play some role.

My thoughts about models and building something with the students were reinforced by the fact that Amanda, whose mother made and sold beautiful one-of-a-kind dolls, was a skilled artist and craftsperson; she had worked on her mother's dolls and her own line of crafts since she was about ten. Amanda could take an idea and create a marvelous physical representation of it. "Dolls" went up on the wall. Through free association, so did notes about masks, social roles, pretense, stigma, and, by extension, role models, socialization, peer pressure, fashion, and popular culture.

I also considered major events that had taken place during 1985 and 1986 and reflected on how they might be used to illuminate the subjects we were studying in class. I noted events like the Tower Commission report, the protests and strikes in South Africa, the coming Bork confirmation hearings, and Surgeon General Everett Koop's congressional testimony supporting condom distribution and warning about the danger of AIDS. These events could spark discussion of important sociological, civic, and economic ideas.

In addition I started stacking up resource materials and pasting up notes on how I might use them for our reading and discussion. Among the dozens of things I posted and gathered were the following:

Plato's dialogues, in particular the following Socratic dialogues, which everyone concerned with democracy and issues of conscience ought to have an opportunity to read and discuss: *Phaedo*, *Crito*, and the *Apology*. I also included the "Allegory of the Cave" section of *The Republic* as a possible reading assignment.

Jefferson's drafts of the Declaration of Independence (from historian Carl Becker's book *The Declaration of Independence*) along with the document as adopted; we'd use these to study the process Jefferson and others went through as they tried to articulate their notion of a democratic society and government.

The Constitution and the drafts of the Bill of Rights. The U.S. Government Printing Office was a prime source for these. For example, they provided a document called "The Making of the Bill of Rights," which reprinted the original drafts, containing fifteen proposed amendments, as well as the final Bill of Rights.

A collection of national constitutions from Namibia, the Soviet Union, and France as well as selected parliamentary papers from England. My idea was to contrast parliamentary democracy with our system of the balance of powers and to illustrate how a country without a written constitution (Great Britain) could develop democratic forms of government.

An assortment of human rights documents, including the United Nations International Declaration of Human Rights, the Emancipation Proclamation, the French Declaration of Human Rights, and the "Declaration of Sentiments" of the 1848 Seneca Falls Convention on Women's Rights.

A similar collection of essays and excerpts from works on sociology and economics, as well as a stack of cartoons, quotes, charts, and graphs and reproductions of posters, paintings, and photos related to the various topics we might consider. I included many essays that examined culture and community from a multicultural perspective.

Poems and short stories, by a variety of writers representative of the many peoples of the United States, that illuminated the subjects we were studying.

Documents from the civil rights and women's movements and from struggles over freedom of speech and other Bill of Rights issues.

U.S. Department of State Post Reports, one for the Bahamas dated August 1985, and the other for Saudi Arabia dated May 1986, which I discovered at the GPO on a visit to Washington, D.C. These documents, produced by the State Department, are given to diplomats and their families being posted to different parts of the world. They provide practical information on how to dress, behave, shop, get settled, treat local people, and understand local government and politics. What made them particularly interesting for my purposes was that they were specifically intended to inform U.S. government officials how to behave in various cultural and political contexts.

I organized all this material into what I called a casebook, by analogy with a legal casebook. Each student was to produce an individual casebook that would include her or his own work, copies of some of the work of their classmates, and the readings we actually used. Instead of having a fixed textbook, we would have an evolving one, specific to what we studied that year.

After a month of accumulating ideas and materials my wall and floor were a mess. Nevertheless, clusters of ideas had begun to develop, and some overriding themes and broad concepts began to emerge. They promised to unify the class while giving it the unpredictable and creative nature of a flowing stream that keeps its identity within difference. My overriding concern for the class was to make sure that my goal of having the students learn about citizenship, society, and economics would not crowd out the students' creative input or take on a didactic character that would prevent them from thinking through important issues and developing their own well-reasoned and sincerely held beliefs. The themes of model building, small systems, autonomous institutions, local power, and conflict resolution recurred over and over in the material I selected. The problems the students faced—AIDS, drugs and alcohol, feelings of alienation and powerlessness, sexual identity, economic security, trust—all occurred in the context of defining a world for oneself, of making a meaningful place in a hostile environment.

The first few weeks of the class were fairly formal. They were run like graduate seminars I had participated in and taught myself. There were no grades, no critical evaluation of the participants. The center of energy and concern was the subject matter itself. All of the students participated and began to feel comfortable being part of an intellectual community, one in which learning became the focus. For some students, fear of being judged dissipated. Others forgot their internalized opposition to formal schooling. The seduction of the subject began to take over. People being driven mad, a man who died for his ideals, a culture whose values were fundamentally different and in some ways more humane than ours were all intriguing things to learn and speculate about. The power of learning about a world larger and more problematic than usually presented in school was my best ally in creating a community of learners.

At the end of September I opened the class up a bit by introducing the project, which was to build a community. The students' response, however, turned a gently flowing creek into a rushing stream. I handed out a small map of the land we were to resettle, as well as a description of our task. Then I suggested that we translate the map into a plaster of paris model of eighteen inches by three feet. That way we could have a visual image of the terrain as we planned the density of settlements, the placement of houses and public facilities, the development of commercial places and farms, and so on. Sean said the idea was dumb and that the model was too small to have fun with. Ian, Josh, Amanda, Abel, and Sage agreed with him. Oona, Dominique, and Ilana thought my idea of a small model was better.

Sean said if we made a model it should be large enough to put in details. Abel followed with the suggestion that we should make small houses and docks and boats to put on the model, as if we had already built it and had planned for them. Ian suggested that Sean's idea was feasible, that we could build an epoxy model on top of a four-foot-by-eight-foot sheet of roofing insulation. Amanda suggested we paint it and maybe even add channels so water could actually flow through it. Sage added that we could build a table for it outside the classroom and even make a shelter to cover it during the rain. Even Ilana, Dominique, and Oona caught the fever. They added that we could experiment with the placing of settlements and land divisions and have many models of what was possible instead of just one.

I had no idea how to work with epoxy, wasn't sure about taking up so much space and time with a model, and wondered if what could be learned from doing this would be worth it. Instead of making a decision, I told the class that I would think through the issue over the weekend.

I spent Saturday and Sunday in an internal struggle, the teacher in me wrestling with the educator.

The teacher had been conditioned from the time I entered kindergarten: School was for learning. Time must be filled up with measurably meaningful activity. Work must be demanding and have an edge that proves it's serious. The goals of learning must be set out clearly and measurably. Part of me has not been able to escape the feeling that if I can't control learning and know what my students are doing, then learning isn't taking place and I'm not doing my job.

The educator in me knows that the teacher is often misguided when it comes to understanding how learning takes place. Trusting students, letting things move toward goals in diverse and frequently digressive ways, following enthusiasms, and responding to events and experiences are not diversions or wastes of time. Rather, they are the essence of substantive learning. From the perspective of the teacher, the four-by-eight model was a digression, a potential waste of time. For the educator, it was an opportunity—indeed, not one opportunity but many. It meant learning about epoxy and model building from the experienced surfers, skaters, and craftspeople in the class. It meant giving the students real ownership of the community-shaping project. And it provided time to speak casually of where we might go with the project as hills, mountains, valleys, rivers, creeks, and streams were shaped.

Leaning toward the educator in me, as I usually do, I prepared for the adventure. However, I could not completely silence the teacher in me, so I tried to think of how the students could do much of the construction outside of class time. That old demon efficiency was still bugging me—but obviously not the class. Josh told me that Sean and Abel had gotten the epoxy and tools, Amanda had come up with the paints and brushes, and everyone had agreed that we would start on the model Monday. Josh just wanted to know if he could take our truck to the lumberyard and charge the insulation board, plywood, and other materials needed to build a table for the model. Abel, Oona, and Ilana would be coming over in the afternoon and they planned to have the table finished by Monday's class.

So much for my decision making. I confessed my hesitancy, and Josh told me not to worry, reminding me that the students had initiated the class because they wanted a learning adventure. My resistance crumbled and on Monday we began to build the model—or, more accurately, the students began to build the model and collaborate on designing the physical world that would frame our planning. My map had indicated only a river with an island in the middle, some flat land, and some forested hills. The model developed to include a watershed, a logical unit for the development of a sustainable environment. This meant studying how a river might actually flow through the land, where its source and its mouth might be. It meant getting specific about the climate and the flora and fauna. And it also meant, for each of us, becoming familiar with the characteristics of the land in a way that I had not anticipated. As the model developed over a week we had a chance to talk about swimming holes, good places to camp, places we wanted to preserve from people's compulsion to develop and overplan. The themes of the rest of the class were sounded informally, without any pushing from me or attempt to organize them.

The next Monday I took advantage of the discussions we were having and the common focus model building had created. I suggested we have a brainstorming session, putting down everything we could think of that might have to be considered when planning a community. We generated a list of variables that represented about a hundred different aspects of planning and then grouped them together into tasks. The next step was to set up planning committees. We formed a Commission of the Whole divided into five planning groups: Surveying, Land Development, and Finding Resources; Laws and Government; Transportation and Housing; Water Usage and Waste Disposal; and Communication, Economic Development, and Entertainment. Each committee generated questions they had to answer, taking account of scientific knowledge and social theory. Then they did the research, reaching out to experts in the field and using library and computer-based resources for suggestions for the development of the community. The committee work took up about half of the class time. During the other half we read resource materials, tackled some shared questions, and read and discussed materials I had selected to enrich our discussions. There also were weeks off to investigate some issues in depth as a group. One of these investigations was on the role of the arts in society. We also took time to read constitutions and bills of rights and to draw up our own governing documents.

After the committees met and sketched out various themes for investigation we all met together. The students read out their lists and I wrote down their suggestions on butcher paper. Soon every wall in our seminar room was covered with the makings of a small community, mirroring the planning process I'd used during the summer for the class itself. The bewildering options displayed by this brainstorming provided us with a vision of the miracle of everyday life, in which the simplest and most ordinary activity presupposes that many complicated structures are in place and functioning. It was a dramatic illustration of how we are surrounded by culture, by social institutions, and by norms of organized behavior, and yet are not explicitly aware of how much we are part of this nexus of structured interactions. The vocabulary word that described these semivisible underpinnings of everyday life was "infrastructure."

As the class reflected on the infrastructures of social life it became clear that we could not adequately deal with everything in the space of one year. We had to develop priorities. I pointed out that this need to make sense out of bewildering complexity is what leads to theory making. Here was a marvelous and unexpected opportunity to dig in intellectually and study some aspects of the relation between theory and practice.

I had had no intention of studying the process of planning and the nature of theory when the class began, so I had to rethink where we were going just when I thought we would get down to working on specific aspects of community development. However, since I think of my teaching as participatory research I felt free to range far in my search for intellectual tools for community planning. With so many factors determining the shape and character of a community, we needed a sensible way to sort them out.

Instead of beginning with a lecture on theory versus practice I asked everyone to read through the lists and look for common themes. I believe it was Josh or Oona who pointed out that some things were contradictory. For example, if we wanted all the houses clustered in one place, people wouldn't be free to choose to live where they wanted. If we wanted to develop agriculture, we would have to destroy some of the natural habitat. If we wanted radios, TVs, computers, and so on, we would have to sacrifice economic self-sufficiency, and also find a way to establish economic relationships with the outside.

During our discussion of these dilemmas the following general points emerged: One, we needed some agreement on overall principles about what kind of life we wanted to have within the community before we could go ahead with the plans. Second, we had to let facts—that is, what is possible according to current science and knowledge—also determine what we included in the final draft.

This latter came out in the vegetarian wars. Josh had managed to include in one of the lists a stipulation that the community would be vegetarian. He was a philosophical vegan and, at that stage in his life, was also a proselytizer for that cause. Sage pointed out that she didn't want to live in any community where she couldn't have a hamburger. Others felt that with a well-stocked river it was foolish not to eat fish, and that with so much land it was equally foolish not to raise chickens. Sean felt that hunting should be permitted as well, and that deer and wild pig should be consumed. The tension over this issue diverted attention from all other planning issues. I decided to let it play itself out as a way to introduce some theory and order.

First, everyone agreed that maximum self-sufficiency should be an overall principle guiding community planning. From there came the problem of hamburgers. Philosophical arguments about keeping cows, slaughtering animals for human purposes, beef and health, a good diet, and the right to eat yourself into the grave went on for a few classes. Then Dominique raised a simple question: Could we afford cows? What would raising beef to feed the population cost by way of resources and the environment? I remember the students turning to me for an answer and I replied that we hadn't raised cows in the Bronx. Research was in order; we needed facts to inform our moral and philosophical musings.

A temporary working committee on cows was set up. I love to use temporary structures in organizing my teaching. A small group for welcoming guests, a committee to solve a problem, a standing team ready to be the research branch for someone writing a paper, a temporary construction or model-building crew, a music or art brigade—all these temporary and usually invisible structures add to the whole group's learning resources. They also make it possible for everyone to have a chance to be the boss, the leader of a team, the expert in a particular task, or the director of a certain activity.

Josh and Ilana were assigned to call the California Department of Agriculture and find someone who could tell them about raising beef cows. Abel, Sage, and Dominique were to visit local dairy farms and find out how much land they used per cow and why they were in the milk business rather than the meat business. Sean was to call the Cattlemen's Association and ask them what was needed for a cattle ranch.

I reminded the students that, if self-sufficiency was one of the main values in our community building, then they had to find out about fattening the cows, slaughtering them, distributing the meat, and so on. At that point I turned to the concept of wayfinding. This is a planning strategy that takes into account both the space in which an activity occurs and the time and processes it involves. When planning a football or baseball stadium, you have to plan for more than the playing field. Among other things, you have to consider how people will find their way from home to their particular seats in the stadium. The path from the parking lot to the seat, if not taken account of in the planning, can lead to frustration and chaos. The same is true in planning airports, transportation systems, and recreation and shopping facilities. One must be specific about such things as what facilities are needed and how paths should be designed. Wayfinding also means paying careful attention to seemingly simple aspects of design such as where signs should be and how they should be designed.

I suggested that the concept of wayfinding should be applied to the production and consumption of beef and that we should draw a diagram of the path from a cow's birth to its consumption, noting all the facilities, resources, and processes needed along the way.

Pursuing the vegetarian wars was much more than a diversion. It gave the students content to wrestle with at the same time that they were struggling to define themselves through diet and philosophy. Food wars are not minor matters; people have killed each other over eating habits. Here was a concrete opportunity to integrate scientific information with struggles over health, style, and culture. The subject involved hard knowledge and research but was shaped by philosophy and tinged with passion.

I have described the work of this class to many teachers and administrators. One common response is hostility to the idea that what could be done with eight students in a rural setting, off campus and with no administrative constraints, is irrelevant to public education and particularly to the problems of urban schooling. Another response is a grudging acknowledgment that many of the ideas and exercises of our class are useful and that in minor ways they can be applied to enrich the regular curriculum.

However, over the years I've concluded that you take the teaching as the opportunity presents itself, that all young people have the same hunger to learn, and that good teachers can take a sensible idea and make it useful wherever they teach.

Part II

Teaching and Learning

The selections in Part II are concerned with the shape of content in learning. It is usual to separate particular aspects of the content of learning from the techniques of teaching. These methods or styles of teaching are imposed upon content no matter what the nature of the content is. Science, math, reading, and the arts are, for example, all lined up and fit into a lecture-test format no matter what the concepts, inner structures, and meanings central to a subject are. For me it is different—reading implies writing; science begs experimentation; mathematics involves puzzles, proofs, and games; and the arts involve imaginative expression as well as historical knowledge. Each of these areas of learning suggests its own kind of teaching and educational environment. One of the great challenges of teaching is to set specific content in a way that encourages understanding, provides pleasure in learning, and develops intellectual discipline and a love of learning. That means teachers will sometimes lecture, set up experiments and step aside, or develop dialogs with students that lead to creative writing and act as literary critics. For me, teaching means having a kit bag of styles and techniques and a willingness to experiment with shaping content through direct classroom action.

Over the years I have written about this shaping of content, as well as trying to uncover the basic aspects of learning that contribute to helping young people develop into intelligent, sensitive, and thoughtful adults. The selections in Part II sample some of what I have discovered and come to think about teaching and learning.

The first selection is from *Basic Skills*. It is an attempt to move beyond a rigid focus on reading and math and extend to the basic skills that contribute to learning not merely in school but throughout life. These skills set the context in which particular knowledge can be mastered and lead to further learning.

The second selection, from *On Teaching*, concerns people's motivation for becoming teachers. It also articulates some of the aspects of a teaching life that have to be developed as one grows into feeling comfortable with creating a classroom that works for the students and for the teacher.

The third selection, from *Reading, How To*, focuses on print literacy and developing a comprehensive program shaped to the context in which one is teaching and the nature of the students. This applies to whole-class teaching, reading circles, tutorials, and even adult literacy programs. It is centered on comprehension and questioning as well as the mastery of specific skills. The goal is to develop intelligent readers, not merely efficient test takers.

The fourth selection, from *Growing Minds*, has to do with loving students as learners—the particular kind of pedagogical affection that drives good teaching. This piece also comments on the suspension of ego in teaching, something that is hard to develop as one comes to terms with being "the authority" in the classroom.

The final selection, from *Math, Writing and Games in the Open Classroom*, is about the importance of playing, modifying, and creating games in the development of thought and imagination. This applies easily to math and science but is also relevant across other areas of learning.

SIX BASIC SKILLS

From *Basic Skills: A Plan for Your Child, a Program for All Children*

There are at least six basic skills that our children must acquire if they are to learn how to function effectively and compassionately as adults. They are:

1. *The ability to use language well and thoughtfully.* This skill implies developing speech that is sensitive to the weight and meaning of words, acquiring the habit of reading intelligently and critically, and learning to write coherently in forms that can be read by others. The struggle to say what one means and the ability to attend to the meaning of other people's words must be central to any educational program that hopes to develop democratic sensibility.

2. *The ability to think through a problem and experiment with solutions.* This skill implies learning techniques of observation, questioning, listening, and experimenting. It also implies that modes of thinking should be taught explicitly and not merely implied through different school subjects.

3. *The ability to understand scientific and technological ideas and to use tools.* This implies learning to use numbers, computers, and hammers, and having opportunities to apply language and thinking skills to scientific, technical, and mechanical problems.

4. *The ability to use the imagination* and participate in and appreciate different forms of personal and group expression. This implies serious attention be given to the arts from historical, performance, and technical perspectives.

5. *The ability to understand how people function in groups* and to apply that knowledge to group problems in one's own life.

6. *The ability to know how to learn something yourself* and to have the skills and confidence to be a learner all your life. This involves learning how to deal with new situations, and to develop new skills and interests throughout your life.

These six basic skills lead to a six-stranded curriculum that suggests ways of reorganizing the structure of public education and making fundamental changes in the way students are treated. I will discuss each of the six basic skills separately and then suggest concrete ways in which, even in these difficult times, positive changes might be made in public education.

Basic Skill 1: The Ability to Use Language Well and Thoughtfully

Reading without critical understanding and writing without the ability to express what you intend are not basic skills: reading thoughtfully and writing with control of content are basic skills. Underlying these basic skills is the ability to use language well.

It is crucial to understand the intimate relationship between content and comprehension. Young people have to learn to attend to the meaning of what they read, to compare it with other material, to question the author, to guess at intent, or challenge conclusions. They need to deal with the substance of, rather than simply pronounce the sounds of, letters on the page. Reading is understanding, not reciting.

The same is true for writing. The mechanical skills are only useful if they serve meaning and content. *Reading and writing as basic skills cannot be separated from understanding.* This implies that *understanding is itself a basic skill* and that it is essential that time be devoted to conversation, observation, analysis, experimentation, and other activities that lead to comprehension. These are not frills, or wastes of time, as some people assert, but are at the very core of developing intelligent reading, coherent writing, and informed citizenship.

Language is a form of mobility. Through listening and reading one can explore spatial, temporal, and imaginative worlds that are beyond what one can observe directly. A major reason to learn to listen and to read is to become aware of the world outside of one's own experience. In cultures that do not use written language, speech is the central means of preserving history and sharing adult knowledge of the world with the young. If a child doesn't learn how to listen, to attend to nuances of meaning, there is the chance that he or she might make a major social error or lack a skill necessary to adult survival. In our society, writing supplements speaking as a source of information and experience. Through books and magazines, et cetera, it is possible to project oneself through space and time, and share the imaginative work (artistic, scientific, and technical) of people one will never hear or meet.

Speaking and listening, and writing and reading, are obviously powerful ways of acquiring information about the world. Yet most school programs discourage speech, pay no attention to the development of sophisticated listening skills, turn writing into mechanical exercises, and impoverish the content of reading. The opposite should happen. Speech, especially student speech, should be encouraged. That's not the same as encouraging talking out in the middle of a lesson or shouting wildly and incoherently, as some fundamentalists would interpret it. Rather it means that students should be encouraged to speak in class about their perceptions of the world, about their ideas and aspirations, about adult politics and religion, about conflicts they experience and ways they've found of building things and enjoying themselves. Equally, students should be encouraged to listen to each other, raise questions, and speculate in class. *Time must be taken for speech.* This should be a major principle of curriculum development and is essential for the development of intelligent reading and writing programs. *The struggle to say what one means and the ability to attend to the meaning of other people's words are central to an education program that has as a goal the development of democratic sensibility.*

The content of speech and books, the stuff one can talk and read about, should be made clear to young people. Information can be gotten from people if one asks, and from books if one reads, and this bit of information itself should be demonstrated in school by the constant presence of people with things to talk about and by the presence in every class of a rich library that students are encouraged to use.

I did not come from a book-rich home, though there were many adults around who told wonderful tales and were willing to share what they knew with young people. For years in school, books were a problem to me. I had no idea what was in them. Reading was something I was forced to do for some mystical adult reasons having to do with my future. Fortunately, in the fifth or sixth grade I had a teacher who loved books for how they expanded her life, and she shared the knowledge of what was in them with us. This may be my fantasy, but I seem to remember her holding up a book a day and asking our class if we knew what was in it. It was like a wrapped toy, a gift that might contain all kinds of riches. We guessed from the look of the cover and the author's photo on the flap of the jacket. Amazingly, she let us spin out fantasies of what could be in books, let us talk and forget about being self-conscious or nervous about getting the right answer. And then she gave us a peek, read some select paragraph or page, and asked who wanted to read the book first. Usually there was a rush of seven or ten people to grab the book. I remember the crazy feeling of rushing to grab a book. There was something in it, it wasn't the print but the content that made sense of reading to me. In a way, the word *information* is too cold and limited to describe what can be learned from books and from other people. It implies a passive receiving of facts, when reading is really more like the process of in-formation: the structuring, questioning, and evaluating of information that is beyond what you directly experience.

Question asking, that is, learning to use other people as resources, is a basic skill that should be encouraged and developed in every subject. Many questioning themes can be worked in, themes such as How do I ask questions about nature? (That is, how do I observe and design an experiment?)

- How can I ask someone to clarify the meaning of what they say or do?
- How do I ask for information from a stranger (e.g., how to get to a place, find out about the resources of a community, et cetera)?
- How do I approach people and find out about them when I'm in a new place?

Everyone at a school might even pause once a year and pose lists of questions to think about. This would be a sensible extension of the language program. Imagine asking fifty or a hundred young people to list questions they would like to see answered, posting the questions at the beginning of the school year, leaving them posted for several months, and then taking time to look at the questions again and discover whether anyone has found answers or tentative approximations to answers for some of the questions.

Language is a resource through books and other written matter as well as a bridge to other people's knowledge. Yet to know books, you must be surrounded by books. It is not enough to have textbooks and workbooks, or even a library you visit once a week. Books should be everywhere in any learning place, lots of books of different kinds. There should be student-made and -printed books, old books, picture books, books printed with different typefaces, books that express different opinions, books that raise questions, books that can transport students into worlds they have never seen or touched. The diversity of books is especially essential these days when large publishing houses are no longer committed to keeping books in print if they don't sell.

It's important to let students know that old books are not necessarily obsolete books, that answers to questions and needs can be found if you know how to search for books. I've found that one of the most useful skills one can have is *the skill of browsing*, of wandering through libraries, bookstores, subject index catalogs, *Books in Print*, in search of books that answer your needs. Research skills, that is, using books to get specific information, are extensions of the skill of browsing. They consist of knowing how to find and use books and involve more random search and intuitions than one would imagine. Contrary to the usual image of book research as looking up something in an encyclopedia, it can be a much more exciting adventure. If you have a subject to research, say, Napoleon, you can go to an encyclopedia. But you can also develop a series of associations with your subject and begin to piece together many different sources to develop a complex understanding of your subject. For Napoleon, for example, here are some of the roads it might be interesting to follow:

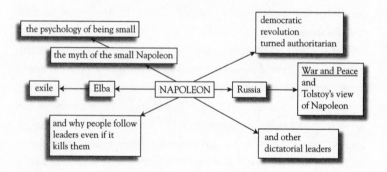

Research and browsing are skills that don't have to be taught separately. In a setting where questions are raised and students are encouraged to piece together answers from different sources, they are an integral part of everyday functioning.

There are some basic sources that every child should master, among them the etymological dictionary, the encyclopedia, and the library. In fact, once a child learned to read, say in the equivalent of the third grade where fluency usually develops, I would give him or her as a substitute for a report card a gift of an etymological dictionary, a one-volume encyclopedia, and a library card.

These gifts would provide students with mementos of their achievements and with tools to use for further learning. An A or B+ can provide some verification of learning, but it leads nowhere and leaves no specific memories. Gifts, tokens of welcome and future learning, can and might become symbols of achievement and tools for future growth. A series of educational gifts might provide young people with an educational toolbox they could use and expand throughout life.

Of course, these suggestions go beyond the language program and can be used in every area of study. There are gifts that can be worked into every aspect of a learning program. However, it is crucial not to confuse gifts with rewards. A gift is given to provide someone else with pleasure. It looks to the future and should be something that can be used. A reward is a token or memento of past performance more bound up with what has happened than with what can happen. All children should be given gifts as they move through different stages of development and these gifts should not be ranked or graded. There should be no A gifts, B gifts, or C, D, and E gifts, but equal tokens of our regard as adults and educators of our children's growth.

Basic Skill 2: The Ability to Think Through Problems and Experiment with Solutions

The ability to think does not develop spontaneously. Thought requires concentration, practice, and the ability to hold many things in one's mind at the same time. Though there may be some children born with exceptional powers of thought and concentration, these skills can also be developed and honed to a remarkable degree. It is possible to teach thinking skills, and it is essential for people who will be faced with choices and decisions all their lives to develop these skills as early and thoroughly as possible.

A separate subject entitled the *Development of Thinking Skills* should become a central part of young people's school experience.

The subject would deal with three basic problems: confronting a new challenge, understanding something or someone who is *different*, and learning how to extract what is valuable in *old* forms. It would deal directly with *the basic skill of learning how to think*.

The *Development of Thinking Skills* would encompass the analysis of systems, the evaluation of alternate solutions to a problem, and the variety of techniques that can be used for organizing a body of information. It might deal with problems like:

- How can one find out what people think about a given question?
- What are ways of analyzing survey data and how reliable are these methods?
- What is the nature of predictions? What kind of information can lead to reliable predictions? What information doesn't lend itself to prediction at all?
- What is the nature of relationship? In space? Time? Between people? Between objects?
- What is the history of thought? How have different cultural traditions (and individuals) gone about defining and solving problems?
- How can numbers be used as a tool for organizing information?
- What is a system? How does one construct one?
- How are buildings, theories, books, TV shows, musical compositions, paintings designed?

The goal of a series of classes on the *Development of Thinking Skills* is to show young people how to think through a problem, gather and organize information, and make hypotheses and draw conclusions about things in the world. It would be as much an integrative program as *Word Definitions of Experience*. It would encompass such subjects as logic, design, architecture, planning, systems analysis, art criticism, mathematics, writing, literary criticism, the history of technology and invention, the history of language and linguistics. The primary goals of the class (which could be taught every year using different and increasingly sophisticated themes and techniques of analysis and criticism) would be to give young people the power to plan a future, to think through a problem, and to create solutions. The class would be an attempt to counteract paralytic thinking with active intelligence, to give young people the intellectual tools necessary to live a decent life in a complex, often nasty, world.

For young children the course can center on queries like: How do people move water? How do you discover the structure of an animal group? How do you fix a bicycle? How do you put it together once you've taken it apart? How can you plan in general to put something back together after you've taken it apart?

For older students, problems can be more sophisticated. For example, one course can center on the history of the book. Who reads? Who controls publishing? How do books get written? How do they get printed, distributed, advertised? What goes into making a book a best seller? What goes into preventing a book from reaching an audience? What is censorship? How is the book industry organized? How does one get enough information to answer these questions?

The subject would also have a personalized aspect. It would help individual students learn how to organize working spaces for themselves, find connections with their own energy and style, and develop a resource library that will be useful to them.

Some of the themes considered over the course of a person's time in school could be:

1. *Approaching new materials.* How to deal with the new, either in terms of moving to a new community, or dealing with a new job, or a new social or family problem, or a new thing to learn.

2. *Figuring out what is wanted.* Understanding what is expected before you decide to comply or not; how to get at assumptions and make them fit in terms of mind, society, politics, intellectual tradition, as well as how they relate to your experience and how you can find ways to decide on how you feel and believe about them.

3. *Uncovering contradictions.* A valuable technique when dealing with any issue or topic or theory or experience is figuring out the contradictions inherent in it. Setting them side by side, solutions often emerge, or at least new directions of research or thought are indicated.

4. *Formulations and reformulations.* Ways of putting down initial ideas, and then organizing them. Writing with different colored pens, using a pair of scissors and a stapler; moving things around, eliminating them or developing new themes. This could also be called working habits.

Basic Skill 3: The Ability to Understand Scientific and Technical Ideas and Use Tools

In addition to being able to use language well and to think, citizens of a democracy need to be able to understand, use, and control human inventions, from hammers to computers. For this reason, the third strand of a reconstructed curriculum should deal with the subject of *Science, Technology, and the Use of Tools.*

School science tends to be twenty or more years behind current scientific practice, especially in the elementary and junior high schools. Part of the reason for this is that most teachers don't know science and depend upon whatever textbooks they have available; part is that science is not considered one of the "basics" and is usually placed just a cut above art and music in order of time priorities.

Technology fares a bit better. There are usually a few lessons on the Industrial Revolution in fifth-grade history and perhaps in American and world history in high school, and possibly some attempts to introduce knowledge about the computer revolution as well. Computers have been tossed into classrooms as backup for a bare-bones phonics and calculation curriculum.

There is no place in the present curriculum for considerations of how scientists and inventors work on an everyday level, or for serious consideration of issues like the social responsibility of science, the different social and political contexts in which technology and science can be used, whether "improvements" improve the quality of life, whether everyone benefits equally from science and technology, and whether the earth can survive their effects.

In addition, the use of tools of science and technology, from the hammer to the loom, lathe, computer, and electron microscope, are either not taught or are relegated to advanced science or vocational education.

Advanced science and vocational education: the two ends of the class system set up in school. Students are able to do one, not the other. Yet citizens of a democracy, people who have power over their lives, should be able to use both computers and hammers. Manual labor and intellectual labor are not incompatible. Moreover, people should have knowledge of how everyday things work and can be constructed, repaired, and improved, as well as professional knowledge. It is important for children of carpenters and children of computer experts to know how to use hammers and computers, to know how to organize information about how a house can be built or repaired, and about how a computer can be used to control inventory of a small business or large corporation. That doesn't mean that everyone will end up being either a carpenter or computer expert or both, but that people who work will be able to respect each other and that our children will be taught how to work with their heads and their hands.

There are a number of implications in considering science, technology, and the use of tools to be basic skills. One is that scientists in the schools, machinists in the schools, inventors in the schools, should be as common as artists in the schools. We simply cannot depend upon teachers to provide adequate information and current means of using the information. We should draw on the people who do the work, and it should be their obligation (as well as a possible source of renewal for them) to offer what they know to young people.

Teachers can, however, help provide history, analyze the political and social roles of science and technology, supervise student projects, et cetera. However, this would require knowledgeable teachers, people who will work at their profession and not be bound to textbooks or what they learned at teachers college. Technology moves fast, scientists disagree, and new discoveries are overthrowing old theories all the time. Teachers cannot be expected to know everything about their subjects but they should be literate and current. I have known science teachers who can't follow an article in *Scientific American*; schools where computers sit in a closet because the teachers don't know how to use them; and worse, many, many students who will never see a computer, run a lathe, machine a screw, handle a press, try out a loom, look through a microscope. Science and technology will be mysteries to them, though some will learn to use hand tools and repair machines at home despite school.

We have to empower young people through command of science, technology, and the use of tools; through an understanding of technical information and the strategies used (mostly mathematical) to organize it and develop applications. We must also not leave out in the process consideration of whom science and technology serves, for it can be used to serve democracy or to crush it. *Science, Technology, and the Use of Tools* would deal with units like the following:

1. *Engines and motors:* Their development, their use and repair, their manufacture, the positive and negative effects of their use, smog and the internal combustion engine, the tools needed to make and repair an engine, and so on.

2. *Weaving:* The role of clothes in history, the cottage industry and the development of large-scale weaving, weavers and unionizations, the technical history of the loom, the biological nature of fibers, plastics and weaving, portraits of a Rochdale weaving cooperative and the J. P. Stevens Corporation, the practice of weaving and the design of fabrics and cloth.

3. *The history of joining things together:* Hammers, nails, screws, bolts, fasteners, and the development of bridges and airplanes.

4. *Cutting:* The social and practical history of knives and saws, from the stone blade to the logging chain saw, including the use

and sharpening of saws, the effects of the logging industry; the development of the laser and of electronic processes for fine cutting; diamond cutting and the agony in the diamond mines of South Africa; cutting coal and the life of a coal miner; cutting stone, and the Pyramids and who built them.

5. *Machines that make machines and men and women who invent machines:* On the development of the tool-and-die industry, practice making tools and creating tools to solve physical problems, and so forth.

6. *Computing and computing devices, from the abacus to the home computer:* With a study of miniaturization and its role in developing the power of computers, as well as a study in the use of base-two number systems, an introduction to data processing, to BASIC and other computer languages, to the limits of computer-stored information; the social history of IBM, as well as the effect of computers on working-class people, et cetera.

7. *Clones:* The study of cellular life, the story of the discovery of DNA, the building of models of DNA, the social dangers of cloning, the definition and understanding of macro- and microbiological levels, with discussion and demonstration of mutations, using electron microscopes, studying and cultivating bacteria, et cetera.

These seven units are just some of hundreds that could be developed. Other illustrations of the range of what could be taught are:

1. model making, physical and mathematical
2. surveys and the use of numbers to organize information
3. agriculture: how to plant and how to maintain the productivity of the earth
4. the building of Chartres Cathedral compared with the building of the Seagram's Building.

All of these classes would involve technical knowledge, practice in gathering and organizing information, and using tools.

They would also deal with social, economic, cultural, and political aspects of science and technology; with history and perhaps most importantly with speculation about the role science, technology, and tools can play in a democracy. Ecological and environmental considerations would not be secondary but, to use a term from weaving, built into the very fabric of learning. The human and earth dimensions of science and technology would not be separated as they currently are, nor would the lines between the technical, artistic, and social worlds.

It may be objected that this is a lot to expect young people to be able to master. I'm not sure; no one knows how much and on what level of sophistication children can learn. The limitations on school learning that are imposed upon most children come from teachers' lack of knowledge, contentless curricula, limited resources, foolish organizational structures, and fear of democracy, not from anything having to do with young people or their capabilities.

Interesting lessons in science, technology, and tools can be done on a classroom and individual level. Nevertheless, many scientific and technical resources as well as tools are expensive and are also beyond what any single classroom or teacher can be expected to provide. Centers for the study of science, technology, and the use of tools should be established throughout the country and be made available to all children.

These centers should be joined with centers of the arts and form seminal places of learning in the community. There is no reason to separate science and the arts. In fact, there are many reasons to combine them and give all children access to technology as well as to arts. The study of computers can encompass graphics as well as programming; the study of printing fits well with the creation of literature, just as painting, and dying cloth fit with the physics of color. Centers for arts and sciences should be established throughout the country, giving arts and sciences equal status, since the ability to participate in and enjoy the arts is a fourth basic skill.

Basic Skill 4: The Ability to Use the Imagination and to Participate in and Appreciate Personal and Group Expression

Painting, drawing, music, film, dance, video, poetry, theater, and other forms of personal and group expression are basic to the development of articulate individuals and cohesive groups. As John Dewey said in 1914,

> Viewed both psychologically and socially, the arts represent not luxuries and superfluities but *fundamental forces of development.*[1]

Experience with art leads to the development of the imagination, to the playful exercise of the mind that leads to the solution of social and technical as well as artistic problems.

The development of imagination is a basic skill. The attempt to express feelings or ideas through art is essential for coming to terms with experience. People come to know themselves and others better through song, dance, and theater. They learn ways of organizing the visual world through painting, drawing, video, and film. All the arts provide ways of experimenting with the possible, of extending oneself and participating with others in fulfilling collective activity. Theater, for example, makes it possible for people to play at being others and become involved in complex, often painful, situations while staying safe. Theatrical distance allows people to rehearse action, a privilege we are not often afforded in everyday life. The visual arts can represent reality, fantasy, or even pure form. They teach control and thought. Classes in life drawing, in perspective, or in abstract painting provide as many useful techniques for organizing information as classes in arithmetic and social studies.

The idea that arts are frills and privileges and not basics is a manifestation of the antidemocratic sentiment that is current in politics. It is a way of saying that the development of the imagination and the pleasures provided by the arts should be luxuries;

and that children must be born into families with money in order to learn music, drawing, dance, filmmaking, video.

It is a way of putting a price on the quality of life and the ability to use the imagination. I feel that some of the recent attempts, in the service of so-called back-to-basics and high-stakes testing movements, to cut art programs from public schools really mask a desire to see that poor people's children are denied the educational opportunities of the more advantaged. Certainly it would be difficult to argue that plane geometry is more basic or useful in adult life than the ability to play the piano or sketch a face.

The arts are basic, and the creative use of the imagination is a basic skill. Schools should have arts programs that are given the same priorities as language and technology. All of these programs should concentrate on developing the creative capacities of children and helping them learn to analyze experience and solve problems. In the arts classes, these should be available to all students:

Drawing, Sketching, and Thinking with a Pencil, a program stretching over several years, encompassing, among other things, life drawing, architectural drawing, the use of thumbnail sketches and other drawing techniques to visualize solutions to problems, technical and scientific drawing, the drawing of faces throughout history, the rendering of human and animal expression, and the explanation of media for drawing, from pen, pencil, and charcoal to computer graphics.

Another art strand could deal with *filmmaking*, ranging from simple stop-action animation, to studying editing techniques, sound synchronization, storyboarding and scriptwriting, studying the history of film, and analyzing current films.

The possibilities of developing art curricula have hardly been explored. By considering the arts to be frills, current educators have often turned their programs into frilly, superficial attempts at self-expression.

Decent programs should incorporate history, technique, performance, and practice, as well as the technical aspects of the art and criticism.

However, I have found that many people confuse an educational program that considers expression basic, with the idea that all children's expression in its raw and undisciplined form is wonderful. This view leads to no growth. Children develop their means of expression through training, observation, and practice; through studying the history of art and knowing what other people have done and are doing; through making mistakes and producing many bad, uninspired works as well as occasionally achieving excellence. A program that includes classes in life drawing, the history of sculpture, music performance in different cultural traditions, the revision of fiction, poetic composition, Greek theater, should not be confused with one that gives children paper, pencil, and paints, and lets them "express themselves."

I have directed performances of *Antigone* and *A Midsummer Night's Dream* with seven- to thirteen-year-olds, have discussed Shakespeare with children as young as seven, have worked on productions of *The Doll's House* and *Golden Boy* with fifth, sixth, and seventh graders. The children were interested in these works because Antigone is about female defiance of male royal authority, because *A Midsummer Night's Dream* is about magic and love triangles, because Shakespeare deals with murder and love, because he can be raucously funny and delicately romantic, because in other words, the stuff of great expressive works is the content of life. Content is the core of significant, motivated learning, and some major ways of organizing and understanding this content are what we call artistic. Art, the many forms of personal and group expression, should be a major aspect of a reconstructed basic-skills curriculum.

Resources must be allocated so that students have opportunities to experience and participate in music, dance, the visual arts, theater. It is foolish to try to do this on a classroom level, for no teacher can be expected to be competent or even knowledgeable in all the arts, just as no teacher can command all of science and technology. Nor can every classroom be a theater, dance studio, art workshop, poetry center, or film lab. Art centers have to be created that are staffed by artists and teachers that serve all the schools. These centers could be attached to school systems or they could serve multiple purposes, such as providing working space for artists, community arts programs, and exhibits and performances. I've mentioned this to a number of people who have pointed out to me that there isn't money these days for such ambitious building plans and for additional salaries. My response is that athletic complexes continue to be built and maintained, that competitive sports are supported in a way that makes them as functionally basic to American education as reading or arithmetic and perhaps more basic than writing. If we were committed to supporting the arts in the same way, we would allocate community resources to building and maintaining art centers, which could also serve as science, technology, and tool centers. At first, local efforts will be crucial. Donated land, a rented storefront, a reconstructed empty supermarket would do. Everything from bake sales to foundation proposals should be explored and community energy should be mobilized the way in which it can be mobilized to support a football team or a cheerleading squad.

It is important to stop thinking of the classroom as the basic unit of instruction. There is no reason why students of all ages couldn't spend a quarter to a half of their time at an art center or, for that matter, why classes in history, math, science, English, and so on couldn't take advantage of such a center to enrich the content of what is being explored in those classes.

A *center of expression* could contain, in addition to space for dance, theater, and music, collections of historical documents, photos, slides, and recordings. It could be a place where the expressive forms of the peoples of the earth can be reproduced, compared, and used as resources to nurture the imagination of young people.

The center could also contain students' work, the work of contemporary artists, community history, photo collections. It could be a source for community renewal. What is crucial, though, is that centers of expression be staffed by practicing artists as well as teachers and archivists. The expressive arts cannot merely be left to educators without becoming stale, textbook imitations of art.

New people, actively involved in creative work, need to be brought into the world of schools, new credentials created if necessary. I'm tired of seeing qualified artists, musicians, and writers involved in artists-in-the-schools programs being forced to work with bored teachers because state laws say that students can't be left without credentialed supervisors in public schools. It's silly, negative, and expensive.

Basic Skill 5: The Ability to Understand How People Function in Groups

Knowing about others, about people in groups, is basic to understanding the rewards and responsibilities of citizenship in a democracy, and there should be a subject studied throughout a student's school years called *People in Groups*.

Groups can be looked at from many perspectives. They can be examined politically, that is, from the perspective of how power functions in the group

- economically, according to the distribution of wealth and work within the group
- historically, as the development of the group over time
- socially, according to relations of caste, class, and kinship
- culturally, according to style, habit, custom, and patterned relationship among individuals or groups.

In current school practice these subjects are covered in social studies in the early grades and in history and geography in the upper grades. The amount of information provided students is meager. Yet, in order to become a responsible and intelligent citizen in a complex pluralistic democracy like ours, there is an enormous amount of political, social, cultural, historical, and economic information people must absorb and analyze. On a minimal level, young people should learn:

1. *How to understand cultural differences without using words like* "*primitive,*" "*dirty,*" "*deficient.*" Cultural ignorance is at the base of much racism and conflict. Recently I heard a dramatic instance of this from some people who were studying racial conflict in the United States Army. It seems that many white officers interpreted certain forms of greeting, walking, and dressing that are signs of friendship and respect in African American communities as defiance and disrespect. This misinterpretation led to African American enlisted men being disciplined for what they perceived as positive gestures. The only sensible interpretation the African American soldiers could make of the white officers' actions was that they were racist.

The same racial misunderstanding and fear exist in school between student groups, and students and teachers. Simple-seeming things like eye contact, handshakes, style of dress, tone of voice, display of hostility and affection differ from group to group, and these differences often lead to misunderstanding and, at worst, violence.

Culture should be studied explicitly in order to give young people a sense of the variety of ways people approach social interaction and organization. They should also be given techniques for observing others without judging them, and for building a picture of a culture that differs from their own. I believe the knowledge of one's own and other people's culture is basic to democratic education.

2. *How politics works, who has power and how it is used.* This is a survival course. Young people have to know how to trace the sources of power, understand indirect manipulation, coercion, seduction, and other forms of control, if they themselves are to take power over their own lives. Looking for where the power is, going directly to the center of power if you want something, developing alternate sources of power, and even knowing something about oppressing those in power are important. Over the past years we have been victimized by abuses of power again and again, have been deceived by leaders, and by control of information, by false words, and we should not wish our children to be as stupid as we

have been. Politics, as I conceive of it, is not simply the study of politicians and government. In some societies power and government may be identical. That is not the case in our society, and the complex interplay of many sectors, each with differing power, determines the character of society more than government does. Of course, once one starts studying politics in this broader sense, one realizes how difficult it is to get information about the sources of power and the relations of power blocs to each other and to the people they supposedly serve. However, the attempt to acquire information about power and to organize the fragments one can obtain will itself be a basic education on the power of information. The Internet helps.

3. *How to gather historical information.* Primary sources should be used wherever possible: people should be heard in their own voices. In addition, the idea that some people, the "civilized" ones, have history and that other people don't should be dispelled. All peoples have history, and so far as I know, all peoples have recorded some of that history, whether through myth, song, oral poetry, or through writing. Moreover, all peoples have ways of interpreting their own history, and it is important to understand that if we are to make any sense of some of the major problems in the world. Language and civil wars, border disputes, alliances and enmities take on their particular characters because of people's interpretation of their own history. A more sophisticated understanding, for example, of the complex perceptions of Asian history that differ from nation to nation and ethnic group to ethnic group might have saved us a lot of grief in the sixties and seventies. The same could be said of our blundering in Iran.

4. *That social relations have their history and are part of culture.* However, they can also be looked at separately, and such topics as family structure, the anatomy of friendship, courtship and marriage, the development of fraternal and sororal associations, clubs, and clans can illuminate history and culture. They can also lead to insight about the behavior of people who are culturally different. In some cultures, for example, a child's mother's brother is as cen-

tral in the child's life as is the father. In others a grandmother is the central figure. I've seen instances where an insult to a grandmother led to serious fights, and others where a sensible appeal to the correct uncle overcame serious discipline problems.

These days when there is much talk about the sanctity of the family, the collapse of the family, the development of alternate families, the demise of the nuclear family, the rise of communal families, and so on, it would be sensible to study family and small group structures and provide young people with information of the range of kinship structures that people have invented.

5. *That economics in its broadest sense is perhaps the most neglected basic*. Teachers tend to avoid discussing topics like the distribution of wealth, the effects of poverty, the struggles to achieve economic equality, class conflict and class interest, the range of economic organizations, from capitalist to socialist and communist, the effects of economic interest on politics, the relationship between capitalism and democracy, et cetera. Economic information is withheld and, as adults, people listen passively and dispiritedly while words such as *depression, recession,* and *inflation* are used to conceal different forms of economic manipulation.

This points to a basic concern that a reconstructed education must have. Life in groups must be examined from at least four different perspectives if we are to provide young people with adequate information to form a just picture of how people live. The study of *People in Groups* would examine group life from *political, cultural, social-historical,* and *economic* perspectives. There are different ways the subject could be organized. For example, a year could be devoted to studying one's local community from those perspectives, another to studying a series of events, like the Revolutionary or Civil wars, from those perspectives. One could look at the lives of United States presidents from historical, political, economic, social, and cultural perspectives, or examine the armed forces. Other nations and cultures could be examined, and perhaps, after a while, classes in gathering and organizing information from different perspectives can be offered. One can take documents like the United States Constitution and ask what social, political, economic, cultural, and historic factors contributed to its construction.

The study of *People in Groups* could also deal directly with democratic values and how they have appeared and disappeared over time, and how they have manifested themselves in different systems. The relation between the study of *People in Groups* and an adequate understanding of democracy should make it basic in a public school curriculum.

In addition, the resources that exist within one's own community should be incorporated into the study of people. Schools should be places where peoples of different cultural backgrounds can meet respectfully and share their strengths. Cultural resources are fundamentally people resources. Older people, the bearers and recorders of cultural history, ought to be welcomed and invited. Schools can make attempts to document the history of their communities; to compose, print, record, and illustrate aspects of the culture and history of the people they serve. Every school should have an archive of photos, tapes, booklets, interviews so they develop a past and a character that can be known to everyone in the community. The *People in Groups* class could coordinate this archive, which would be one way a school could define and celebrate its uniqueness. As a bonus, such an archive would help new teachers who are not from the community learn about the people they have been hired to serve.

The notion of community needn't be interpreted narrowly and confined to a few blocks, a part of a city, or even a county. A learning program can build in student mobility. Students could have a chance to touch rural and urban environments, to spend time (on exchange programs or overnights) with people unlike themselves. It is important to help young people experience the marvelous complexity of our nation so they can learn not to be afraid of diversity. They should understand the joys and sorrows of different peoples, see land that has been devastated and land that has been nurtured, see rewarding work and hard, unrewarding labor. In particular, this might mean that the study of *People in Groups* might also involve

- pairing urban and rural schools and exchanging visits
- having children go to work with their parents and other people's parents
- having two teachers work together, an inside teacher and an outside teacher, one who travels away from the central learning place with some children while the other works with the rest of the children
- setting up apprenticeships and learning so that (for older children) about half the students are out working and learning in the community at any time
- developing long-range exchanges of students from all schools similar to those supported by the National Association of Independent Schools. (The association identifies high schools that have special learning programs, such as in music, marine biology, theater, or filmmaking. It then coordinates year-long student exchanges among those high schools.)

Basic Skill 6: Learning How to Learn Throughout Life and to Contribute to the Nurturance of Others

We all run down occasionally, get weary of the daily round, and need sources of renewed strength and learning. As individuals we need to continue learning new things to stay fresh. We need times to play and forget the stresses of our usual lives. We also need the renewal provided by passing on what we know to others, and by serving our communities. In addition to learning, play, teaching, and service, we have to contribute to the renewal of the earth, which is our major resource and the source of our lives. We become strong by giving as well as taking and consuming. Ecology, environmental action, and the recycling of resources is both an obligation of being a citizen of the earth and a source of personal renewal.

The basic skills, though acquired and practiced through school, are basic because of the power they provide us as adults. Young people need to understand this and know that what they are learning will be useful and empowering throughout life. They also need to anticipate the need for renewal and to understand that learning is not merely a school matter, but a source of growth and vitality throughout life. There are a number of ways techniques for personal and group renewal can be part of a learning program devoted to keeping language, imagination, invention, thought, and sensitivity basic throughout life. Here are some of them that could be organized through a subject called *Learning to Learn and Teach.*

Renewal Through Lifelong Learning

If one identified learning with school-learning, it would be difficult to make a case for the notion that lifelong learning can be a source of renewal. Who would want to go to school all one's life? Luckily school-learning is a small part of what one learns and it often doesn't prevent us from learning new skills, crafts, arts, concepts, and ideas throughout life.

In a decent school situation learning would not take any single form, nor would it be boring or excessively mechanical. It would be an extension of life outside of school and pass naturally into life after school. Lifelong learning would be constantly referred to, and perhaps every topic studied or class taken would end not with a grade, but with a personal evaluation and a series of suggestions of how what has been learned could be expanded on and how students can pursue additional learning themselves. The purpose of taking time to suggest ways students can continue to learn on their own and initiate new learning is not to encourage students to act immediately. It is a way of giving them strengths for the future, when they might become bored with what they're doing, tired of old ways, and hungry for some new content in their lives. It is not the specific suggestions that are important so much as the constant reminder that it is always possible to learn. Teachers in all subjects should leave their students with a sense

- of where they can go to learn more about a subject
- of what techniques are valuable for self-teaching (which is not the same as having good study skills in school)
- that it's never too late to pursue a subject or learn something new
- that it's perfectly all right to learn something because you care to even if you may never use it.

Lifelong learning doesn't have to be an individual activity. There are times, especially as one grows older, when community and culture are important, and learning and working cooperatively with others is a source of renewing personal energy.

In the past there were many different kinds of schools adults set up in order to teach each other and learn together. These schools didn't need to have grades and report cards, or to separate different areas of learning. Reading and writing were important but so was singing, dancing, building, creative art. Most important perhaps was talking and being together. These schools ranged from labor schools to settlement-house schools, took place in apartments, in churches, in the backs of stores. They existed because they gave the learners power, joy, and comradeship.

Young people need to learn how to initiate and conduct classes if they are to bring people together for purposes of learning as adults. Every school should provide for student-taught and -initiated classes. They could range from a simple fifteen-minute class on how to do magic tricks, to classes on particular books, to classes on computers, or on music, or motorcycle repair. The sum of what is known by all the people in a group should be the strength of the whole group. There does not have to be one teacher and many students. Even five-year-olds have things to teach, and the sooner they learn that what they know can be of value to others, and that others can also offer them something valuable, the quicker respect and the pleasures of being part of a community will grow.

Play as a Source of Renewal

Some scholars and students of play have asserted that play is serious business. I'd like to take an opposite position and assert that play in that part of life that is deliberately not serious. When games become professional or too emotional, play becomes life; the pleasure of participation turns into the grief of defeat and the gloating of victory.

This is particularly true of child's play, which can easily be overinterpreted and can be turned from pleasurable activity to performance for adult approval.

A good example of contrasting ways of understanding play is the attitudes toward long-distance running held by African and American athletes. Of course there are exceptions. Americans run seriously and feel terrible when they lose. They are condescending toward the losers when they win. The crucial thing for many African runners is a good race. If you win by such a large margin that there was no race at all, you've lost the pleasure of racing. A race needs winners and losers and they need each other in order to have a good race. Therefore, winners and losers respect and congratulate each other for the pleasure of racing they have provided each other. The same is true of a game of basketball, football, and even chess, or Go. Winning by fifty points or in ten moves is no fun, no game.

The essence of competitive *play* is a well-played game in which the contestants respect and challenge each other and the goal is pleasure, not merely victory.[2]

The concept of well-played games should be integrated into the games children play, not merely for the pleasure it can provide in their immediate lives but also because playing well and for pleasure can be a constant source of renewal all of our lives.

Handicapping systems often help to make games equal. Constant shifting of sides, games with no score kept, games where the rules change every time they're played, should all be experimented with. Physical activity, both for individuals and groups, has to be a part not merely of school life but of adult life as well or we shrivel up. Play in the larger sense, that is, activity without judgment or consequence, is necessary for survival. We need a time free of the stress of competition in our adult lives in order to renew our energy to face the pressures of living. And we need to learn when we are young how to take this time. I find it distressing that in most schools play is turned into bitter competition; the pleasure of participating turned into the pressure of performing.

Play should be a basic part of the curriculum, and playing well, rather than winning, should be the goal. This means that young people should be taught a wide variety of field and board games, exposed to dozens of different kinds of exercises, and given the opportunity to organize and create their own games. They should also be introduced to noncompetitive games and understand that playing does not always involve competition.

One of the most important consequences of teaching play might turn out to be giving young people opportunities to organize themselves to participate in group activities that provide them with pleasure. I've been quite distressed recently talking to bored youngsters between the ages of ten and sixteen. They complain that there's nothing to do and often get in trouble doing nothing. They tell me they are waiting for some adult to come along and organize a game or a tournament or a community center, and when I suggest they do it themselves, they shrug and close up. If there is any comment it's usually, "We're kids, we can't do anything." That attitude doesn't provide one with much positive feeling about the future of our democracy.

Renewal through Teaching and Service

Helping others get strong and learn new things can be a source of personal energy. It is a matter of one's attitude toward the learner or the person that is served. It's interesting to take an inventory of all the people in a community who choose to teach for their pleasure and not as a job. In our small community there are Little League and basketball coaches; people who teach knitting and crocheting, weaving, computer programming, and writing on an informal level. There are several men's and women's groups where people try to teach each other how to cope with personal stress. In addition, there are Boy Scouts, Cub Scouts, Brownies, and Girl Scouts, and the 4-H Club. I, personally, have been taught how to use a chain saw, to recognize and collect good firewood, and to repair roofs, among other things, by neighbors. In exchange I have offered to teach people how to use our letterpress, how to write, and how to help their children read and write. Sharing one's skills and being involved in a community where certain skills and services are part of a natural round of exchanges provides one with a sense of participation, of belonging somewhere. The use and exchange of skills other than in the service of making money is a binding force in the development of decent community. It is important for children to understand that teaching, that sharing what one knows, is a potential source of personal strength and friendship and not merely a loss of competitive advantage.

It is also important for them to learn the difference between charity and service. Charity consists of taking a little time to give something you can do without to people in need. Charity does not deal with the fundamental problem of empowering the needy or of changing the competitive nature of society, which creates an unbalanced distribution of resources that leads to poverty and disability. Service is different from charity. It is an empowering activity and its goal is to enable those served to become strong enough to lead full lives and offer services in exchange. In my experience, no one wants to be helped without returning a service, and if you know and value people's strengths it is unlikely that an occasion for the return of a favor will not arise. All you have to do is ask for help. Asking for help is the other face of teaching and providing services to others. Unfortunately, many people are too shy or too proud to ask for help. It is considered bad manners:

an internalization, I suppose, of the competitive ideology of our society, where the strong win and weakness is a sign of deserved inferiority.

Young people are not encouraged to ask for help and in highly competitive classrooms are simply afraid to show their ignorance. I remember observing a second grader who transferred into my class during his first week. It was clear he didn't understand what we were studying and I waited the first week hoping he'd ask for help. By Friday he was not merely confused but angry, a budding discipline problem. I finally took him aside and asked him if he was confused. He denied it but I went ahead and explained things to him anyway. After an hour together he thanked me for the help. I finally asked him why he didn't ask me or one of the other students for help before. His answer was that you're not supposed to ask for help in school because then the teacher will know what you don't know and give you a bad grade and the other children will think you're dumb.

We have to share what we know, in the classroom and in our adult lives. I believe students should become accustomed to teaching others as well as asking for help from students and teachers. Asking for and offering help should be a part of school life from a child's earliest days. In addition, children should have occasion to serve the whole school and the community at large. This can mean anything from cleaning up a dirty lot and turning it into a garden or park, to making regular visits to people who are not mobile and cooking, cleaning, shopping, and reading for them. Perhaps the class on *Learning to Learn and Teach* or a part of the class should be devoted each year to the subject of how to serve others and the community. This class could deal with themes like:

- identifying community problems
- developing strategies for solving problems
- organizing others to help you
- helping people without insulting them

- helping people acquire the power to help themselves
- styles of teaching and styles of learning
- what trust in your student means
- devising new teaching methods
- designing solutions to an educational problem.

It is not far-fetched to imagine that a group of six-year-olds can spend a half hour a day for several weeks studying the various ways in which people have tried to teach reading and trying the methods out on each other. Nor is it impossible for junior and high school students to mobilize themselves to build a greenhouse and maintain a garden or assume the responsibility for the safety of older people on the streets in communities where police protection is inadequate. Moreover, learning to act for others provides a confirmation of one's own strength that can renew a commitment to live decently and vigorously at times when one is tired of the competitive grind all of us are exposed to no matter what our intents.

Renewal and the Earth

I have seen a number of school recycling programs begin with enthusiasm and then fade out. Collecting cans, bottles, and papers can become boring however sensible and necessary it is. It is a bit like washing dishes. We all know that it is a futile cyclic activity because the dishes will become dirty again. The reason most of us manage to clean the dishes most of the time is that we have to eat, can't afford new dishes every meal, and are not particularly inclined to eat off dirty dishes or the table. The consequences of not recycling materials or taking better care of the earth are not so immediate, nor do we see the larger consequences of our personal waste and carelessness. When people toss a beer can out of the window of their car or leave a beach littered, they don't think in terms of 100 million beer cans and square miles of plastic wrappings. But that is the magnitude of the problem: the tons and miles of waste and a geologic environment unable to produce new resources at the same rate as they are being depleted.

The habit of linking individual actions to consequences within groups and on the scale of the earth has to be developed if we are to have much of an earth left to pass on to our grandchildren and their grandchildren. Sometimes we have to think over generations and not just of ourselves and our children. Contributing to the maintenance and renewal of the earth may not lead to immediate pleasures and might even cause inconvenience as we cut down on the things we own and the energy we consume. Yet there is a global pleasure that it is possible to experience, what could be called metaphysical or spiritual pleasure, from contributing to the maintenance of the earth and being a positive part of a whole of which your own life and actions are an insignificant part. That pleasure is a source of renewal, a small affirmation that we are trying to live decently and respect the whole.

It would be a good idea to devote time through integrated study in the rest of the curriculum to study cycles and systems. The study would consist of consideration of:

- life cycles
- geological cycles
- the use, depletion, and renewal of resources
- the nature of systems: social, cultural, political, and natural
- the structure of systems
- energy within systems: running down, exploding, and providing new energy to continue operation
- the relationship between parts and wholes; for example, between individuals and nations or between people and the natural environment
- the fit between a system or action and the environment it exists within, for example, the fit between strip mining and the human and natural communities in which it occurs, or the fit between the development of a particular community and its surroundings
- the study of changes over time, which is not necessarily the study of progress. This would look at how parts of the earth

changed and affected each other over various time spans: over 10; 100; 1,000; 10,000; 100,000; and 1,000,000 years.

- the imaginative study of the future, the analysis of current trends, and the projection of future developments, as well as the imaginative construction of decent futures.

These subjects can be joined with action: recycling with the study of cycles; care of the local environment with the study of development. It is possible for five- and six-year-olds to run an entire recycling program with the help of a few adults and for high school students to participate in the development of community and regional general plans.

The habit of understanding cycles, wholes, and the part one's actions can play in creating a decent self-renewed life, as well as the habit of acting itself, can be developed and sustained throughout life in school. It can also help people come to a sense of the meaning and importance in their lives of what they can do as individuals and within groups. This feeling of empowerment, of each person's sense that he or she can be an effective part of the whole, is a basic contribution public education can make to the continuation and renewal of democratic ideas in our society.

The principles and ideas for renewal suggested here are:

1. Help students become lifelong learners.
2. End studies with suggestions for future learning and exploration.
3. Continued learning in groups should be encouraged through student-initiated and -taught classes.
4. Playing well should be a value in the curriculum and there should be many different opportunities to experiment with play throughout school life.
5. Students should be given opportunities to teach and serve the school and community.

6. Classes on how to teach, ways of being of service without being condescending, how to tackle a problem with your friends, and so on, should be offered.
7. Ecological action should be accompanied by the study of systems, cycles, energy, and the renewal of resources.

These are all ways of preparing young people to apply the basic skills they learn in school throughout their lives.

NOTES

1. John Dewey, *John Dewey on Education: Selected Writings*, ed. Reginald D. Archambault (New York: Modern Library, 1964), p. 351.
2. Bernard deKoven, *The Well-Played Game: A Player's Philosophy* (Garden City, NY: Anchor Press, 1978).

WHY TEACH?

From *On Teaching*

There are many reasons that lead people to choose elementary and secondary school teaching. Some people choose teaching because they enjoy being with young people and watching them grow. Others need to be around young people and let their students grow for them. Teaching for some is a family tradition, a craft that one naturally masters and a world that surrounds one from childhood. For others teaching is magical because they have had magical teachers whose roles they want to assume. Teaching can be a way of sharing power, of convincing people to value what you value, or to explore the world with you or through you.

There are some cynical reasons for going into teaching which were much more prevalent when getting a job was not difficult. For example, for some people teaching becomes a matter of temporary convenience, of taking a job which seems respectable and not too demanding while going to law school, supporting a spouse through professional or graduate school, scouting around for a good business connection, or merely marking time while figuring out what one really wants to do as an adult. For others teaching is a jumping-off point into administration, research, or supervision.

Many student teachers I have known over the last five years are becoming teachers to negate the wounds they received when they were in school. They want to counter the racism, the sexual put-downs, all the other humiliations they experienced with new, freer ways of teaching and learning. They want to be teachers to protect and nurture people younger than they who have every likelihood of being damaged by the schools. Some of these people come from poor or oppressed communities, and their commitment to the children is a commitment to the community of their parents, brothers and sisters, and their own children as well. Others, mostly from white middle- or upper-class backgrounds, have given up dialogue with their parents and rejected the community they grew up in. Teaching for them becomes a means of searching for ways of connecting with a community they can care for and serve.

There were a number of reasons that led me to choose elementary school teaching. For one, I never wanted to put my toys away and get on with the serious business of being an adult. I enjoy playing games, building things that have no particular purpose or value beyond themselves, trying painting, sculpting, macramé without becoming obsessed by them. I enjoy moving from subject to subject, from a math problem to a design problem, from bead collecting to the classification of mollusks. Specialization does not interest me, and teaching elementary school makes it possible for me to explore many facets of the world and share what I learn. My self-justification is that the games I play and the things I explore all contribute to making a curriculum that will interest and engage my students.

I guess also I became a teacher of young children initially because I thought they were purer, more open, and less damaged than I was. They were the saviors—they could dare to be creative where I was inhibited; they could write well because they didn't know what good writing was supposed to be; they could learn with ease, whereas I was overridden with anxiety over grades and tests. I never forgot the time in high school when I was informed that I missed making Arista, the national high school honor society, by 0.1 of a point. I went into the boys' bathroom and cried, the first time I had cried since being a baby. Neither Hitler's horrors nor the deaths of relatives and friends could cause me to cry because I was a male and was too proud to show sadness and weakness. Yet 0.1 of a grade point could bring tears and self-hatred and feelings of inferiority. And what if I'd made it—would

I laugh at my friends' tears because they missed by 0.1 of a point just as they did at me? There is no reward on either side of that cruel system.

When I became a teacher, some of my dreams of free development for my own students came true—they could be open and creative. But they also could be closed, destructive, nasty, manipulating—all the things I wanted to avoid in the adult world. It was important to sort out the romance of teaching from the realities of teaching and discover whether, knowing the problems, the hard work and frustration, it still made sense to teach. For me the answer has been "yes," but there are still times I wish I'd chosen some easier vocation.

Everyone who goes into teaching, even temporarily, has many reasons for choosing to spend five hours a day with young people. These reasons are often unarticulated and more complex than one imagines. Yet they have significant effects upon everyday work with students and on the satisfaction and strength the teacher gets from that work. Consequently, it makes sense, if you are thinking of becoming a teacher, to begin questioning yourself and understanding what you expect from teaching and what you are willing to give to it.

It also is of value to understand what type of children, what age, what setting is most sensible for your temperament and skills. Simple mistakes like teaching children that are too young or too old can destroy promising teachers. I had a friend who was teaching first grade and having a miserable time of it. The class was out of order, the students paid no attention to what she said, and she couldn't understand what the children were talking about. One day in anger, she blurted out to me that her major frustration was that she couldn't hold a good conversation with her class. She wanted to talk about civil rights, racism, about ways of reconstructing our society, about poverty and oppression. She wanted to read poetry with the children, expose them to music. She prepared each class for hours, put herself into the work, cared about the children—and yet things kept on getting worse.

What she wanted and needed from her six-year-olds was simply beyond them. I suggested that she try junior high if she wanted dialogue and challenge from her students. First grade was a mistake. The next year she transferred to one of the most difficult junior high schools in New York City, where she immediately felt at home. She was in the right place—what she offered could be used by the students, and therefore they could reward her with the exchange she needed.

There are a number of questions people thinking of becoming teachers might ask themselves in order to clarify their motives and focus on the type of teaching situations that could make sense for them. These questions do not have simple answers. Sometimes they cannot be answered until one has taught for a while. But I think it makes sense to keep them in mind while considering whether you actually want to teach and then, if you do, during training and the first few years of work.

1. What reasons do you give yourself for wanting to teach? Are they all negative (e.g., because the schools are oppressive, or because I was damaged, or because I need a job and working as a teacher is more respectable than working as a cab driver or salesperson)? What are the positive reasons for wanting to teach? Is there any pleasure to be gained from teaching? Knowledge? Power? As an elaboration on this, there is another similar question:

2. Why do you want to spend so much time with young people? Are you afraid of adults? Intimidated by adult company? Fed up with the competition and coldness of business and the university? Do you feel more comfortable with children? Have you spent much time with children recently, or are you mostly fantasizing how they would behave? Before deciding to become a teacher, it makes sense to spend time with young people of different ages at camp, as a tutor, or as a playground supervisor. I have found it valuable to spend time at playgrounds and observe children playing with each other or relating to their parents or teachers. One day, watch five-, ten-, fifteen-year-olds on the play-

ground or the street, and try to see how they are alike and how they are different. The more you train your eye to observe young people's behavior, the easier it will be to pick up attitudes and feelings and relationships in your own classroom.

Elaborating on the question of why spend so much time with young people, it is important to ask . . .

3. What do you want from the children? Do you want them to do well on tests? Learn particular subject matter? Like each other? Like you? How much do you need to have students like you? Are you afraid to criticize them or set limits on their behavior because they might be angry with you? Do you consider yourself one of the kids? Is there any difference in your mind between your role and that of your prospective students?

Many young teachers are not sure of themselves as adults, feel very much like children, and cover over a sense of their own powerlessness with the rhetoric of equality. They tell their students that they are all equal and then are surprised when their students walk all over them or show them no respect. If students have to go to school, if the teacher is paid and the students are not, if the young expect to learn something from the older in order to become more powerful themselves, then the teacher who pretends to be an equal of the student is both a hypocrite and a disappointment in the students' eyes. This does not mean that the teacher doesn't learn with or from the students, nor does it mean that the teacher must try to coerce the students into learning or be the source of all authority. It does mean, however, that the teacher ought to have some knowledge or skills to share, mastery of a subject that the students haven't already encountered and might be interested in. This leads to the next question:

4. What do you know that you can teach to or share with your students? Too many young people coming out of college believe that they do not know anything worth sharing or at least feel they haven't learned anything in school worth it. Teacher training usually doesn't help since it concentrates on "teaching skills" rather than the content of what might be learned. Yet there is so

much young people will respond to if the material emerges out of problems that challenge them and if the solutions can be developed without constant judging and testing. I have found that young people enjoy working hard, pushing and challenging themselves. What they hate is having their self-esteem tied up in learning and regurgitating material that bores them. Constant testing interferes with learning.

The more you know, the easier teaching becomes. A skilled teacher uses all his or her knowledge and experience in the service of building a curriculum each year for the particular individuals that are in the class. If you cannot think of any particular skills you have, but just like being with children, don't go right into teaching. Find other ways of spending time with young people while you master some skills that you believe are worth sharing.

Here is a partial list of things one could learn: printing; working with wood, plastic, fabrics, metal; how to run a store; making or repairing cars, shoes, boats, airplanes; playing and teaching cards, board, dice, ball games; playing and composing music; understanding ways of calculating and the use and construction of computers; using closed circuit TV; making films; taking pictures; understanding history, especially history that explains part of the present; knowing about animals and plants, understanding something of the chemistry of life; knowing the law; understanding how to use or care for one's body.

These subjects are intrinsically interesting to many students and can be used as well in teaching the so-called basic skills of reading, writing, and math, which are themselves no more than tools that extend people's power and make some aspects of the world more accessible. Too often these basic skills are taught in isolation from interesting content, leaving students wondering what use phonics or set theory could possibly have in their lives. It is not good enough to tell the class that what they are learning now will be of use when they are grown-ups. Six-year-olds and ten-year-olds have immediate interests, and reading and math ought to be tied to these interests, which range all the way from learning to make and build things to learning to play games and master comic books and fix bicycles and make money and cook and find out about other people's feelings and lives—the list can go on and on. The more time you spend informally with young children, the more you will learn about their interests. Listening carefully and following up on what you hear are skills a teacher has to cultivate. If students are interested in paper airplanes, it is more sensible to build a unit around flying than to ban them and assume police functions.

5. Getting more specific, a prospective teacher ought to consider what age youngster he or she feels the greatest affinity toward or the most comfortable with. There are some adults who are afraid of high school– or junior high school–aged people (thirteen- to seventeen-year-olds), while others are terrified at the idea of being left alone in a room with twenty-four six-year-olds. Fear of young people is neither unnatural nor uncommon in our culture. This is especially true in the schools, where undeclared warfare between the adults and the children defines much of the social climate. As long as young people feel constantly tested and judged by their teacher and have to experience the humiliation of their own or their friends' failures, they try to get even in any ways they can. Teachers who try to be kind often find themselves taken advantage of, while those who assume a strict stand are constantly tricked and mocked. It takes time and experience to win the respect of young people and not be considered their enemy in the context of a traditional American school.

It is very difficult to feel at ease in a classroom, to spend five hours with young people and not emerge wiped out or exhausted at the end of the day. This is especially true if one is mismatched with the students.

Great patience and humor, an ease with physical contact, and an ability to work with one's hands as well as one's mouth are needed for teachers of five- and six-year-olds. A lack of sexual prudery is almost a prerequisite for junior high school teachers, while physical and personal confidence and the love of some subject make work with high school students much easier.

This does not mean that an adult shouldn't take chances working with students whose age poses a problem. I know this year has been one of the most fulfilling of my teaching years, and yet I was full of anxiety about my ability to be effective with five- and six-year-olds after working with twelve- to eighteen-year-olds for twelve years. I taught myself to be patient, learned to work with my hands, to play a lot, to expect change to develop slowly. The students' ability to express affection or dislike openly and physically moved and surprised me, and initially their energy exhausted me. I must have lost fifteen pounds the first month, just trying to keep up with them.

One way of discovering what age youngster to begin working with is to visit a lot of schools. Try to find teachers you like and respect, and spend a few days working alongside them. Don't visit for an hour or two. It is important to stay all day (or if you have time, all week) to get a sense of the flow of time and energy working with that age person involves. Of course, your rhythm as a teacher might be different, but it is important to have a sense of what it is like to be with young people all day before becoming a teacher.

6. Before becoming a teacher it is important to examine one's attitudes toward racial and class differences. Racism is part of the heritage of white Americans, and though it can be mostly unlearned, it manifests itself in many subtle ways. Some white teachers are overtly condescending toward black and brown and red children, give them crayons instead of books. Others are more subtly condescending—they congratulate themselves on caring enough to work in a ghetto, choose one or two favorite students and put the rest down as products of a bad environment. They consider themselves liberal, nonracist, and yet are repelled by most of their students while believing that they are "saving" a few. There are ways of picking up racist attitudes in one's own way of talking. When a teacher talks about his or her pupils as

"them" or "these kind of children," or when a favorite pupil is described as "not like the rest of them," one is in the presence of a
racist attitude. Accompanying this attitude is usually an unarticulated fear of the children. I have seen white kindergarten teachers treat poor African American five-year-old boys as if they were
nineteen, carried guns and knives, and had criminal intentions at
all times. Needless to say, this sort of adult attitude confuses and
profoundly upsets the child. It also causes the adult to ignore acts
that should otherwise be prevented. Many white teachers in
ghetto schools claim they are being permissive and believe in allowing their students freedom when it would be closer to the
truth to say that they are afraid that their students will beat them
up and that they are afraid to face the moral rage their students
have from being treated in brutal and racist ways. When a student destroys a typewriter or brutalizes a smaller student, that is
not an acceptable or humane use of freedom.

Young teachers have a hard time knowing how and when to be
firm and when to be giving. This becomes even more complex
when the teacher is white, of liberal persuasion, afraid of physical
violence, and teaching a class of poor children who are not white.

However, fear is not limited to white-nonwhite situations.
Many middle-class people have attitudes toward poor people in
general that are manifested in the classroom in ways very close to
the racist attitudes described above. Poverty is looked upon as a
disease that one does not want to have contact with. Many
teachers have a hard time touching poor children, as if somehow
the poverty can be spread by physical contact. Then there are the
condescending liberal attitudes toward "saving" a few good students from the general condition of poverty, as if the rest got
what they deserve.

Prospective teachers, especially those who might choose or be
assigned to work with poor or nonwhite students, have to examine their own attitudes toward class and race. If these people
come from isolated white middle-class communities, I would suggest they move into a mixed urban community and live and work

there before becoming teachers. Then they might be able to see their students as individuals rather than as representatives of a class or race. And they might also develop insight into the different ways people learn and teach each other and themselves. Good teaching requires an understanding and respect of the strengths of one's pupils, and this cannot develop if they and their parents are alien to one's nonschool experience.

7. Another, perhaps uncomfortable, question a prospective teacher ought to ask him or herself is what gender-based motives he or she has for wanting to work with young people. Do you want to enable young boys or girls to become the boys or girls you could never be? To, for example, free the girls of the image of prettiness and quietness and encourage them to run and fight, and on an academic level, mess about with science and get lost in the abstractions of math? Or to encourage boys to write poetry, play with dolls, let their fantasies come out, and not feel abnormal if they enjoy reading or acting or listening to music?

Dealing with gender is one of the most difficult things teachers who care to have all their students develop fully have to learn how to manage. Often children arrive at school as early as kindergarten with clear ideas of what is proper behavior for boys and girls. The teacher has to be sensitive to parentally and culturally enforced gender roles that schools traditionally reinforce, and be able to lead children to choose what they want to learn, free of those encumbrances.

There are other problems teachers have to sort out that are sexual rather than gender-based. Many male teachers enjoy flirting with female students and using flirtation as a means of controlling the girls. Similarly, some female teachers try to seduce male students into learning. All these exchanges are covert—a gesture, a look, a petulant or joking remark.

Children take adult affection very seriously, and often what is play or dalliance on the part of the adult becomes the basis of endless fantasy and expectation on the part of the child. The issue exists in the early grades, but is much more overt on the high school level, where young teachers often naively express affection and concern, which students interpret as sexual overtures (which in some cases they might actually be, however unclear to the teacher).

A final question that should be asked with respect to gender in the classroom: do you need to get even with one gender, as a group, for real or fancied injuries you experienced? Do you dislike boys or girls as a group? Do you feel that the girls were always loved too much? That the boys brutalized you and need to learn a lesson? That somehow you have to get even in your classroom for an injury you suffered as a child? There are many good reasons for not becoming a teacher, and the need to punish others for a hurt you suffered is certainly one.

It might seem that I'm being harsh or cynical by raising questions about motives for teaching and suggesting that there are circumstances in which a person either should not become a teacher or should wait a while. If anything, these questions are too easy and can unfortunately be put aside with facile, self-deceiving answers. But teaching young people—i.e., helping them become sane, powerful, self-respecting, and loving adults—is a very serious and difficult job in a culture as oppressive and confused as ours, and needs strong and self-critical people.

There are other questions that ought to be considered. These might seem less charged, but are not less important.

8. What kind of young people do you want to work with? There are a number of children with special needs that can be assisted by adults with particular qualities. For example, there are some severely disturbed children—children whose behavior is bizarre, who are not verbal, who might not yet be toilet-trained at nine or ten, who might be engaged in dialogue for hours at a time with creatures you cannot perceive.

These same questions should be raised by people thinking of working with deaf, blind, or physically damaged people. Who are they? What is the world they live in? How can I serve them?

Let me illustrate a perverse way of going about deciding how to serve people in order to point toward a more healthy way of func-

tioning. For a long time most schools for deaf children were controlled by nondeaf teachers, parents, and administrators who advocated the oral, rather than the manual, tradition. The oral
tradition maintained that it was necessary for deaf individuals to
learn to speak instead of depending on sign language. Many oralist schools prohibited their students from using sign language,
and some professionals within that tradition maintained that
sign language was not a "real" language at all, but some degener-
ate or primitive form of communication. All these prohibitions
were to no avail—deaf children learned signing from each other
and used it when the teachers' backs were turned. Many deaf
adults trained in oralist schools ended up despising the language
they were forced to learn and retreated into an all-deaf world
where communication was in signs. Recently things have begun
to change—sign language has been shown to be an expressive,
sophisticated language with perhaps even greater potential for
communication than oral language. A deaf-power movement has
developed which insists that teachers of the deaf respond to the
needs of deaf adults and children. It is no longer possible to tell
deaf people what they must learn from outside the community.
To teach within a deaf community (and, in fact, in all communities) requires understanding the world people live in and responding to their needs as they articulate them. This does not
mean that the teacher should be morally or politically neutral.
Rather, it means that being a teacher does not put an individual
in a position of forcing his or her values on students or community. A teacher must engage in dialogue with the students and
parents if he or she hopes to change them—and be open to
change as well. Many teachers have been educated in communities they initially thought they would educate.

9. Some people get along well in crowds and others function
best with small groups or single individuals. Before becoming a
classroom teacher, it is important to ask oneself what the effect is
on one's personality of spending a lot of time with over twenty
people in the same room. Some of the best teachers I know do

not feel at ease or work effectively with more than a dozen students at a time. With those dozen, however, they are unusually effective. There are other people who have a gift for working on a one-to-one basis with students no one else seems to reach. There are ways to prepare oneself for individual or small-group work—as a skills specialist, remedial teacher, learning disabilities specialist, and so forth. There are also schools where it is possible to work with small groups as a teacher. Once you decide how you want to begin to work in a school, then you can look around and try to discover a situation in which you can be effective.

EXCERPT FROM *READING, HOW TO*

Condition 1: Who Is Qualified to Teach?

Anyone who reads with a certain degree of competency can help others who read less well. This is the case regardless of age or previous educational training. However most people in this culture are not accustomed to thinking of themselves as teachers. This is especially true of students in school who undervalue each other's capacity to share knowledge and skills and look to the adult teacher as the source of all learning.

Teaching is supposed to be a professional activity requiring long and complicated training as well as official certification. The act of teaching is looked upon as a flow of knowledge from a higher source to an empty vessel. The student's role is one of receiving information; the teacher's role is one of sending it. There is a clear distinction assumed between one who is supposed to know (and therefore not capable of being wrong) and another usually younger person who is supposed not to know.

It is possible however to think of teaching in another way, as more akin to guiding and assisting another person than to pouring knowledge into him or her. When a baby is learning how to talk, he or she is surrounded by innumerable guides who have mastered the skill to a greater degree than the baby, but none of whom know all there is to know about talking.

There are four people in our family in addition to me: my wife Judy, my daughters Antonia who is five and Erica who is three-and-a-half, and my son Joshua who is a year and a half. Josh is learning how to talk and he has four teachers on different levels of competency with the language themselves. Because Judy and I have a greater mastery of spoken English than Erica or Antonia does not mean however that we are more effective teachers of Josh. The girls spend a lot more time playing with Josh than we do and he follows them around and talks to them all the time. They sometimes seem to understand him a lot better than we do.

I notice they correct him every once in a while or name objects for him and ask him to repeat the words. It is a game for the most part but they want to communicate with him and he wants to communicate with them, so there is a natural reason for them to guide and assist him with language, and for him to accept their help.

The girls are also learning how to read in a natural manner. There are a lot of books around our house and the kids see the adults reading and want to do it too. Josh picks up a book and pretends to read. So do Antonia and Erica, only in different ways. Tonia knows which side is up or down, how the pages turn, and how the writing moves across the page. She's heard us read some books so often that she feels she can read them herself and does in a way—moving her finger across the page and reciting the story she knows by heart.

She also knows the alphabet and some words.

Erica knows which side of the book is supposed to be held up, but forgets which way the pages turn and the writing goes. Tonia helps her and sometimes reads the stories she has memorized to Erica who follows avidly.

Erica on the other hand helps Josh turn the book right side up, talks to him about pictures, imitates Judy or me reading a story.

Whenever there is a question about a picture or a word the kids bring the books to one of us and we tell them.

Judy and I in turn are still learning how to read—she has begun to read texts in ethology and has a new technical language to figure out. I am trying to make my way through Paolo Freire's *Pedagogy of the Oppressed* and have to learn his special use of some words as well as the meanings of some of his statements in the original Portuguese, a language I do not know. I have to deal with a translation and learn whether the translation distorts Freire's thoughts.

With the exception of Josh, we are all teaching and learning reading at different moments in our lives. There is no one of us who is always a teacher or always a learner. In fact the children often teach us to look at something differently—a story or picture, which they see more clearly than we do.

The other day I came upon Tonia and a six-year-old friend sitting in her bedroom reading a simple comic book. He was teaching her what he learned in school—pointing out words, reading sentences, explaining the story. He remembered what he picked up in school and being just a first-grader saw nothing wrong with sharing that knowledge.

Many of us underrate what we know or forget how we learned ourselves and therefore do not believe in our capacity to teach. We are trained to believe that professionals are the only ones who can teach, and that teaching requires a school. We are afraid to teach our children to read, or to teach other people's children to read, because we might mess up the work of professionals. We deny that professionals fail even when we see it happen and allow ourselves to believe that, rather than the professional being wrong or incompetent, our children are failures.

Of course professionals, in order to maintain their special claim to teaching or law or medicine, encourage our feelings of inadequacy and incompetence. They even develop ingenious ways of covering up their own mistakes as well as the hollowness of many of their claims to expertise. For example, there is a new category of diseases that doctors have chosen to call "iatrogenic diseases." Translated into simple language "iatrogenic" means doctor-caused. The iatrogenic diseases consist of health problems people develop because of doctors' mistakes and include ailments ensuing from side effects of drugs or aftereffects of surgery or mistakes in diagnosis. To call those ailments "doctor-caused" is to place responsibility where it belongs—that is, with the doctor. To call them "iatrogenic" legitimizes the doctor's errors and assimilates them to other disease categories such as cardiovascular diseases. Instead of a doctor's admitting that he made a mistake or didn't have adequate knowledge, he can tell his patient, "I'm afraid you have an iatrogenic disease," thereby locating the problem with the patient and creating the impression that he has a professional understanding of what is wrong.

I am surprised that educational professionals haven't followed their medical cousins and avoided dealing with problems they create for children by creating a new category that would appear to explain away teacher-caused learning problems. It would be easy! The Greek for teacher is *didaskalos*. "Genic" is the suffix used to express the idea of "being caused by" or "giving use to." Put them together and neaten it up a bit and we have "didagenic learning problems." Imagine parents being told when their child is failing to learn how to read, "I'm sorry but your child has a didagenic learning problem" and then being assured that the same professional who caused the problem can cure it.

The process of "professionalizing" ignorance is very common in our culture, which is obsessed with credentials and the power they can provide. Teaching need not be the province of a special group of people nor need it be looked upon as a technical skill. Teaching can be more akin to guiding and assisting than to forcing information into a supposedly empty head. If you have a certain skill you should be able to share it with someone. You do not have to get certified to convey what you know to someone else or to help them in their attempt to teach themselves. All of us, from the very youngest children to the oldest members of our cultures should come to realize our own potential as teachers. We can share what we know, however little it might be, with someone who has need of that knowledge or skill.

If you are in a position to help someone, it frequently helps to remember how you learned something yourself. This doesn't mean imitating your teachers so much as looking at the process of learning you went through, often despite your teachers. It also helps to listen to the learner's questions carefully, to discover the kind of help someone wants from you. For example, people may want you to tell them how to read a particular word because they want to learn how to sound out complicated words in general, or they may want to know it because the meaning of a story they are reading hinges on the sense of that word. In one case they are asking for a lesson, in the other for a quick answer.

It is important for the person who teaches to learn how to respond appropriately.

Occasionally you should take inventory, think about what you know how to do, and about ways of sharing those skills. People complain of isolation and powerlessness in our society. Teaching is a form of connection for the teacher as well as a gift to the learner. One doesn't have to become a "teacher" in order to go about teaching. Look around and devise ways to share what you know.

I remember a fantasy I had on the subway in New York when I was in the fifth grade. I was reading some complicated book that had some words I couldn't pronounce or understand. There were many people in the car reading the *Daily News* and the *New York Times*, and I wanted to ask someone to help me with the words but was scared. My fantasy was of being punched, stomped, laughed at, ignored, and ridiculed for daring to ask a stranger for such help. I don't think I'm alone. We are accustomed to asking strangers for directions if we're lost, but to ask for help with reading or the mastery of some skill is often looked upon as an invasion of privacy and a threat or challenge.

Somehow we must all open up to the possibility of being teachers, of assisting each other and not holding on selfishly to the little we know or undervaluing that knowledge. Students in schools can teach as well as learn—we all can—and without elaborate or expensive training. Reading can be taught by anyone who has learned up to the level of his competency.

This is not to deny, of course, that some people will be more obsessed with reading or the teaching of reading than others, nor to deny that there are different levels of competency. However one need not be an extraordinarily gifted reader to bring others to the point of being able to teach themselves on as complex a level as they want.

Condition 2: Knowledge as an Expensive Commodity

Learning to read is often just an incidental by-product of what traditional schools attempt to teach. A main goal of schooling in our society is to get the young to the point of conforming to a competitive mode of functioning in which being first is identified with being best and in which the failure of some is considered a natural event in human history. Consequently, students have to learn not to share what they know because that might lose them a competitive edge over other students. They also have to learn to compete for the teacher's attention and affection and turn the acquisition of skill and knowledge into an elaborate game in which there are winners and losers.

The traditional American classroom is governed by the teacher with the aid of an elaborate series of controlled so-called learning devices that enable the teacher to know at every moment what every student is supposed to be doing.

It is up to each child to learn for him or herself. No student is responsible for the learning of any other person and students are encouraged to look down upon the slowest or least compliant learners. The teacher's methods, which usually come from a prepackaged development or basal reading program,* are assumed to be effective for the "serious" student. If a youngster fails to acquire the skill or comply with the rules for learning, he or she is considered retarded or criminal, that is, in more polite school language, a learning or behavior problem.

Failing to keep up with the pace prescribed by the program and set by the teacher is an indication of inferiority. Because the

---

* The same critique applies to completely individualized structured reading programs as to group programs. They all predetermine what a student must do and attempt to manipulate the student into following directions and trying to move faster and faster along a prescribed path. Their goal is generally to produce students who make good scores on standardized reading tests rather than develop sensitive, socially and politically aware readers.

teacher has a rigid notion of the rate of progress, it is natural to form reading groups with moral biases built in—a "slow" group, a "normal" group, and a "fast" group. The notion that different individuals learn *normally* in different ways and at different paces is difficult to fit with the notion that there is a right way of learning.

There are other moral biases built into the traditional, teacher-centered classroom. Not only is the good student one who performs well for the teacher, but also the child learns to read in order to show he or she is a good student (and by association a good person). The central motivation for learning is not the acquisition of the skill and the self-fulfillment reading and writing can bring. Rather it is the approval of the teacher and of one's parents. Good readers are often good citizens, though of course in many traditional classrooms there is the bizarre phenomenon of some students reading too well—that is of moving faster than the teacher wants and asking too many penetrating questions. A teacher-centered classroom turns issues of learning and the development of skills into questions of approval and rejection. It is no wonder then that many students who conform and learn as they are told end up resenting the price they have had to pay and avoid using the skills they acquired in schools. This is especially true for white middle-class kids who acquiesce to the demands of their teachers and parents and believe in the rules:

> I am a good student
> Therefore I am loved (good).
> I am loved (good) because
> I am a good student.
> I will be a good student
> so I can be loved (good).

and fear the consequences of nonconformity:

> I am a bad student
> Therefore I am not loved (bad).
> I am unloved (bad) because

I am a bad student.
I will be a bad student.
so I can prove that I am unloved (bad).*

When love, approval, moral status, competitive ability, and the acquisition of a skill are so compounded in the classroom, it is no wonder people come away from the experience of schooling resenting what they learned.

Since most of our schools are middle class in culture and dominated by white middle-class values and people, it is no wonder that many poor white and nonwhite people fail to learn the basic skills of reading. If a student is not ready to play the love/hate game with the teacher, if the teacher does not identify with the student and therefore doesn't care if he is good (that is, doesn't care to love him or her), if in addition the whole system of learning is based on a series of rewards and punishments that denigrate the values and lives of the students' parents, then it is no wonder that many of these students reject the whole business of confusing acceptance, rejection, competition, loving, and learning.

Some students (predominantly from the middle class) do learn to read within the traditional classroom and others learn despite it.† For the former, the pace the teacher sets is natural and the love offered for conformity to the teacher and competition with one's peers rewarding. The substance of the reading program probably doesn't matter much for them—any one that keeps them working regularly and rewarded periodically will do. The problem is what happens when the teacher disappears—will there be any other reason for them to read, or will they feel, as many American adults feel, that reading is a chore rather than a source of pleasure and a vehicle for learning all one's life?

---

* With apologies to R.D. Laing and his *Knots*.

† Many people who learn despite school are quickly engaged in reading outside of school once they master some minimal skills in school. Comic books and romances specifically written for the young become their texts and reading becomes an activity that they engage in for themselves and not for the sake of the teacher or the grade.

The question of how reading is to be taught is a moral one, and not just a matter of finding the proper technology. This can be seen even more clearly by looking at the remedial reading clinic, which is a good illustration of what the traditional school system does with students who are considered failures.

The remedial reading clinic fits within the moral world of the traditional classroom. A remedy according to the *Oxford English Dictionary* is "a cure for a disease or other disorder of the body or mind" or a "means of counteracting or removing an outward evil of any kind." In many of our schools students who have not learned to read by traditional methods are considered to have a learning disease or to be vested with some form of evil that must be removed or remediated. These students are removed from their classrooms for a few hours a week and sent to a special room designated as a reading clinic and staffed by someone who is supposed to be a specialist in reading—the educational equivalent of an internal medicine man or orthopedic surgeon or psychiatrist. The clinic is set up differently than a classroom. In many remedial reading situations there are a few chairs or desks placed around a teacher's desk. A well-stocked clinic will have many books, programmed reading material, workbooks, material designed to develop perceptual skills such as hand-eye coordination and left-to-right orientation. There will be a wide variety of resources available so that the specialist will be able to develop an individual or small-group program that will make the sick student well by getting him or her to read on grade level and therefore be able to return to the classroom and fit into the regular reading program. The prime goal of remedial reading is to prepare the student to fit back in, not to enable him or her to read well. Therefore the "good" remedial reading teacher must believe in the culture of the school. If not, he or she will be considered a disruptive maverick whose attempt to help the kids read well will be taken as an attempt to disrupt the culture of the school.

Students are "referred" to remedial reading as patients are "referred" to mental hospitals. They do not go by choice and are not released until they are deemed well. In the public elementary schools at which I have taught the kids going to remedial reading felt they were dumb, or at least they felt that other people thought they were dumb. Some welcomed the opportunity to get better and return to compete with the rest of the class. Others gave up on themselves altogether and looked at remedial reading as an hour's release from the constant humiliation they experienced in the classroom. None of them thought very much about reading as a skill to acquire for their own strength and purposes— they were that much caught up in being the victims of the social and moral system we build around the acquisition of the simple skill of reading.

Many remedial reading teachers use an elaborate diagnostic procedure to analyze everything from the student's reading ability to his or her dietary habits to the state of the soul. The only thing left out is an analysis of what the student's teacher had been doing to induce failure. For example, the Gates reading diagnostic form includes the following information:

Age, grade, intelligence
   Chronological age
   Grade status
   Binet IQ
Silent reading tests
Oral reading
Vocabulary
Reversal test
Phrase perception
Visual perception techniques
Auditory techniques
Tests of vision
Tests of hearing
Observations or tests of speech
Eye movements; use of finger; lip movements; head movements, etc., in silent reading

Evidence of emotional tension, fear, irritation, lack of confi-
dence, etc.
Evidence concerning special interests and distastes
Influence of home, parents, and other out-of-school factors
School history

Some useful information can be acquired by using this elaborate procedure, but the medical setting—the implication that the
student is sick—tends to create nervousness and encourage some
of the psychological problems it is meant to cure.

The assumption that a student needs remedial help if he or she
has not learned to read needs to be examined. First of all, if someone has not acquired a skill there is nothing to remediate. To
need remediation, strictly speaking, the skill must be either acquired in a confused manner or acquired then lost. If a person
who has not learned how to read is simply considered as someone
to be taught or helped for the first time, the whole problem of
guilt or failure disappears and with it the need for a special place
to deal with failures. There are some cases where there is a genuine need for remediation, such as cases where people lose previously acquired ability to read through head injuries. Even these
cases can be confounded by overreligious adherence to a medical
model and to the school's notion of success and failure.

Several years ago I worked with a sixth-grade girl who had a severe reading problem. She was referred to me by a doctor after many
reading specialists had given up on her. The girl had read perfectly
well during her first four years of school, but when she was ten she
was involved in a serious car accident. Her head was thrown against
the dashboard and she had suffered severe headaches ever since.
Also, she seemed to have forgotten how to read, though her verbal
and mathematical abilities were completely intact. This seemed a
clear case of someone who needed remedial help.

When I first saw Lillian she was thoroughly demoralized. She
had recently scored 2.7 on a reading test and had to score at least
5.0 to be promoted to the seventh grade, and thus go on to jun-

ior high school with her friends. She was sure she would be left behind in the elementary school and put in a "dumb" class to boot. That was what her guidance counselor had told her.

I asked Lillian to read Maurice Sendak's *Where the Wild Things Are* (Harper), one of my favorite diagnostic tools. The language is simple; the story is sophisticated; the pictures are interesting and a bit scary. In the middle of the book there are six pages that contain only illustrations, no words. This gives me an opportunity to ask questions about the story and the pictures, which can lead to an interesting talk about wildness and the symbols Sendak uses to embody it. After a little talk I can get a sense of how much interpretation and elaboration the reader is used to.

Lillian read the first few pages with no trouble (there are only a few lines per page). On about the fifth page she made a simple mistake, read "mild" for "wild," a word she previously had no trouble with. Immediately after making the mistake she panicked and read every other word on the page incorrectly. I noticed she looked away from the page, wrinkled her brow, and began to make sound associations that had nothing to do with the story. For example, she read "more" as "four" and then said "door," "boor," "coor" and finally trailed off into some inaudible sounds.

I asked her to stop for a while and rest. She began again and was fine until she made another mistake. Then the same flight from the written page occurred.

Lillian didn't have any problem with phonics. She knew how to read in a technical sense. Only she could not sustain herself for more than a few sentences. She had no stamina and didn't know how to help herself when she made a mistake.

I spoke to her about my observations, and she was surprised. She was used to going to remedial reading clinics, getting a "work-up," and then being given a reading treatment. No one had ever spoken to her about the process of reading, or about what they felt were her problems. She had been treated as a sick child, incapable of understanding her own problems, and was usually told to do exercises that made no sense to her.

I worked with Lillian for two hours a week over a period of three months. She wanted to learn to read again, and I saw no reason she couldn't learn. For the first few weeks we talked about her problems. Every time she made a mistake we stopped and talked about how she could check herself. After a while she could stop when she made a mistake and start again. She found that slowly counting to five helped calm her down after a flight of sound associations. There was nothing mystical about her problem or "professional" about its resolution.

It turned out that Lillian had a problem focusing her eyes on the written word. I didn't need a test of perceptual skills to see that, it was only necessary to look at her. I suggested she follow along the page with her finger, and it seemed to work during the lessons at home. It created serious problems at school, however. Her teacher refused to let her use her finger while she read. Somewhere he had picked up the notion that it was a bad thing to do. The remedial reading specialist agreed. I spoke to the teacher about it. He could not give me any reason why reading with one's finger on the page was wrong or harmful, so he referred me to his supervisor, who took the same position in the same irrational way. Finally, I had to get a doctor's note and threaten a lawsuit to enable Lillian to read in school in a way that was obviously helping her.

Lillian and I did a lot of stamina training. I explained to her almost everything I knew about reading, and together we planned out a reading program she could follow by herself. She learned to control her nervous habits and her tendency to panic disappeared. She used her finger and sometimes a piece of paper to help her focus. Together, we practiced taking reading tests. By the end of a few months she could read again and could also understand what reading problems were all about. She could, and did, help other students with reading problems.

In June she was given a reading test again and scored on a sixth-grade level. The teacher and the reading specialist refused to accept the results. They said that progress could not be made that quickly and therefore Lillian and I must have cheated.

They retested her, and she scored the same. They refused to accept the second test results either. They gave her a third test, and she scored on the fifth-grade level. Some of her nervous habits had begun to return. The school was beginning to create a new reading problem for Lillian. Again, with the help of a doctor and the threat of a lawsuit, we got the school to accept the results of a fourth testing on which Lillian managed to score on the fifth-grade level. She was promoted to junior high.

Lillian's story illustrates how school can actually inhibit young people's learning how to learn. The example, though dramatic, is not such an exception as it might seem. Lillian was nervous because of her accident. But she was even more nervous over the prospect of not being promoted. She was separated from her friends and put into a class for "special" students because she couldn't read. She took tests, and nobody believed her results, thereby undermining her confidence and making reading more of a problem. And there was no way for her to escape the situation because the law says that she has to go to school, and her mother cannot afford a private school or a special tutor.

In this case the remedial reading clinic was no more successful than the regular classroom. That's not surprising since their goals are the same—fit the child to the system of learning without bothering to find out how the child learns best.

I have thought a lot about my experience with Lillian and about what specifically helped. Nothing was done to her in a medical sense. No technical knowledge was employed though I had some experience watching young people read and helping them develop programs based upon what I could perceive about their approach to written material. There was no way Lillian could fail so far as I was concerned. As long as she wanted to learn how to read we would keep on exploring strategies together. Eventually, we were bound to hit on something that worked. If not, I would ask a friend to help. Lillian was not a failure, she was just seeking a way to learn how to read again.

The attitude of the person who assists another is crucial in the teaching/learning situation. Teaching a skill such as reading is not a phenomenon that can be abstracted from the values of the teacher or the institution the teacher works for. If you believe that learning is a competitive phenomenon that is bound to produce failure, some people must be put in the position of being designated failures in order to justify your beliefs. If, on the other hand, your concern is to help people acquire the power necessary to control their lives, failure is your failure as a teacher and not the pupils'. In our culture there is a competitive elite. That is, a group of people who succeed in beating others at academic or financial games. The victorious have no responsibility to share their knowledge or wealth with the defeated. In fact, they need the presence of the defeated to justify and verify their victories.

If one cares to help people read, to share one's own skills, then the phenomenon of failure on the part of students is out of order. You can help some people; others you may not be able to assist but some other person might. To separate reading from competitive gaming implies a generosity toward others, an offering of one's own skills and wealth to people who do not have them. It implies that the other has a right to refuse the gift without being considered inferior or a failure; it also means that the person who learns is not expected to be in the obligation of the teacher or the institution that employs the teacher. When people learn to read, the only responsibility one can hope of them, and the greatest at the same time, is that they will assume the obligation of teaching someone else to master what they have achieved.

Condition 3: Respecting the Language and Culture of the Learner

If there is to be a natural transition from speaking to reading, the learner's voice should be present in writing as well as speech. However, in our intolerant culture some variations of the English language are judged to be superior to others. For example, so-called Standard English is said to be more expressive, abstract, powerful, proper, and correct than the dialect African Americans or Chicanos or East Europeans or Italians or Chinese speak. The grammatical forms of Standard English are looked upon as "the correct way of speaking and writing" and other forms are considered primitive and incorrect by many teachers. For example, "I am happy" is considered "correct" and "I be happy" or "I happy" are supposed to be signs of illiteracy. However, all three sentences are equally clear and expressive. There are certain myths about standard and proper language that must be set aside once and for all:

Myth 1. There is a single correct way of writing and talking. This myth translated really says that the people who make the rules in the culture want to regulate language and insist that the way they speak is better than the way others speak. One frequently hears people claim that everyone *must* learn to read and write Standard English. That statement is true only insofar as the people in power insist that official documents, job applications, business letters, etc., must be written in Standard English as a sign of conformity to the basic competitive values of the culture.

Myth 2. Some languages are more complex, abstract, and expressive than others. This is just false, though it comforts some people to believe that their way of speaking is more abstract and intellectual than that of other people. All known languages are capable of the same expressiveness and have similar structural complexity. However, how people use their language is a social and moral matter. The way people choose to use a language and the capacity of the language itself should not be confused.

Myth 3. Within a language some dialects are superior to others. This again expresses the need of one group of people to feel superior to others. Actually there is probably not even a functioning "standard dialect." There are a wide variety of ways people use and pronounce the English language within our society and these variations have to do with the original languages people spoke as well as the social class of the speakers and the part of the country they came from. It is important to eliminate linguistic imperialism and understand that the imposition of a standardized language is just another form of oppression. This is not to deny, however, that people ought to compromise enough to make their writing comprehensible to the audience they want to reach.

Myth 4. If people learn to read and write in their own dialect they will never learn the standard language. This again is a major put-down of poor or minority people. It is no big deal to be able to read and write in so-called Standard English as well as in one's own natural voice, especially for someone who understands something about reading and language. After all one can understand many dialects with ease, imitate them in speech, and consequently in writing. Anyone, for example, who has been exposed to television has heard a lot of so-called standard ways of talking and can imitate many television characters. One can learn to read and write in a number of dialects at the same time.

Respecting the language and culture of the learner implies taking a nonelitist attitude toward language.* It implies that one does not believe that one's own way of speaking is superior as well as that one is curious about understanding the structure of other dialects. These last remarks are specifically addressed to white middle-class people. It is fashionable to be interested in so-called non-Standard English, in African American or Chicano or Puerto Rican dialect in a condescending paternalistic way. I have seen many young teachers who say they believe that kids should be allowed to speak and write in their own dialects. The tone these teachers take implies that the natives should be indulged a bit before being raised to the level of "our language." One has to listen to how people speak, to think about language, to be aware of how one's own values slip into so-called objective statements about language, in order to undo the racist sense of the superiority of

---

* *Black English* by J. L. Dillard (Random House, 1972) substantiates the points made in this section with respect to the speech of African Americans. It should be read by anyone who thinks about language and culture.

white middle-class language that is part of the legacy of American education.

Let me say once more: To respect someone's language does not merely mean to tolerate it or condescendingly accept it. Respect is an attitude that exists among peers, equals. It is the basis of dialogue between different peoples and different cultural traditions. Without respect in this sense it is not possible to avoid master-slave mentality.

A note on basic skills, natural learning, and different cultural traditions:

Many people make the argument that poor and minority people cannot afford humane, open, cooperative education. They claim that the basic need for poor people is to acquire the skills of reading, writing, and math, and that any nontraditional schooling will deprive them of skills needed to survive and therefore perpetuate their powerlessness. I find this attitude condescending and patronizing. Poor students, minority students, people in general, respond when they are respected. One of the main points of this book is to show that the skills of reading and writing can be obtained by all people in humane, natural, open ways. Another point is that the learning situation has to be tailored to the cultures and lives of the students. There are and should be open learning situations that exist within the setting of African American, Chicano, Puerto Rican, Appalachian culture. There is no question in my mind that it is necessary for people in our culture to be able to read and write. The question is how people acquire those skills and what else they learn on the way.

An interesting situation developed in Berkeley a few years ago. According to the test results taken as a whole, Berkeley was a bit above the mythical national norm. When the scores were broken down, as they were three years ago at the insistence of a few members of the African American community, it was discovered that there was a bimodal distribution of scores within the city. The white kids were well above the norm, and the African American kids were below. Whatever one's feeling about testing, the results indicated one thing clearly—in terms of the school and society the white kids were making it, and the African American kids were not.

The test results also revealed in a crude way something else which could not be ignored—the white kids could read and the African American kids couldn't. Something had to be done, and here is where the conflict came in.

There was a cry for a reemphasis on basic skills within the school district. Many white kids and parents did not favor this since their kids already had those skills and needed other things from school. However, there was another and unfortunately little noticed contradiction: Some conservative members of the African American community were asking the teachers to reemphasize the basics when, in fact, the way they had been emphasized in the past was precisely what had led to failure. In the panic over scores, issues like teacher accountability were bandied about. Finally, a formula (later not enforced) was developed and approved by the school board, where each teacher was to be held accountable for one year's growth in reading for each student in his or her class. There was naturally a general panic and a harsh reemphasis on phonics and all the other pseudoprofessional paraphernalia of the teaching profession. Failure was built into the situation, for African American kids do not easily succeed in the cultural world of white middle-class schools.

At a meeting of administrators I was asked what the school I ran would do about the board mandate. I replied that there was no problem for me in getting our students to read as long as it was left open as to how it was to be done.

The question of the need to acquire basic skills is often confused with the question of how these skills are to be acquired. I know many people who equate open education with indifferent education and believe that a teacher in an open situation does not care whether young people learn or not. Nothing could be farther from the truth. I would even go so far as to say that open education grew out of a concern for the way in which young peo-

ple learn and an awareness of how present school teaching dis-
courages learning. I want all kids to read and write, but I do not
believe that all young people should be forced through a develop-
mental reading program at the age of six and should be considered failures if that way of learning how to read is not natural to
them. Young people will learn to read and calculate when the
need is obvious to them, when the atmosphere in which they
learn is comfortable, and when the culture of the school is natural to them.

THE CRAFT OF TEACHING

From *Growing Minds:*
On Becoming a Teacher

Faith in the learner leads some teachers to find strengths where others see nothing but weakness and failure. Such faith, which is a component of teaching sensibility, is a form of what I call the love for students as learners. It is important to pause over the idea of *loving students as learners*, which is not the same as simply loving students. Each of us has only a limited amount of love we can offer, for love is not cheaply won or given. I care about all of my students, and respect them, but love grows slowly and requires attention and effort that cannot be spread around to twenty or thirty people simultaneously. Love also engages all parts of one's life, and teaching, for all its demands, is still just a part of one's total life as a parent, lover, citizen, and learner. I don't trust teachers who say they love all their students, because it isn't possible to love so many people you know so little about and will separate from in six months or a year.

Yet a certain kind of love is essential to good teaching, and that is what I choose to call loving students as learners. I once worked with a fourteen-year-old boy who could not read at all. He was very big and often defied his teachers. Occasionally he would explode with an uncontrolled and undirected violence that made people afraid to go near him. His parents came to me in despair. I promised to work with him two days a week after school. I was afraid of him too, though I considered being alone with him one of the risks and challenges of teaching. Since he had little sense of humor and seemingly no affection, I didn't particularly like him. Still, I responded to the teaching challenge, and as we worked together, I loved the way he came to master first his energy, then the alphabet, and then later books and writing.

I believe the turning point in our relationship came after about a month. He had been remote during that time, politely bored with my attempts to help him read. On this day, however, he was clearly angry. I could sense an impending explosion from the way he held his thumbs tightly in his fists and looked straight down at the floor instead of at me or at the book I was trying to get him to read. After a few minutes he did explode and knocked the manuscript of a book I was working on off my desk. I exploded quicker than he did at that. Next to the people I love, my manuscripts are the most important things in my life and I told him so. I ranted on about how important writing and books were to me. He tried to pick up the manuscript, but I let him know that at that moment I couldn't trust him to do it. As I calmed down I noticed for the first time that he was afraid, almost in tears actually trembling. I put the manuscript together and explained that books and writing were not small school things for me but central to life and understanding, that it was no joke not to be able to read, that it was a form of poverty, and that he didn't have a right to not read. I doubt that he had ever experienced an adult express so much care for learning and books—not for some relationship to a reading test or grade, but for books themselves. Anyway, his whole attitude toward reading began to change. I felt that my love of learning and my pride in teaching him gave him a very different perception of himself as a learner. For the next few weeks we talked about what was in different books. I read sections from books that dealt with subjects he was interested in, such as sea adventures and animal life. Slowly he took up phonics and simple books again, and after a while he could read. I loved to see him learning and, of course, to feel that I was some part of that process. Yet when he no longer needed my help, we parted no better friends than we began and I didn't miss our lessons, as I sometimes do. However, I took great pleasure in seeing him focus his previously undisciplined energy and learn to read. I loved him as a learner: it was a job-related affection. That affection led me to study him carefully and build on the strengths and personal interests I could tease out of him. It required that my personal feelings about him be subordinated to my feelings about him as a learner.

Teachers have preferences and can't be expected to like every student equally. And though teachers want to be liked by all their students, they shouldn't expect that to happen, either. Nevertheless, a teacher has an obligation to care about every student as a learner, just as every student should respect a decent caring teacher whether or not he or she likes that teacher.

I remember a context in which the suspension of ego enabled me to turn a potentially chaotic situation into a pleasant learning experience. I was substitute teaching for a friend who had to take care of a family crisis. I was called at eight in the morning and arrived at school at eight forty-five. The students had been in the room since eight-thirty and had managed to organize several games, dismantle a bookcase, turn over chairs and a large table. I knew my friend was having trouble with the class and intuited that his absence had released even more chaos. When I arrived, the door was open and I stood watching what was going on. It was clear that I'd have to step in and act in order to get through the day. Where to begin, though? How to step in and convert the disorder to some form of positive activity? I looked for details that would indicate who the class leaders were, listened to get a sense of the language the children used with each other, watched for clusters of children to estimate how many different things were happening simultaneously. I had to suspend my ego, and not jump in too soon or worry about whether I would be liked or successful, but rather gather as much information about the class as I could, as quickly as possible.

The largest group of students was playing around with a basketball, shooting it toward the teacher's desk, bouncing it off the ceiling, passing it wildly around the room. I decided that taming the basketball game would refocus the class's energy and establish enough structure so that I would be able to talk to the whole group and plan a full day together with them. I waited for a downcourt pass that was coming my way and stepped inside the room and caught the pass. Everyone froze for a moment—who was this stranger with their basketball?

I told the group that I was going to be their teacher for a day and turned to a boy whom I perceived to be a leader and asked, "Does your teacher always let you play basketball in the room?"

He said, "Yes."

I knew he was jiving me and I could have pretended to be angry and sat everyone down and proceeded with a lecture on classroom decorum. But lectures like that are no fun to give and don't produce results unless they are backed up by coercive force, which I had no intention of using. Better to go with the energy of the basketball game and use it as a positive focus. My response was:

"Where's the basket?"

He looked at me as if I were crazy.

"A basketball game has a basket and rules. If you play in here all the time, I wouldn't want to change anything. Where's the basket?"

One of the students caught on that I was willing to play along and let everyone save face rather than punish them, and she brought me the wastebasket. I accepted that as the basket, drew a scorecard on the chalkboard and a foul line on the classroom floor and set up a foul-shooting contest. Ten shots for everyone from the foul line to the wastebasket. Three scorekeepers at the chalkboard, two students retrieving the ball, two holding the basket, the rest on line waiting to shoot, unless they wanted to read a book or play a quiet game somewhere else in the room. Those were the first activities for the day. The next was to talk about what usually went on in the classroom and plan a day together.

My goal was to shift the focus of group energy away from taking advantage of their teacher's absence to helping me contrive to find a pleasant way to pass the day together. It would have been impossible if I responded by taking charge right away and laying down the law because my ego as a teacher was threatened.

Children pick up on their teachers' weaknesses and sometimes use them to shatter classroom authority. They can make fun of your clothes or breath or nose or walk or voice. In my case, students seem to pick on my flyaway hair, as one youngster called it. When I first began teaching, I wasted energy worrying about whether to cut my hair or defend myself against some student's snide remarks. That energy would more profitably have been invested in making the content of my teaching more interesting. After a while I learned how to make casual fun of my own hair and move on to more important things.

Another way students had of undermining my confidence was to make fun of lessons I had meticulously prepared. For example, during my second year of teaching, the theme of the fifth-grade social studies curriculum was the Industrial Revolution. I had spent the summer studying ways of building a working model of an early factory. I built or bought miniature models of factory tools and connected them through a series of belts and pulleys to a small steam engine. My idea was to demonstrate a simple version of a working factory to my class and then build a large, fairly accurate scale model of a cotton mill while studying the psychological, social, and economic effects of industrialization. Sometime during the first week of school I brought in the steam engine and a simple piston press that was powered by the engine. I was proud of my teaching plans and sure my students would be excited by them. One of the students filled the engine with water and another lit the can of Sterno under the boiler. As the water began to heat, we could hear sputtering and rumbling inside the engine, and a bit of steam escaped through the safety valve. Suddenly a voice from the back of the room proclaimed, "It's farting," and everybody started laughing and holding their noses. I was shattered, my face became red; my wonderful ideas had been turned into nothing but a silly joke. I blew out the fire, put the engine away, and insisted that everyone get out their workbooks and do an extra assignment. It took me several days to recover enough confidence to do something interesting again and try to get my students out of the workbooks that I used as a punishment.

If a similar thing happened to me these days, I'd laugh with my students at the farting engine and show them how the force created by such a blow-off could be used to run a machine. I would go with their energy and refocus it on learning, without destroying the good feeling created by sharing a joke.

I remember another instance where a similar twist on a planned lesson occurred. It happened a few years ago, after I'd had over fifteen years of teaching experience and learned how to control my ego and laugh with my students. I was teaching a combined kindergarten and first-grade class and had prepared a week's worth of explorations of the phenomena of light. The subject was introduced by giving each child a small mirror and some three-by-five cards that had capital letters written on them. My intention was to introduce the notion of symmetry and have the class discover which letters were symmetrical and which weren't, using the mirrors. As I explained the meaning of symmetry to the class and demonstrated it with a larger mirror and some drawings I'd prepared, there was a slight commotion in one corner of the room. I ignored it for a few minutes and went on. It got louder and as I turned to say something I found myself blinded. Four students had discovered how to use their mirrors to reflect sunlight into people's eyes and found that much more interesting and challenging than learning what symmetry was.

I went with the energy released by the students' discovery and reflected the sun back at them, using my mirror. Then I suggested we all try to focus the sunlight we captured on one spot on the ceiling. After managing that, one student suggested we have sunspot races and before long there were reflected spots of sunlight racing around the room, chasing each other. I joined in the games and at the same time reformulated my teaching plans. We'd start with reflections and angles, maybe move to shadows, and eventually find our way back to symmetry. Actually it didn't much matter to me how (or even whether) we got to symmetry. What was much more important was experimenting with the nature of light and trying to devote energy to understanding that phenomenon. The homework assignment for that day was to draw a picture explaining how someone managed to blind me. The picture had to show the sun, the mirror, me, and the path of light from the sun to my eyes.

GAMES AND MATHS

From *Writing, Maths and Games in the Open Classroom*

I go to toy stores the way other people go to bars, bookstores, garage sales or thrift shops. Several times a week I wander through toy stores in Berkeley looking at games and models and dolls, reading instructions and experimenting with the toys whenever the salespeople allow me to. I love observing children deciding upon birthday presents or cajoling adults into buying things for them. I also watch parents trying to convince children to buy what they as adults feel they missed as children. The children's resistance to their advice is usually serious and "grown-up"—they insist that toys are their business.

From toy stores one can get many teaching ideas, for they make clear what interests young people outside school. This doesn't mean that commercial toys are fine and sensibly designed learning materials. On the contrary they often embody the worst in our culture—violence, competitiveness, sexism, racism, and deceit. Most toys are packaged to seem grander than they are. Everything is displayed in boxes that are twice as large as necessary on the assumption that the bigger the box the more people can be tricked into paying for it. Yet there still remains so much of experimentation, fantasy, love, and the sheer pleasure of learning in games and toys that they draw children to them.

Certainly toys have a powerful effect in training children to take their place in the adult world. GI Joe is designed to have children practice violence, or at least to admire uniforms and get accustomed to technological warfare. It is no accident that laser guns, space modules, electronic bugs, and missile systems are sold as birthday presents for young children. However, toys lend themselves to many uses and often the intent of the adults making the toys is thwarted by the ingenuity of children and by their repugnance toward some of the more dehumanizing aspects of our culture. Kids have to be taught to observe the habits of their elders and unless they admire what the adults do they often have to be forced to do so. Imitation of adult culture is not to be taken for granted, especially in cultures like ours where so many adults seem so often discontented.

I do not like Barbie dolls or what they represent. The dolls themselves are not so expensive. But they are surrounded by possessions that are meant to mobilize the greediest sentiments of young children. In the Barbie section of a toy store one can find Barbie clothes, Barbie wigs, Barbie cosmetics, a Barbie house, and even a Barbie camper complete with sleeping bag and camp stools. Still, my daughters love Barbie dolls. I broke down last Christmas and got Erica a Barbie camper. The camper is central to many of my daughters' most elaborate fantasies and games. It has been everything from an actual camper to an ice cream truck to a mystery car carrying superheroes and heroines to a boat, a plane, a raft. Barbie is Barbie one day, Wonder Woman the next. My wife and I don't buy Barbie's elaborate costumes, so the children create their own. The other night the Barbies in our house even had a political meeting on the top of the camper to decide how to create kid power.

It is probably true that there are children in this country who believe there is only one way to play with Barbie dolls. However, most children know how to discard the rules and create their own.

I have seen dozens of versions of chess, checkers, Monopoly created by children; seen musical instruments played in the most unexpected ways; seen children merge dinosaurs, stuffed animals, Barbies, and knights and soldiers as they experiment with all the combinations and relationships they can imagine.

Watching children play, I decided that if one presents young children with the components of games, they will generate games themselves. Children experiment with different ways of doing things whereas adults get accustomed to believing there is one right and one wrong way to do things. Creating a game is much like discovering how to write in one's own voice. Making games, writing, building are all ways young people can discover that they can put things into the world, that they can have some control over life.

The other day I ran into some children who were playing their own version of chess. The knights jumped two squares at a time, since they galloped like horses. The queen, rooks, pawns, and bishops moved in their regular ways, though the king was given the mobility of a queen. When I came upon the game, a young student teacher was telling the kids how wrong they were in daring to change the rules of the game. He pointed out that there was only one way to play the game, that they would never be "real" chess players if they didn't play by the rules. One of the kids said that she didn't want to be a real chess player but was curious about what happened when you changed the rules. The new game was interesting but the student teacher insisted it wasn't a game and forced the kids to play by the standard rules. When I mentioned to him that there were dozens of variations of chess played throughout the world, he claimed that the only justification for letting children play games in school was to accustom them to learning to play by the rules. I disagree. It is important to learn how to play by other people's rules but it is also important for young people to understand that all rules are not sacred or universal, that they can often be modified or discarded or replaced. Creating new games or modifying old ones is one way young people can explore things for themselves. It is an indirect yet powerful way of accustoming people to build for themselves and not to accept traditional forms as inevitable and timeless.

For the past few years I've been experimenting with ways of teaching games, creating new games, and modifying old ones. During this time I have developed a scheme which breaks most games down into different components which can be modified and examined in some depth.

From my perspective games can be examined according to:

1. their *themes*, the ideas they embody or the images that give rise to them;

2. the *playing board*, the space used to play the game, the environment specifically created for the game;

3. *the pieces*, the tokens or elements out of which the game is built, as well as the *moves* assigned to these pieces and the *captures* or *changes in status* that occur during the game.

Related to the moves are

4. the *decision devices* (such as dice and spinners) that are sometimes used to determine specific moves.

Overriding all of these considerations are

5. the *game's goals*. Is there to be a winner or loser, or are collective goals set? Does one need points or have to trap an opponent's pieces or clear the board? How is the game scored?

Finally,

6. *teaching the game*. How do people learn to play games, or teach others to play? Which teaching strategies work and which fail to get students involved in games? How would a games center in a classroom look? What kinds of skills and learning are involved in playing games and how can these be evaluated and documented? How could games be introduced into all areas of the curriculum? What are the resources a teacher can draw on and the materials he or she ought to have available to begin a games program?

I. Game Themes

Themes suggest games. It is easy to imagine games centered about any of the following subjects:

—founding a city
—borders and boundaries
—bees
—pollution of a stream, a city, a park
—confrontation
—collective action

—dinosaurs

—rebuilding a devastated world

—the solar system

—discovering a new planet

—the meeting of two cultures that previously had no contact

—pigeons and people

—advertising a product in order to seduce people into buying
   what they don't need

—making it in a hierarchical system

—life in a mental institution

—life in prison

—war

—falling in love

But why teach games anyway? What do the kids learn and how
do you evaluate it?

Let me try a somewhat indirect answer to these questions by considering one of the clichés of contemporary education: begin where
the students are; start your program with what they know.

Beginning where the students are is usually interpreted by
teachers as learning, through various "diagnostic instruments,"
how much of the standard curriculum each student has mastered,
and then starting them at their own levels. This is referred to as
"individualized instruction" and is little more than channelling
students through the traditional curriculum at different rates.
New words like "individualized instruction" generate new programs, or rather the repackaging of old programs.

For example, IBM under the trademark of SRA sells individualized learning kits which are little more than traditional reading
materials organized into a system by which each child works
alone from level to level rather than with the rest of the class. In
this setting the teacher's role shifts from conductor of the whole
class to systems manager. The manager has to be sure that each
person enters the system at his or her appropriate level and pro-
ceeds through it in an orderly manner.

But there is a completely different way of interpreting where the students are that focuses on what the students bring with them to school and what they learn at home or on the streets, from the adults on television, or in the playground. Most students who are failures in school, who, to judge by the results of standardized tests and teachers' reports, appear stupid, know all kinds of things that are never considered important in school or used as the foundation upon which to learn new things. Over the last few years I've heard teachers, and have occasionally caught myself, saying things like:

"Put that comic book away. It's time to do reading."

"Stop playing cards. It's maths period."

"Shut off your transistor. It's interfering with the choral music lesson."

In other words:

"Stop reading. It's time to study reading."

"Stop using maths. It's time to study maths."

"Stop listening to music. It's time to study music."

Beginning where the students are implies knowing your students, not just as they appear in school, but how they are during most of their day. Teachers, especially those who work in communities they did not grow up in and do not live in, generally don't know enough about their students. It is necessary to spend time in the community, to learn what parents teach their children, to observe the games the adults or the adolescents play, to know something about gambling, about the verbal games people play, about jump rope games and street rhymes—in other words to know the culture not as an anthropologist from an outside community but as a participant and celebrant.

In learning who the student is, what the community is like, one comes upon games everywhere. People throughout the world learn through play, practice through play, and relax through play. By beginning the learning process in school with the games of the community, a teacher permits the students to remain in contact with a familiar world while they reach out to more abstract issues. Playing a game can lead to analyzing the game, to research embodied in the game, to historical investigations about the origins of the game, to modifying the game, etc. I don't mean to imply that games are the only, or even the central, aspect of people's lives. However they do provide a good starting place.

Recently I've explored the mathematical skills and knowledge that play a part in everyday life and translated them into learning experiences that can extend into the classroom and then back to the community.

I've developed a list of different areas of knowledge that can be used as a guide to studying what mathematics the students have and therefore to generating starting points for units in math. Not surprisingly, games can be found in almost all of these.

Mathematics are embodied in everyday life through:

1. *The way people locate themselves and others in space*, through the territory they claim both within their homes and in the community; through the boundaries they draw and those they respect; through the games of hide-and-seek and chase they play; through the places they gather to play cards or dominoes, to meet members of the opposite sex, to take babies out for a stroll, to play ball, or to go to the movies, a bar, or a restaurant. People also define themselves by whether the territory is foreign or dangerous. Knowing some of this information, and using it in the classroom, can lead to the study of maps, boundaries and boundary games, topology, measurement of areas, making floor plans, replanning a community, etc.

2. *People moving ground*, getting from one place to another by foot or train, bus, car, or plane. Different modes of transportation are appropriate to different forms of mobility. It doesn't make sense to fly to your friend's house next door, or to walk 3,000 miles if you can fly. What is the shortest way to get from one place to another in the neighbourhood, in the country, in a game? What is the quickest way? Is the quickest way always the shortest? How far can a person walk, run? How about animals—dogs, cats, pigeons? How about machines? Is speed always a virtue? These and other questions arise naturally from considering how people get around.

3. *Locating oneself and others in time.* Work hours, the moral issue of being on time, birthdays, anniversaries, holidays, time as indicated by the sun, moon, and stars, astrology, and the effect of celestial movement on human personality, the development of the clock, the internal clock, twenty-four-hour rhythms, personal rhythms, rhythm in music, in life, biological rhythm, measurement of rhythm and time, winning, racing, timing events, non-Western calendars, white man's time—one can explore all these social and mathematical questions, starting with a study of how people divide up the day—when they get up, eat, go to sleep, work—when they get to places on time and when they take their time.

4. *Family relationships.* How many relatives do people have? How many generations back can they project? How many cousins, second cousins, aunts, uncles can they name? How many different branches of the family can be traced? How can family trees be diagrammed, relationships represented abstractly? How are other relationships (in logic) represented? Which relationships are symmetrical (I am the cousin of my cousin), nonsymmetrical (I am not my father's father), transitive? (If I am a relative of X, and X is a relative of Y, am I Y's relative? This of course depends upon how my culture defines relatives.) Is it possible to make up family games? To study family relationships in other cultures or the range of family structures in our culture? What are the variations of kinship structure throughout the world? Can they be represented algebraically?

5. *Sharing.* What resources in the community are shared? What is the child's share, the mother's, father's, relative's, friend's? How are things shared or budgeted? What fraction (or percentage) of the resources available are used and in what way? How do teams share responsibilities during a game? How do young children learn (or not learn) to share? What is the devil's share? How are our natural resources shared? How are cards or dominoes dealt out so everyone gets the same number at the beginning of a game? How are food, clothing, sleeping space, living space shared?

6. *Accumulating.* What is saved or hoarded instead of shared? How is it done, how are resources counted, what are they weighed or measured against? What is the value of a dollar? How are points accumulated in a game? How do you add or multiply large sums? How do you know you're not being cheated?

7. *Exchanging.* How are things traded? How is value set? How many dolls are worth one bike? How are trading cards accumulated or exchanged? How do you weigh goods, balance them against one another? What systems of weights and measures are used throughout the world? Is it possible to get along without money as a medium of exchange? Is there anything that is so valuable that you would never exchange it?

8. *Gambling.* How is fate dealt with? How are odds set? Why gamble? What is there to lose or gain? What gambling strategies do people use? Do you know anybody who has won? How much? What are the chances of winning? What do people feel about winners and losers? How are the winnings used? How do you play the numbers, the craps, the horses, cards, roulette, Monopoly?

9. *Making, building, and fixing.* How do people in the community make clothes, build houses, fix plumbing, paint, plaster, rewire an apartment? What can you build yourself and what do you need help with from outside the community? Are you sure? How do you fix a car, rebuild one, scrounge around and build one yourself? How have other peoples solved the problem of building their own communities? How can other people's solutions be rethought in your own circumstances? How can you make your own basketball court? Chess or checker game? Wari board? Create your own game? How can you gather together the skills already available in the community, record them, and teach them to others?

10. *Dealing with machines.* What machines do you come into contact with every day? How can they be understood? What is the power of people who command the knowledge of how to build and fix machines? How can that knowledge/power be acquired? What games or toys exist that help understand principles

involved in broadcasting, television, understanding and using computers? How does one get hold of resources? Is technology beyond the understanding of most people or is knowledge withheld deliberately to keep people with little power awed?

11. *Curiosity about numbers and relationships as abstractions.* What puzzles do people set for each other or try to solve? How does one go about exploring thoroughly unfamiliar material, trying to solve traditional puzzles or paradoxes?

This last category leads back to the teacher who, by respecting and knowing a community, can offer it unfamiliar material and have the gift accepted rather than suspected—accepted because it helps people to better understand the world and gain control over their lives. The teacher is not a judge of his or her students but rather a worker whose role is to serve their needs and broaden their options. The community and the classroom must help each other.

Part III

Being a Parent

Judy and I have been parents for four decades now. Our three children are forty-one, forty, and thirty-eight. Erica, our middle child, has just had a baby, so now I'm a grandfather participating in the growth of a child all over again. It is a refreshing and exhilarating experience. One of the main things I learned as a parent was that as your children grow you also have to grow. Your ideas as a parent must be modified if not totally changed by the day-by-day experience of being with your children.

My hope as a parent is to encourage my children to become compassionate, caring, politically sensitive adults who are living rewarding lives they have chosen for themselves. When my children were just entering school, I wrote *Growing with Your Children* in order to share what I had learned growing with my children. I also speculated on what might be useful to parents who would like their children to develop self-discipline and their own intellectual and artistic skills as well as a commitment to equity and social justice. The book was meant as a progress report as well as a manual for parenting; excerpts from it begin this part.

The second selection in Part III is an essay I wrote on being a father. It addresses the specific challenges men face in learning how to be compassionate, caring parents. They encounter their own fathers and their desires not to duplicate some of the less effective ways they were treated as children.

The final selection is from a recent book, *Painting Chinese*. It is about aging and how being with young people can become a vital part of feeling youthful in old age.

EXCERPT FROM *GROWING WITH YOUR CHILDREN*

Being a Parent and Being a Child:
A Personal Introduction

When Judy was pregnant with Antonia, our first child,* I spent a lot of time imagining how I would act as a parent. There were hours of fantasizing holding, feeding, and changing a baby, of worrying about colic and croup. I remember reading and forgetting Gesell and Spock a dozen times, thinking about asking my parents and grandparents about bringing up infants and then shying away because I didn't want to treat my children the way I'd been treated as a child. Beyond these practical anxieties over how to care for an infant, I found myself confronted with problems of values: What would I do about discipline? Would my children respect me? What limits should they be given and what should they be expected to learn? Would they get as angry at me as I sometimes did at my parents—and would they be justified?

I was concerned about the kind of adults they would become and agonized over how to enable them to be compassionate and concerned with justice while at the same time being competitive enough to survive. As these speculations evolved it became clear that these moral and social problems weren't that much different from those faced by my parents and grandparents, though their worlds were different from mine. Though I had more choices open to me, they too worried about the roles respect, discipline, strength, justice, and love would play in their children's lives. The more I thought of myself as a parent the more I remembered

---

* She is now forty-one.

my parents and grandparents and the choices they made about how to raise children. And I began sorting out what they did that was nurturing and what they did that tore me down and made me resent them. Coming to terms with their actions and values has been and continues to be helpful to me in learning how to be a decent and nurturing parent.

I grew up in a two-family house in a working and lower-middle-class neighborhood in the Bronx. My grandmother and grandfather and two uncles lived upstairs. I lived downstairs with my brother, sister, and parents. The smell of wet sand, two-by-fours, sacks of nails, bags of plaster, and cement reached my bedroom from the garage beneath, where the Herbert Construction Company truck was parked every night. Everyone in the family worked for Herbert, which made me feel awkward. My parents told me that when I was four I used to go around saying, "Me Herbert Construction." I'm not sure that it was an assertion so much as a question.

I remember my grandfather pacing in front of the house at 5:30 in the morning, muttering to himself about the stupidity of the world, waiting for Rogers, the truck driver, who wasn't due until 6:30 but would be cursed for being late whenever he arrived. There was no being early or being on time in Pop's world. Everything and everybody was always too late.

He came to the United States some time around 1905—no one was quite sure of the exact date. Before that he spent a year in Whitechapel in London. He remembered every detail of his stay in that ghetto, and over fifty years later, in 1959, on my return from a trip to England he described that part of London with amazing accuracy. In fact, as he got older he remembered the details of his life in Poland and the passage to New York with increasing clarity while his sense of the present faded. Just before he died he told me that he remembered every detail of the mill in Bialystok and of Hamburg and the boat to Liverpool but couldn't remember what had happened last week.

Pop's passage to the United States was not motivated by any

desire to seek a new life in the land of golden opportunity. He was drafted into the Tsar's army, as were many other poor young men. The fact that he was Jewish and poor meant to the Tsar's officers that he was doubly expendable. He was put in a crew whose role was to haul a cannon from Moscow to Vladivostok. When he learned from other soldiers how far Vladivostok was from Moscow, much less from Bialystok, he managed to escape and find protection in the Jewish underground. It isn't clear how he managed to get away, but the facts seemed too harsh to detail for grandchildren like me who were well on their way to joining the American middle class.

All I can piece together is that he was hidden from city to city, given train fare and lodging with Jews or sympathetic Christians until he reached Hamburg, where other exiles from Polish Russia, some of whom were relatives, received and helped him until he could earn passage to Liverpool. From Liverpool he went to Whitechapel in London, where he repeated the process until he somehow managed to earn steerage fare to New York, where he met my grandmother, who had lived no more than twenty miles from him in Poland.

My grandmother earned her way to New York on the underground railway too. She took other people's infants from Warsaw to Hamburg, pretending at least a half-dozen times to be a mother. She's told me how she managed to slip off trains with the babies before reaching the station and connect with people who would protect them until they caught the next train.

A few years ago a friend of mine told me about his great-grandmother's escaping to Canada through the underground railroad from Georgia. His African great-grandmother's experience was no different from that of my grandmother. And her pride and strength were just what I have known from both of my grandparents.

I remember my grandfather as tough, somewhat wild, yet very gentle with me, the oldest son of his oldest son. He smelled of the construction jobs he worked at twelve hours a day. He was a framer—a rough carpenter—who built walls and partitions for over fifty years. He received a gold card to commemorate fifty years as a member of the carpenters' union. The union itself couldn't have been much older than that at the time he received the card. Unions and the Workman's Circle were a central part of his life. He was socialist as a matter of nature rather than intellectual conviction. He shared what he had and expected his fellow workers to do the same. This often led to trouble. He would give away everything he had to friends in trouble and then have to work even harder to support his own family. However, his generosity was frequently and necessarily tempered by my grandmother's shrewd understanding of American culture and fierce determination to see that her children made it on American terms. It is almost no exaggeration to say that my grandparents lived a continent apart in the same apartment. Pop never came to the United States, and to emphasize this he refused to learn how to read or write English and never signed his name in over fifty years in this country. My grandmother went to night school briefly to learn to read and write and did manage to learn to sign her name. However, before her lessons progressed much, my grandfather invaded the class and forced my grandmother to withdraw. He was convinced that the teacher, a man, was trying to seduce his wife. Mom barely restrained Pop from beating up the teacher and reluctantly gave up her dream of educating herself.

Pop was strict and possessive when it came to his wife and children. He believed that life was a struggle and you had to be prepared for difficulties and protect your family. It was as if he believed that the Cossacks might descend at any moment and that one always had to be ready. His conception of the United States was both political and personal. This was not a land of opportunity for him so much as a place to work with less oppression.

He was also full of fun, a trickster in many ways. Neither work nor politics made him grim. There was in him a love of living and an ability to put aside all his problems and play when he was with his family. The ability to work for justice and still live with a joy that flowed to others was his most special characteristic.

Pop worked in construction as he had worked as a peasant in Europe, and was proud of his labor and his class. He was a misfit in the United States because though he knew how to work he didn't know how to compete. He was too trusting and generous to be a successful businessman, and he left it to his wife and children to learn how to make it.

Recently I asked my father what kind of a father Pop was. My father began negatively—Pop never tried to be a pal or companion to his children. He left their education to the schools, though he insisted his children do their homework. Since he couldn't read English, he couldn't help with their homework, which he didn't think was his job anyway. All he had to do was see that they spent time seeming to do their assignments.

He never took his children to museums or movies or shows. Whenever he wasn't working he was resting or at the Workman's Circle, or out partying with *landsmen*, men who had also escaped from eastern Europe. He liked to go to the Russian baths, to drink a bit and play cards, to fool around. I have a photograph of Pop and his cronies dressed up as cowboys looking wild and funny. It seems that one Friday night they stumbled into a photography store and had their pictures taken in costumes.

Every day after work Pop would come home, wash the smell of construction off, have a few shots of Canadian Club, and settle down at the kitchen table and wait for dinner. He would joke around a bit, sometimes fall asleep—he wasn't to be bothered with taking care of children. He was physically exhausted from working from 6:30 A.M. to 5:30 P.M.—something he did until he was well over seventy. After we got a TV he spent evenings watching wrestling—screaming and cursing, scaring me until I realized that wrestling was an act and that Pop's response was theater too.

Pop defined certain duties for himself as a father. He had to support the family, no matter how hard he had to work. He didn't want my grandmother to work, though early in their marriage she had taken in piecework. He also assumed the role of upholder of respect in the family. If any of his children cursed, threatened, or talked back to my grandmother, he could become irrational and violent. There was no negotiating or bargaining with the children or investigating the facts. My grandmother was always right. In his way he instilled respect in his children for himself and for my grandmother and taught them something I see in my own parents—loyalty to another human being and the strength to share hard times with someone else.

From a contemporary perspective, a lot of my grandfather's manner can be seen as sexist and uncompassionate toward children. However, that is a way of misunderstanding and putting him down. He did not look upon women as unequal, as weak or helpless or dumb. He didn't even look at women as a group. Central to his view of the world were the notions of family and *landsmen*, tempered by a bitter awareness that simple survival was never guaranteed. One had to work and had to nurture the family. There also were responsibilities to *landsmen*—to relatives and countrymen, to Jews from one's hometown and to family left in Europe. There was more to be done than could be done by one person, and men and women had to assume responsibilities—he worked as hard as possible so my grandmother would have time to nurture the children. My grandmother regretted not being able to finish school and not having time to grow and learn about the world. She regretted having to flee Europe (though she was far from romantic about the pogroms that forced her to leave) and having to work so hard taking care of five children and numerous relatives. She didn't resent my grandfather so much as the social forces that made life such an unpredictable struggle. I remember her fierce pride in the way she maintained and controlled our house. She held things together, guided and supported her children's education even though she couldn't read or write English. There were times when she was severe and demanding, when she forced my grandfather to say "no" or to drive a hard bargain with his *landsmen*. But with her grandchildren she was always kind and indulgent—she let us know in many ways that our lives were to be the fruits of her struggles.

Both my grandparents did what they felt had to be done to survive. They did not expect of life the gift of personal fulfillment. They never had time or the security to think about fundamental changes in the conditions of their lives beyond their struggles to establish unions. They always felt that living with greater ease and developing one's self were gifts they would provide for their grandchildren through their work and love, and through the opportunities they gave their children. They were aware that it would take two generations of work to produce one generation who would have the time and security to grow without struggling for necessities. That was why grandchildren were so special for them. We were to be the first free children. And they weren't wrong in the case of my family. The fruit of their and my parents' labor was the leisure it afforded me to go to college, travel, and choose what to be, both professionally and as a person. When I was younger, I resented their inability to understand me. Now I often feel foolish for not understanding the gift they offered me. Perhaps part of that resentment came from my bewilderment at the freedom I had—the burden of being able to choose where to live, whom to become or to love, what to work at, and choose with no guidelines or tradition since my parents' and grandparents' worlds were not the same as mine.

Work, the job, was the main bond between my grandfather and his sons, just as the house and the market were the main bonds between my grandmother and her two daughters, who lived across the street from us. The men and women spent a lot of time in separated worlds, and, as a child, not surprisingly it was the men's world I identified with and the women's world I spied on. One of the first toys I remember being excited by was a miniature toolbox, which I carried around while pretending to be my grandfather.

My father described to me the experience of working with his father during the summers. He remembers first how hard Pop worked. It was profoundly affecting. Though Pop came home tired every day, it was another thing to see him work, carrying lumber all day, throwing up partitions, walking up and down the half-built frames of buildings carrying tools and lumber, keeping at it for nine and ten hours with only short breaks. My father worked alongside his father and told me that it was one of his most profound, difficult, and yet joyous experiences. He came to understand his own father, to know what he did with his time and the world he lived in most. He learned to work himself and came to understand and share the knowledge generated by years of intuitive building accumulated by my grandfather's genera-tion. Later, when my father graduated from Cooper Union as a civil engineer and, along with my grandfather, formed Herbert Construction Company, he was able to combine that intuitive knowledge with some of the more technical knowledge he picked up in college. Working with my grandfather also taught him re-spect for the work of the elders, which I too learned forty years later when I worked several summers with my grandfather.

The qualities my grandfather embodied—respect for family, loy-alty and generosity towards *landsmen*, a hatred of bossism, a need to work to exhaustion, and a teacher's concern with passing these val-ues on to his own children—are things I value too. As a parent I am not libertarian—there are values, both personal and collective, that I want my children to respect. I realize now that many of these I learned by watching my grandfather. And from my grandmother I'm sure I acquired that love of a home full of people that makes me center so much of my life and work about the house I live in. Of-ten I catch myself in the middle of a meeting around our kitchen table and remember my aunts, my mother, and my grandmother in the kitchen at Grand Avenue in the Bronx.

My mother and father tried to be different kinds of parents from my grandparents. Choices were opening up to their generation, and when I was born in 1937 my parents already had a sense that the old ways had their limits. Physical punishment was out except for outrageous behavior or when adults simply lost their tempers. Children were seen as more delicate, needing care and attention, perhaps a little pushing. The emphasis was psychological—see that the child was happy and give him or her enough attention and training to succeed in school. Perhaps the nervousness about academic success was unique to Jews, but I doubt it, for I've seen the same feelings in African American, Chicano, and Puerto Rican communities I've worked in.

My mother was somewhat of a stranger in my grandmother's house. All the other adults around spoke Yiddish; my mother didn't. The Cohens (that was my father's name before it was changed to Kohl) were all in construction; my mother's family were cab and truck drivers, printers, and artists. The Cohens worked for themselves and were moving into the middle class. My mother's family was less ambitious and more aesthetic. My mother's sisters were lovely, fairly low-pressure people who seemed more concerned with people than with success—I enjoyed being with them, since to me as a child they seemed to enjoy themselves more than the Cohens did and to demand less from me. Certainly their lives weren't easy. Two of my aunts suffered the consequences of marrying out of Judaism when doing so wasn't common; none of the family ever became wealthy. Still, they had and have a flair for life, a curiosity about things in the world that seems to have been put aside by my father's family in the pursuit of economic success.

Both sides of the family came together on formal occasions and were polite to each other. I grew up with two worlds and as a child had to sort them out. What of the Cohens' was valuable? What of the Jacobses'? Like most children I didn't imitate the adults around me so much as watch them and sort out what was worth learning and what I should reject.

My mother was right in the middle of these two different families. She once told me that her mother, my Grandmother Rose, who died when I was six, was a militant feminist, a friend to everyone in need, and a negligent parent. Evidently she had a passion for social issues, enormous compassion, and an inability to keep her own house in order. My aunts' niceness and concern for people obviously was influenced by her. However, my mother reacted to her mother's looseness and, from the time she was four-teen, ran the house and raised her three younger sisters. She taught herself how to manage money, to work and maintain a home. In these ways she was the equal of my Grandmother Co-hen. She met my father when she was chief buyer for a restaurant firm and he came to her office about a construction job he was doing with his father. She was making more money than he was at the time. However, for all her drive and orderliness there was something of my Grandmother Rose in my mother—she could be soft and irrationally generous, overindulgent, incapable of saying "no." I have a feeling that she spent a good part of her early life proving herself to the Cohens, and a good part of her later life trying to figure what was the right way to behave in the middle class. She seemed scared and inconsistent to me when I was a teenager, as if she wondered continually how she got to be where she was. The most relaxed I've seen her was when she was with her sisters, unwinding, laughing, being silly, and paying no attention to money or success.

If my mother was hesitant and confused sometimes within the family, she wasn't when it came to fighting for her children's place in the world beyond the family. There she and my father acted in unison. For example, the attitude of my mother and father toward the school as an institution was very different from that of their parents. They were literate in English, could and did help their children with schoolwork, and developed working relationships with their children's teachers. One of my earliest memories is of having trouble learning how to read in the first grade. When my mother saw that her son was behind in reading during the first half of the first grade, she just about fainted. When my father came home from work, he read the report card and brooded about it all evening. The next morning he took off from work and went to school with me. His not working was so unprecedented that I re-alized for the first time that reading was serious business.

I remember sitting in an office with my teacher on one side of me

and my father on the other. The teacher held up words I was supposed to know. For "BOY" I said "girl," for "THE" I said "to." My
mind was heavy and slow; I had to go to the toilet. My father looked
alternately angry and humiliated. He left me at school. By the time
I got home he had been to Barnes and Noble and bought all of their
beginning reading workbooks. He also bought some magazines and
set me to work cutting out words, then doing some worksheets. My
mother made sure I did them when I came home from school. I very
quickly learned to read. In fact I was afraid *not* to learn.

My grandfather also made occasional trips to school for his
children, the results of which would be a beating instead of an av-
alanche of books and worksheets. But the value he placed on education was no different.

There were no limits to what my father would do to further his
children's learning. He would buy chemistry sets, get resource
books. When I was about ten he even bought a set of the *Ency-
clopaedia Britannica* because it was the best encyclopedia on the
market. It made no difference that it was too complex for me to
read until I was in high school and needed it less.

I knew how much was sacrificed for my education—my parents talked about it, my aunts and uncles told me how grateful I
should be. It made me quite nervous—the obligation to perform
well because others were making sacrifices to insure my successes.
There were times when I felt so driven to perform academically
that there seemed to be no time to learn anything. Only perfection would satisfy my father—there were no rewards for B's or
even for A's, since they were expected. Anything less than A indicated a need to improve.

The sacrifices my parents felt they made for their children also
became justification for planning their futures. Not surprisingly, I
was to become a doctor. It wasn't until I was thirty that my father
told me that he had always wanted to be a doctor, but that the
need to work to help his father support the family made it impossible. I was to embody in my life what he had wanted to be. We
fought foolishly for years over my total lack of interest in medi-

cine, and I am not sure that he still doesn't believe we would both be better off if I had just given in.

My father struggled and worked, not to remake the world, but to make a small part of it livable for his family. At one time I resented his obsession with work, but now it seems that there was nothing else he could have done but quit and become resigned to poverty. All of his life he worked as hard as my grandfather and now, at sixty-seven, still runs from one construction job to another from 6:30 in the morning to 6:00 at night. He is not a laborer but does everything else—estimates the cost of work, supervises construction, gets new jobs, does quality control on the work of his men, and generally runs a successful middle-size construction company.

As a child I noticed how work drained him. He came home at night exhausted, went to bed early, lived and ate and drank construction. Often during the evening we tiptoed around him after dinner. If something was wrong at home—if one of us fought with my mother or stole something or had a fight—my mother did her best to deal with it herself. She didn't like to bother him with home problems since he worked so hard and came home so tired. Often, if she needed his help, she told him of the problem, and we all waited for his response, which was unpredictable and determined by the magnitude of the burdens he brought home from work. If it was a good day, he could be kind and firm and reasonable, protecting my mother just as his father had protected my grandmother, reasoning with my brother or sister or myself, listening to us and letting the problem be talked away. More often he responded to the problem by brooding, refusing to talk but just sitting in the middle of the living room looking pained. We children suffered from the grief we caused him after a hard day's work. On occasion, if something serious had happened and he lost his temper, one of us would be physically threatened, but this happened very rarely. Psychological tension and silence were the most characteristic modes of response. This behavior made me jumpy, so I tried to conceal as many of my transgressions as possible or keep them between my mother and myself. Because of the continual possibility of a brooding response, I confined personal talks between my father and myself to aspects of my life that I knew beforehand he would approve of. It got to the point that for several years I communicated with him through my mother. I couldn't bear the thought of hurting him and causing so much pain and frustration and at the same time couldn't relinquish my life. And I had choices—I could have become just about anything I wanted, could choose my college and major. The choices facing me at the time were much greater than those that had faced my parents.

Weekends were very different from weekdays when I was growing up. That was when my father consciously gave time to my brother, sister, and me. He tried to be our pal and companion, both out of a desire to spend time with us and because he understood that Dr. Spock said that it was a healthy and important thing for fathers to do. Whether Spock had written any such thing or not was irrelevant. The feeling in the late forties and early fifties was that men had to become friends with their children, something that would never have occurred to my grandfather. It was a way of integrating men into the everyday functioning of the family and, from the perspective of an older generation, seemed a pretty radical thing to do.

On Saturdays and Sundays my father and mother would take us to a museum or the Gilbert Hall of Science or the aquarium. Occasionally we would go swimming or to a ball game or a movie. Some of these times my father enjoyed himself. I know for me trips to places he liked, such as the Gilbert Hall of Science, were wonderful, and a sense of companionship and apprenticeship developed. He could take me some places and explain what was there. I liked his explaining things to me as much as being at the places.

Other experiences were more complex. Our family visits to the Metropolitan Museum of Art never provided unmixed pleasure. We stayed away from rooms with paintings of crucifixes; my parents didn't know very much about painting or sculpture, and often I felt that they didn't like them but felt it was necessary to give their children high culture despite their tastes. They wanted us to be better than they were, Americans for whom the specters of poverty and pogroms didn't exist.

The desire to have children who were "better" proved a very mixed blessing in my case at least. I didn't become any better but did become different, and it has taken years for us to come close again.

Being a pal of young people was a hard role for my father to sustain. He was much more comfortable being an authority, an older and wiser counselor to his children. This was his role when he took my brother and me to places where he felt at ease, especially to his office or one of his jobs. There it was somewhat analogous to the way he developed closeness to his own father. We did not work alongside him, however. At most we played while the men on the job (including my grandfather) worked. We ran errands, and when I got older and worked summers, I brought beer and sandwiches and knocked down walls with a sledgehammer. There was no need for me to work or contribute to the family budget. It was made clear to me that our family had enough and that physical labor was not to be my fate. Still, I learned so much by understanding my father's and grandfather's work. I saw them transform buildings, build new stores and banks—I got a sense of how my father planned and developed a job and how my uncle and grandfather transformed the plans into reality. It saw them improvise, come up with solutions to construction problems caused by architectural plans that ignored the actual structures of buildings to be renovated.

Work seems to me to be a crucial medium of communication between the generations. My brother and I were taken into a man's world where we were honored guests and, more important, where as children we could see how work made sense. It was impossible for me as a child not to admire people who could build and change things, who used tools, understood how to make walls, install doors, move windows, build cabinets.

It was more difficult for my sister to develop that bond with my father. There were no women on the job, and it was inappropriate for her to visit jobs. All the women who worked for Herbert Construction Company worked in the office. Initially my mother was bookkeeper, paymaster, secretary, clerk, receptionist. The office was in our house just as the company supply depot was in our garage. As the company grew, my mother gave up her role and devoted herself to taking care of her children and educating herself. Evelyn, a secretary/bookkeeper, was hired to do all those things previously done by my mother and soon became indispensable to the company. She was the cement in the office—she held things together, knew where everything was, knew whom my father and uncle wanted to talk to on the phone and whom to put off. She knew all the workmen and job superintendents and contributed to making the whole operation feel like a family affair. It was to Evelyn that Roz, my sister, was introduced. Sex roles were clearly defined in the company, and when she was in college Roz worked in the office typing and answering phones—the female equivalent of my knocking down walls and buying beer.

My brother, Ted, after graduating from college, joined the company and eventually became a partner. That route was simply not available to a female, and I think it made it very difficult for Roz to get close to the men in the family. The sexual biases in work go deep into determining family relations.

But even among the male family members, the direct expression of tender feelings and compassion was difficult. My father and I have always experienced a certain awkwardness in expressing our affection for each other. One incident stands out in my mind. It happened on the day I came home from camp when I was eleven or twelve. That summer was the first time I had been away from home, and it was a good independent time. I walked into the house nervously. My brother and sister had made welcome-home banners; my parents had made a cake. Everything was warm and welcoming, but to me it all seemed smothering and small—that summer I had learned about sexuality, had my first girlfriend, played ball, and learned to swim. I came home feeling big and independent and the homecoming made me feel small and dependent. I burst into tears and couldn't control my feelings of sadness and powerlessness. My mother and brother and sister tried to console me, but nothing worked. My father suggested we take a drive. I remember driving down the West Side Highway pouring out my feelings in between sobs. It was a matter of my independence, an understanding that my parents made love to make me and my brother and sister, a fear of what I had learned over the summer and an urge to try it out. I was struggling with whether to grow up or not. My father kept his eyes on the road, trying to decide how to respond. He was kind yet tough, listened, then tried to assure me that everything was all right. He was struggling with how to express his understanding and support, how to reassure me in the kindest possible way.

Somehow he couldn't bring himself to talk about anything that was on my mind. Nevertheless, he was there to accompany me through the storm, divert me if possible so I could get back to normal. We drove to the Gilbert Hall of Science and he told me to pick out a microscope or chemistry set—I don't remember which. After hesitating, somehow I put my feelings aside and turned my attention to the objects, selected one, and returned home to the welcoming party, which I was able to manage. It was through that gift that he found a way to express his affection and reaffirm the bond between us as father and son, though I didn't understand it at the time and resented him for replacing feelings with a thing. I have tried to be more direct with my children and not shy away from expressing affection. However, I had to learn how to do that both as a teacher and a parent, and it has taken time.

I became a father myself in the most traditional and cliché way. About one in the morning that Antonia was born, Judy's labor pains began. We rushed over to Doctors Hospital in Manhattan. I was terrified and excited—wanted to embrace Judy and was afraid to touch her. Fortunately the cab ride to the hospital took only a few minutes.

As soon as we entered the hospital we were separated. Judy was whisked away by a nurse, and I sat and filled out forms and fumbled with my Social Security number and home phone number. Nothing stayed in my mind.

The obstetrician came out to talk to me after a while. It was the first time we had met, and I can't remember his face. He informed me that Judy would be in labor for at least three or four hours and walked me to the elevator. He said to come back at 5 or 6 in the morning. I had intended to wait at the hospital but let myself be directed downstairs and made my way to the nearest bar.

I found myself buying drinks for strangers who, once they heard my wife was in labor, became philosophical and full of advice and jokes, many implying that a father could never tell if a child was his, others suggesting that children were nothing more than financial burdens. Occasionally, someone hinted that with all the grief there was some joy. Especially if it were a boy, they told me. I listened and felt sick—Judy was somewhere else almost with a child, our child, and I was sitting around drinking in the cynical goodwill of bitter people. I left the bar and walked and walked until dawn and returned to the hospital just as Judy was being wheeled from the delivery room. She looked tired—no, rested—and beautiful. We had a girl. I squeezed her hand, then the nurses pushed me aside and told me she needed to sleep. I sat down in the waiting room, relieved and tired myself. One of the other waiting fathers asked me what it was. "A boy," I blurted out and then collapsed into confused silence, afraid I'd cursed our child with my previously unarticulated desire to have my firstborn be a male. At that moment the birth of a child seemed like something that happened behind closed doors to someone else despite yourself. There was no joy in the first minutes of being a father. I resolved to be with Judy for our next child, to be part of the event for my own sake as well as to help Judy and to know our child from the beginning of life.

There were many other ways I stumbled into a traditional fatherly role despite my desire to share the responsibilities and joys of nurturing Tonia with Judy. It was comfortable to play at being a father and avoid most of the little but exhausting attentions infants require. I let feeding, changing, burping, walking, and com-

forting Tonia become woman's work. The baby frightened me. I
hadn't been around infants for twenty years and had to force myself to relieve Judy when she was fatigued. Otherwise I enjoyed
Tonia when she was laughing, playing, sleeping, or being shown
off to relatives and friends.

I don't care much for infants and yet love being and working
with elementary school children. Teaching is one of the great
joys in my life, yet for the most part I was reserved and nervous
around my own child for the first five or six months.

I watched Judy care for Tonia and assumed initially that she
liked infants better than I did, or at least that some psychological
or instinctual mechanism was at work that enabled her to give so
much to such a passive and unformed being. As it turned out,
Judy didn't care for infants any more than I did. We both loved
the signs of growth and independence in our children and never
wanted them to stay as babies. She did the nurturing because Tonia needed to be nurtured and I seemed shy, somewhat reluctant,
and scared. It simply had to be done.

With Erica, our second child, whose birth I experienced alongside Judy, I was less scared and able to be more useful. By the time
Joshua was born, I no longer was afraid of infants, knew the feel of
them, understood their strengths, and intuited some of their needs.
It was possible to learn how to share caring for him as an infant.

Over the past eleven years, as my children have grown, I've
had to grow too and respond to needs they articulated and problems that arose in our lives together. Many of the conditions we
face as a family are different from those faced by my parents and
grandparents. Judy is from the Midwest and isn't Jewish. We don't
live in a culturally homogeneous world as my family did, and we
don't live near relatives. Antonia was born in New York City and
we moved to California when she was five months old. Joshua
and Erica are native Californians.

Most of our friends have been as mobile as we and are as cut off
from traditional family life. We are involved in creating our own
social and family lives rather than fitting into our parents' worlds.

We have greater freedom than our parents and grandparents did in deciding where and how to live, in choosing lifestyles and experimenting with values. That freedom, however, has been a mixed blessing—we have lost the organic connection with tradition and the certainty about what was the right and the wrong way to bring up children that my grandparents had. There are times when we try out values and ways of behaving and other times when we simply don't know what to do with our children. Sometimes we become too permissive, other times too strict. We spend a lot of time and energy trying to discover, invent, reinvent, or possibly create a centered and nurturing family existence that also embodies the social values we believe in and try to live.

This search for value has another dimension too. Judy and I both graduated from college. We have been involved in the civil rights movement and the antiwar movements. We don't have the same uncritical faith in the values of competition and acceptance of authority that my parents had. We want a more caring and authentic life for ourselves and our children than the lives we have seen our parents lead. And we don't trust in professionals and experts the way our parents did, or believe there is one best way to raise children or some simple formula for conflict-free child-raising. That's probably because we went to college with many people who became experts and professionals and see them facing the same problems with their children as we face with ours. For my parents, professionals were a class apart, not friends whose lives one shared.

The social disparity between generations, however, doesn't mean that there is nothing we can learn from each other. In thinking about myself as a parent I've found values in my parents' and grandparents' lives that I reject and others that seem essential for a compassionate and decent life. There are also things I believe in that I hope my children will value. The questions of what to keep of past values and how to transmit values to one's own children are central issues parents have to face.

There are many aspects of life with children where values are constantly at issue and there is no objective "best" way to act as a parent. The way you act depends upon what you care about, what you believe in, what control you have over your own life, and how you have come to terms with your parents', grandparents', and other older adults' ways of raising children.

Consider discipline, for example. The proper way to discipline children is not a scientific question but rather a question of how you believe people should treat each other. In deciding upon how to discipline one's own children (and I've never known a child who doesn't get out of hand sometimes) there are certain questions that one has to answer for oneself. For example, who has authority? Is there any behavior that needs to be controlled? If so, what should the goal of control be for the child? The adult? Who has a right to tell someone else to do something? Should anyone control another's behavior? Should the goal of discipline be obedience or the development of self-discipline?

Related to discipline and equally dependent upon personal decisions about values is the problem of strength and violence. Are there times when violence is necessary? Is it possible to prevent or avoid violence? Are violence and strength the same? What kinds of physical, intellectual, and emotional strengths should be valued and how can they be developed?

Going along with discipline and strength is another problem we all face—respect. Can respect be legislated or earned? How does it develop and what is the meaning of mutual respect between parents and children? And why should respect be important?

Fairness is as important in our lives with children as is respect. However, what is fair? What is our share of the world and what should belong to our children? Can a sense of justice be developed and lived in a complex and often cruel world? Can our children be expected to be just if we don't act justly ourselves?

And lastly, what of joy—of the things we value and take pleasure from? What are ways in which we can enjoy things with our children as well as take pleasure in what they enjoy doing that we can't be part of?

These five themes, *discipline, strength, respect, fairness*, and *joy*, are the major ones I've had to come to terms with as a parent and teacher, and as an adult trying to understand and learn from Judy, my children, and my own parents and grandparents.

Discipline and Self-Discipline

Giving Up the Strap

My grandparents, specifically my father's parents, with whom I grew up, didn't have problems dealing with discipline. They were clear about how they wanted their children to behave and clear that my grandfather had responsibility for punishing misbehavior. My father and his brothers and sisters knew what was expected of them and knew they would be hit if they were caught doing something wrong. Physical punishment was not looked on by my grandparents and their friends as horrible or damaging. If anything, it was looked upon as healthy preparation for life, especially for boys. Pop worked with his hands, and lived in a pretty tough world. Men and boys were supposed to know how to fight and how to take physical punishment. Spanking was merely an extension of street fighting, an ordinary fact of life, nothing to be concerned about.

It was more difficult to spank girls than boys, but they were not immune from physical punishment, especially if they were disrespectful toward their parents.

My grandparents' attitude toward physical punishment didn't imply cruelty or lack of love. They were fair people and never hit their children arbitrarily or with the intent of injuring them. My father didn't like being hit and resolved not to hit his children, but he accepted that mode as natural for his parents. I know many people who grew up in similar situations, whose parents used physical punishment in a fair way, simply as a settling of accounts for things done. These people didn't like being hit and don't hit their own children. But they don't feel damaged from being spanked, nor do they feel that their parents rejected them. In fact, they wish they could find some nonphysical equivalent of spanking so that when something bad is done they could punish their children and make an end of the affair instead of talking or brooding about the act and dragging it out for days.

This is not meant to romanticize spanking, nor to deny the reality and magnitude of child abuse in our society. There are people who hit and hurt their children out of their own bitterness and despair; who resent the existence of children in their lives; who hate themselves and see in their children their own misery. What has to be pointed out, though, is that not everyone who spanks a child means to damage the child, and that not every case of an adult hitting a child is child abuse. Many people like my grandparents believed that physical punishment was a necessary burden that they had to assume in order to help their children grow to be successful and respectful adults. For them, children had to learn to be respectful and obedient. The idea of a child having choices or being the equal of adults was not part of their experience. Children were not to be reasoned with so much as taught what was right.

My parents saw things differently. I believe that they didn't have such a clear vision of the right way to behave that my grandparents acquired growing up in a small town in eastern Europe. My parents were mobile, from a working-class community but not fully part of it. My father was a college graduate and my mother had a responsible and well-paying job. They were moving into the middle class, and though they weren't sure what that entailed in terms of their behavior, they knew it meant giving up the roughness and physicalness of working-class life. In terms of their children it meant giving up the strap. They wanted to be progressive parents and hoped their children would be even more successful than they were. This meant substituting words for physical punishment, encouraging intellectual development, and treating their children more as equals, as friends almost. I'm not sure how clearly my parents thought out the differences between their generation and their parents' generation. I know they looked around for new models of behavior and tried to treat their children differently from the way they had been treated as children. They read Spock and Gesell and tried to be as reasonable and verbal with their children as possible.

However, giving up the strap caused unexpected problems. When adults give up using their physical superiority over children, they also free the child to talk back, argue, and debate. Giving up the strap has the unexpected effect of giving children power that adults have to deal with. My parents faced this problem continually. For example, my father tried to be close to me in a way that his father couldn't be with him. He gave up the strap with no real guidance as to how to replace it, nor with any articulated set of limits he wanted observed. I remember doing things that upset my mother. She could tell my father about them. Sometimes he would look pained, go in the living room, and sit brooding. I fantasized he didn't love me. He wouldn't talk to me, and I was never sure exactly what he was angry at or how angry he was. It took years for me to understand that that brooding silence which I took as rejection represented an internal struggle on his part. He wouldn't hit me, wasn't sure how angry he was or what to do about the anger.

Sometimes he came home and instead of brooding he would call a family meeting to talk over a problem my mother had with one of us. The meeting always ended inconclusively. I accused my mother of being unfair, she defended herself, accused me or perhaps my brother. My father, exhausted from work, tried to mediate the opposing views and usually succeeded in having everyone apologize. Only nothing was really resolved by those attempts to develop a family democracy. I often went to bed unpunished and guilty—there were times when I actually wished my father would simply hit me and make an end to my guilt.

Occasionally my parents tried to use a completely different strategy to control our behavior when we were bad. They threatened to deprive us of things we liked. However, these threats always caused my parents conflict and were often not enforced. For example, they would threaten to send me to bed without dinner yet felt I needed nourishment; would threaten not to take me to the museum on Sunday yet believed that as middle-class parents they owed me the trip. They wanted to give their children every opportunity they missed as children and at the same time have their children obey their wishes. It was a neurotic system they were trapped in—they felt compelled to indulge their children while at the same time controlling them and turning them into well-behaved, nonphysical, middle-class children. I remember a certain scared look that came into my mother's eyes when we did anything wrong. She didn't know how to handle the situation, didn't know how to punish us without damaging us, and usually retreated from the situation in despair.

Discovering Limits

All these attempts to set and enforce limits of acceptable children's behavior forced my parents to articulate what they wanted from their children. This often led to unexpected problems, since my parents didn't always agree on what was to be expected of us. I've seen the same problem arise in families of friends of mine who also moved rapidly from working-class families into a professional middle-class world.

Moving into the middle class in our culture is more than simply having more money. Usually it involves moving away from a neighborhood and a culture one grew up in. This is as true for people who grew up in an African American or Chicano or Italian or Polish community as for people who grew up in a Jewish working-class community as I did. It also means being free of traditional patterns of rearing and disciplining children. However, this freedom is usually mixed with anxiety over how to function in ways that won't be embarrassing in one's new world.

Moving into the middle class isn't, however, the only way traditional child-rearing patterns are broken. For some people, simply moving to a new community where there are no relatives or old friends forces them to define their values at the same time that it frees them to experiment with different ways of approaching their roles as parents.

As people become free to set limits based on the way they feel children should behave rather than on traditional ideas, differences often develop within a family. One parent turns out to be more lenient than another; one cares more about what the neighbors say than the other does. As these differences emerge, people discover that they don't respect each other's limits, leaving the children torn between two emerging sets of values.

This confusion occurs over little things as well as big ones. For example, a child asks for a toy. One parent says no, the other yes. Or one parent says they cannot afford it and the other brings it home as a surprise.

One parent sets a time for the children to go to bed, the other parent ignores it; one says the children must stay home after school and study, the other lets them go out and play; one says there are to be no sweets between meals, the other brings home gifts of gum and candy.

This makes it difficult for children to know how to behave. Children are not born with an innate sense of the limits of health, sanity, and safety. On the physical level, they explore the environment without a prior knowledge of what is dangerous and have to be protected from heights, fire, electricity, and so on. On an economic level, they don't know what their parents can afford or understand the social, racial, or class circumstances they have been born into. Nor do they know what makes their parents angry or pleased. They have to explore and one way to do that is to push everything until limits are set for them. It is normal for children to be unreasonable and sometimes seem outrageous in their behavior. They push things to see how adults will respond to their behavior; this gives them a sense of what adult limits are and what they need to do in order to survive in a world of other people.

Three sensible limits on behavior have emerged in my experience:

Some Minimal Limits

Limit 1: Don't be violent or tolerate violence except in self-defense.
People should not kill or hurt other people. This is a principle of
self-defense, of protecting oneself from violence and working to
stop violence when it occurs. With respect to children, it means
not tolerating bullying; breaking up fights between unequal and
unwilling partners (sometimes a fistfight between willing peers is a
healthy action); stopping people from torturing each other psy-
chologically. This involves direct "no" saying, separating people,
making judgments about who is hurting whom, and acting on this
judgment. It does not involve punishing anyone, however, or
making moral judgments about their character or rejecting people
or hating them. This will become clearer through some examples.

Occasionally my children fight with each other. Usually the
fighting is not serious. Tonia and Erica will push Josh around, or
Josh and Erica will make fun of Tonia, or Josh and Tonia will pick
on Erica—any permutation and combination seems possible. The
problem usually dissipates by itself—one of the children leaves
the room, a friend comes over, something funny or unexpected
happens, and they forget what they were fighting about. However,
there are times when things seem to get serious, and the children
don't know how to get out of the situation. The tone of a serious
fight is unmistakable. If I'm around and hear that sound, I simply
move in and separate the children, either by telling them to go to
different parts of the house, telling a joke to distract them, offering them a snack if they seem hungry, or by taking one of them
away by force as a last resort. Usually if I'm not tired or irritated
over something else, I can do it without getting angry or upset myself. Once the fight is defused, that is the end of it—no moralizing
from me, no punishment—a simple and unambiguous enforcement of that limit on violence. When the incident is over, it is
over, no psychological residues left behind to clutter up our lives.

Sometimes things are more complicated.

The crucial thing about enforcing limits is that the enforcement itself does not provide someone with pleasure. When an adult (or child, for that matter) enjoys being an enforcer, the issue is no longer protection or nurturance of the individual or group, but one of control and power. The enforcement of a limit does not imply a moral judgment of the character of the person who violates it. It is simply a matter of stopping destructive activity which all of us occasionally engage in through thoughtlessness, frustration, or the desire to control others.

Limit 2: Don't interfere with other people's activities if they are not oppressive. There is a second limit that is as necessary as the limit on violence—people cannot arbitrarily interfere with the activities of others. This simple principle functions in many ways. Just the other day I unthinkingly barged into my daughters' bedroom without knocking. They were outraged. I had interrupted a private game, one that was not an adult's business. They yelled at me, told me that they didn't bother me when I was writing, that they knocked when Judy's and my bedroom door was closed, that if they had to respect my privacy, I had to respect theirs. They were right; there was nothing to do but apologize, close the door, knock on it, and begin all again. Because they were right, it was crucial to have them experience the power *they* had to enforce the limit on me.

Many adults, especially men, seem incapable of allowing children the power to say that an adult is wrong. In situations like school or therapy, the young person is virtually powerless to question the adult. At home it is often no better. Saying an adult is wrong is considered an offense per se, regardless of the truth of the statement. Yet for limits to be respected and discipline to exist as a matter of course, limits must be applied consistently and equitably to all people in the group. This implies that children as well as adults can raise questions about the rules and their applications.

Limit 3: Don't destroy things to show you are in control. There is a third limit on people's behavior that makes for a nurturing personal and collective life—no person has the right to confiscate arbitrarily or destroy what belongs to another person or group. This may seem hardly worth saying, yet in our society many adults act as if children have no right to own anything or to have control over the products of their work. Parents assume the right to prevent their children from playing with their toys or, as a punishment, to take back what they have given.

The same attitude can be seen in the way adults often deal with children's art work or their collections of stones or bottle tops or marbles. A few paintings are considered cute; a large pile of them is unnecessary clutter. No matter that a child may treasure what he or she produces or collects. So long as it is not considered of value in the world of adults, it is treated by adults as if it has no value.

My children draw and paint a lot. They write books of their own. The amount of paper they use sometimes seems overwhelming, and it would be easy to throw out a lot of their work, especially since they probably forget most of what they've done. However, I write too and never throw out a page of my work, whether it be random notes, sentences, a sketch for a story, a random thought. The work that doesn't seem to have immediate application or is too embarrassing to show to anyone is filed away. Every few years I go through this collection and retype some of the material and keep the rest in a "miscellaneous" folder.

I decided to do the same thing with my children's work. Each has a large folder to hold their work. Every few months we go through them, and they decide what to keep and what to throw away. Tonia is very much like me in that she can't seem to give up any of her material. Erica picks a few pieces she likes and disposes of the rest without anxiety. Josh forgets his work, and each time he looks through his folder it is an act of discovery. He likes series— a set of pirate drawings or fish drawings. Individual pieces seem of less value, and often he weeds out my favorites among his work. Each of the children relates to his or her own work differently. They are free to keep, destroy, or give away what they choose.

Giving away things is a problem in our culture, where possessions are often taken to be a sign of personal value. Children are much more generous with their possessions than are adults, and so adults often try to train them to place value on things according to their dollar value. This can be seen when children trade possessions with each other. An expensive doll might be traded for a comic book or an old worn-out stuffed animal; a set of skates for a cap gun; a Barbie doll for two pieces of bubble gum. Often these trades are nullified by parents who know the "real" value of things and worry about their children being cheated. The right to nullify a trade, however, is just another indication of the way adults deny children the right of ownership.

The situation can become complex when it is clear that one child is exploiting another's ignorance. For example, I know of a case where some older children tried to get younger children to trade their bicycles for candy or cap guns. The older children then tried to sell the bikes. It was a clear case of exploitation. In a situation like that, adults have to intervene both to protect the younger children from exploitation and to protect themselves from being badgered into buying a new bike after a perfectly good one has been swindled away. No matter how the adult ends the transactions, I feel that it is crucial to explain as directly as possible to all parties involved that the younger children were being cheated. The exchange of candy for a bike was not an act of mutual respect, but a cynical seduction of the younger children by the older ones. However, this is an extreme example, and most exchanges among friends are entered into by mutual agreement and considered fair trades from the children's perspective.

In most cases, to place a money value on things and insist upon getting equal money value in a trade is one way of preparing children to take their place in the marketplace. It is a way of denying value that is based on affection and sensibility and replacing it by an external assessment of numerical worth.

The conflict between preparing children to survive in the "real" world and trying to help them develop humane and sensitive ways of living is embodied in this simple matter of children exchanging gifts. I believe that the only way this paradox can be dealt with is by talking with children about the difference between cheating someone and genuine exchange. I've found that my children have quickly understood gross examples of cheating and have forced me to broaden my view of what fair exchange means. For children it is not a matter of dollar-for-dollar so much as affection-for-affection. Trading something you hate for something someone else loves is considered an unfair exchange.

Enforcing Minimal Limits

It is one thing to acknowledge certain behavioral limits and another to enforce those limits without using physical coercion. It is hard to walk the line between being too indulgent and being too restrictive. Some of us have to learn when and how to say "no," while others of us have to learn not to say "no" too much.

For some people, saying "no" to a child raises the fear of being rejected by the child. I have a friend who lives alone with her son. She needs and treasures his companionship and is also probably afraid that he'll reject her just as his father did. For several years she has indulged him terribly at the same time she has become increasingly distressed at the way he never seemed happy and kept on asking for more. Recently she decided that she had to say "no" to some of his more outrageous demands. He insisted that she stay home every night, that he come on dates with her, that she buy him everything he saw, even though they were living on a small budget. One night she decided to call a baby-sitter and go to a party. She needed to be out by herself, free of their relationship. She needed to assert that there were limits to how much she could be possessed by her child. She told me that before the baby-sitter came she and her son had a terrible time. She had fears of his rejecting her the next day and she experienced almost uncontrollable anxiety. He accused her of not loving him, tried to make her call the baby-sitter and ask him not to come. She refused, and the baby-sitter, who was also a friend, said that the first few moments with the boy were awkward but that then they got along fine. His mother, despite her fears, didn't spend the evening agonizing over her son. She felt confident that she had done a sensible thing and didn't start worrying again until the next morning. However, her son woke up more curious about what she did and eager to share what he did with her than angry or rejecting.

This may be an extreme case, but for people who are unaccustomed to saying "no" to their children, the first time they do and stick by it can be full of anxiety. I remember the times I have said "no" to my children, to refuse them toys or sugar-coated cereal or the right to have six friends over and stay up all night when the next day is a school day. Something in me clutches, I forget that children are strong and resilient, that their love and affection isn't dependent upon their getting their own way all the time. That fear of being rejected by my children as well as an uncertainty about whether I'm depriving them of something important for their growth never fully disappears. It's part of my own insecurity—in my experience "no" said directly and fairly is taken as just that by children. What I have to do is protect myself from saying "no" in a too hostile way, from adopting an aggressive tone rather than being direct, firm but supportive. "No" in the service of minimal limits is an act of love and support.

Not everyone has trouble saying "no." It's probably true that more people have to struggle with their own impulses to control children's behavior than have no problem letting children do whatever they want. Little things like how children dress or sit at dinner or wear their hair can become occasions for power struggles. Many parents have images of how their children should look and behave, and they try to force these images on their children. One Sunday I was sitting in a park reading the newspaper. I was only peripherally tuned into the parents and children around me, but the word *don't* kept slipping into my consciousness. I put the paper down and started copying down all sentences containing negatives. Here's a partial list:

"Don't dirty your pants."

"Don't talk back to me."

"Don't put your hand in that dirty water."

"Don't suck your thumb."

There's no point in going on with the list. Sometimes it is very hard for adults to resist bombarding children with prohibitions, even silly ones.

Adults have to face times when their children oppose and confront them for good reasons. At those moments children discover whether the grownups are rational and consistent or just a bunch of hypocrites who like to control others but can't bear sensible criticism. It is important to remember times when your children confronted you and to try to understand whether they were right or not. A way to develop a symmetric and just relationship with your children is to allow them the same freedom to criticize you and help you curb your excesses as you assume with their behavior. When all parties can enforce limits it becomes in everybody's interest to have minimal limits in order to keep the group as harmonious as possible.

Limits and Self-Discipline

Limits should not exist in and for themselves. They do not dictate what should be done so much as provide a series of hedges against self-destruction. Within this basic structure it is possible to encourage and nurture self-discipline, which is what enables people to take control of their lives and live harmoniously with others.

Self-discipline is crucial for both parents and children. It implies a sense of self, of knowing that one can initiate actions, can learn new things and tackle problems. It also implies that if one is weak or ignorant or scared it is possible through personal action to overcome these conditions. Self-discipline underlies the whole development of personal strength.

One can see the beginnings of self-discipline in the efforts infants make to walk and talk and grab things, in their drive to do things for themselves. On an adult level self-discipline makes it possible for one to carry a project through from beginning to end, to bear pain while working through a difficult personal or social relationship, to plunge into a new situation and teach oneself how to cope with the conditions it presents. It is what makes it possible for people to resist being ordered about arbitrarily and to be able to create new forms of living.

Self-discipline can be undermined in children by too rigid limitations on their behavior and by no limitations on behavior. If children are continually bossed around, told what to do and how to do it, there is no space to experiment or feel responsibility for actions. Often a well-disciplined child falls apart when the authority disappears. There is no strength underlying the obedience. On a group level this can be seen in what might be called the "substitute-teacher syndrome." Classes that have had strict disciplinarian teachers go wild in the presence of a substitute teacher. There is no internalized discipline in the group nor usually any self-directed activity by the students. When the source of authority is absent and when the students know there will be no subsequent repercussions, they behave in ways that, on reflection, would repel them.

Similar problems develop when no limits exist. Children get trapped in their own mistakes, become fearful or unmanageable. Their lives sometimes run away from them. It is exhausting to try to find a place to work, to protect your work, to find other people unpredictable because they never respond to or make demands on you.

It seems to me that self-discipline is most likely to develop when there are limits on violence, on interfering with others' activity, and on destroying personal or collective property. Beyond these limits on behavior there are also other aspects of self-discipline that provide the ground for the development of personal strength.

Being Alone

One of the main components of self-discipline is the ability to be alone and get to know oneself. For many people, however, being alone is no different from being lonely. When there is no work to be done or no person to gossip with, there is always TV or the radio to make one feel the presence of others. There is no time for the self unless it is forced, unless one seizes some solitary time for reflection and meditation. I suspect that the current popularity of Transcendental Meditation is an indication of the need people have in our society to be shown how to take a little quiet, internal time.

Young children do not usually have that much difficulty being alone. Babies seem to enjoy lying back and looking and listening. Two- and three-year-olds enjoy piling blocks or rolling balls over and over. I've often come upon young children lost in thought and fantasy, speaking softly to themselves and acting out some private world.

With my own children I've found that after they've had friends sleep over or after we've had a siege of people staying at our house, they go off by themselves. If Judy or I try to interrupt their solitary play or reveries, they get extremely annoyed—they act as if some part of their being is violated.

Yet many parents and, later in life, teachers do violate their children's privacy and destroy their ability to be alone. There are a number of ways this happens. One is to turn every random act of exploration by a young child into a testing situation. I remember visiting an old friend's house. He had a three-year-old daughter who he felt was the smartest and most special child in the world. He showed her off to me, applauded as she made a house out of blocks, as she sorted shapes and named colors. She was very precocious and pleased with herself. After a while her father and I turned away from her and began to talk about old times. I kept my eyes on her, however. She lost all attention in her objects and started agitating to get our attention. After a while her father became annoyed and yelled at her. She cried, he melted, paid some attention to her, then turned away to talk to me, and the whole procedure began again. Finally, out of frustration he turned the TV on in the next room and placed her in front of it. The frenetic and seductive sounds of cartoons lured her into a passive silence.

Many insecure people worry that they are not worthy of being parents. They believe that their children will find them out and therefore are always attuned to signs of potential rejection. One act that is easily misinterpreted in such a situation is a demand for privacy. "My child wants to be alone, he (or she) doesn't love me anymore" is a terrible hurt cry one hears from lonely adults who feel rejected and out of control of their own lives.

The ability to be alone implies the ability in a certain part of your life to be free of the judgments and categories imposed upon you by others, and therefore the ability to explore and invent and create; to see and organize things in new ways; to discover strengths and insights that are beyond culture and moral judgment. To be alone in the sense that I am trying to convey is to stay young and fresh in part of your being, and to value and preserve that unique and unpredictable part of yourself that is private.

Being Patient and Encouraging Mistakes

There is another aspect of self-discipline that is important for children and adults: the ability to be patient, to slow time down, to plan and practice and not have everything delivered here and now. Patience also involves the willingness to make mistakes, to take an imperfect idea, plan, sketch, or essay and work on it until it becomes what one wishes.

If a child feels that it is always necessary to be perfect, the smartest response is to attempt little, limit the imagination, and become expert at doing many small, mechanical tasks well. This attitude has its rewards, not only at home, but when one reaches school. The "good" student is the mechanical child who does as instructed and repeats many small tasks without the intrusion of fantasy or imagination. This behavior often passes as patience, whereas it is actually submission, which is the opposite of patience.

Patience is the ability to work at something, to come back to things one doesn't understand, to let ideas and images and thoughts grow in one's mind, and then to express them imperfectly. It is the ability to work on these imperfect forms and shape them. It involves, above all, the absence of a fear of failure.

I've noticed that my children used to worry a lot about messing up a drawing or a building or a sculpture. They would become angry at themselves and tear up the paper or tear down the building. I couldn't understand that attitude—quitting rather than doing something over—until Erica inadvertently explained to me what it was all about. At one moment of frustration she picked up one of my books and said, "You don't make any mess-ups—look how perfect your book is." She believed that the finished product sprung whole from my mind. She believed that cars were made with no mistakes, that things in the adult world somehow emerged in their final form without flaws, without effort, and without improvisation. And why shouldn't she believe that adult creation was flawless and complete? She never saw people working, only the products of labor and invention. In our society few children grow up in the midst of adult work. Most children grow up in residential communities, go to schools or child care centers. They are not situated so they can experience adult mess-ups firsthand. Moreover, adults don't like to expose their mess-ups to their children any more than they like to expose them to their bosses.

When Erica showed me my book, which she thought emerged so perfectly, I saw how unreal production in the adult world was to her and to Tonia and Josh. On my desk was another book I was working on. The pages were all written in longhand. There were cross-outs and mess-ups on every page. In some cases, pages were cut up and stapled together in a different order. My children looked at the manuscript in astonishment. How could that mess ever become a book? The word *become* was the key. The final work went through many stages before anyone ever saw it, much less published it.

Josh asked me then if I liked to make mess-ups. I tried to explain that it wasn't "like" or "not like." Books and all complicated works grow and get better because people have the patience to look at their mess-ups and work on them.

I then tried to show my children how other things are made, how a painting emerges from sketches and ideas; how the car they see on the street has to be designed and tested; how buildings get planned and often changed as they are built. From that time Tonia, Erica, and Josh seem to be more able to work at things, to correct and start over again when necessary, to understand the meaning of patience and process—that is, to understand that work develops and that it is possible to return to the same thing many times as your ideas change and your skill develops.

There are a number of ways to help your child develop patience. The most obvious is for you to be patient yourself. Let him or her play while you stop looking for gifts and talents. Let the child's abilities emerge. Try not to judge your child or to judge yourself by what your child does.

Another thing you can do is take your child to work with you, not once but many times. Show her or him what you do, and what other people do also. Talk about the long-term projects you have as well as the short-term ones. Don't try to make everything look perfect and conflict-free. Your child will learn more by being let in on the process and seeing the patience, persistence, and approximations you go through in order to complete some work.

Also, the way you deal with mistakes—yours and your child's—is crucial. If you panic or feel inferior when confronted with things you've done wrong, or if you put down your child's mistakes, he or she will close up and attempt less. If, on the other hand, you act insincerely and praise what is obviously a mess-up, your child will see the lie and might learn that serious work is not worth the effort.

Commenting on a mistake without overlaying those comments with moral judgments or implying praise or rejection is difficult. A method of developing this ability is to look at the things you mess up in your life and try to face them without praising or rejecting yourself. If you can come to look upon your mistakes as the material out of which you can build a creative life, you probably will be able to look upon your child's mistakes in the same way.

Learning to Observe

Closely related to the development of patience is the ability to deal with unfamiliar experiences and to learn from other people. Children are constantly encountering new situations in the physical world and in the world of people. They have to develop ways of dealing with things and skills and people that are new. When a child becomes fearful of unexpected occurrences or feels constantly menaced, he or she finds it difficult to learn how to master a skill or understand a person. Yet it is not uncommon to find adults who are fearful or closed, who spend their lives protecting themselves and are incapable of observing things without involving their egos. Such self-conscious people tend to focus all their attention in a new situation on the role they are playing and the impression they are making. The questions they ask in unfamiliar situations are: How do they feel about me? How can I develop power in this situation? How do I look to them? Who is it best to get close to? How can I see me through their eyes? Questions too often unasked in these self-conscious encounters are: Who are they? What can be learned from observing them? What is new and different here and what is familiar? What can I learn from listening?

These latter questions lead away from the self to a more heightened view of events and people. They lead to learning and growth, to the discovery of things that don't directly relate to one's feeling or position. The ability to step back from one's ego, to observe something in order to understand it, is a very important component of being able to relate to the world without feeling a need to control it. It can also sometimes provide useful information that can help one work out social and personal problems. For example, recently a friend came over to talk. She was obviously upset, and after a few minutes her problem came out. Her five-year-old son had come home from kindergarten in tears complaining that nobody wanted to be his friend. Laura was particularly sensitive to the problem of making new friends, since she and her son had moved twice in the last fourteen months and she had had to reestablish herself each time. She tried to console her son, do everything she could to support him, but the situation seemed to get worse and worse. Just that morning she had practically had to drag him to school and it hurt her to see him so unhappy. As it turned out, the situation wasn't any better in the neighborhood—her son felt equally isolated and friendless. I have known David since he was two and he seemed to me charming, intelligent, and attractive. He was at ease with adults, easy to play with. He wasn't shy or overly aggressive. If anything, he seemed too adult. I mentioned to Laura my feelings about David's sociability with adults. She had noticed the same thing and explained that it might be because he had been with adults so much during the past year when they were trying to get settled. All of her friends liked David and spent a lot of time with him. As she talked it occurred to me that David might be having trouble with his peers for precisely the same reason that he got along so well with adults. When he was with adults we all played the game he brought out, followed his leads in conversation, and were delighted by the attention he paid to us. However, this behavior when projected into the world of children might look very selfish. My intuition was that David tried to do with his friends what he did successfully with adults and was rejected by children his own age for reasons he didn't understand.

I asked Laura to describe what happened when another child came over to her house to play with David. She described a particularly unpleasant time that had occurred the week before. Another boy, Paul, came over with his favorite racing cars and wanted to play with them. David, on the other hand, wanted to play with his squigglies and rubber monsters and Paul gave in for a while. However, after half an hour Paul took out his cars and said it was car time. David refused to go along and said that it was his house and therefore they had to play with monsters. Neither of them budged, and after a while Paul asked Laura to take him home.

David, who had so much experience with getting adults to play his games, didn't have much experience in learning to join in someone else's game. As it turned out, this problem with Paul wasn't unique. David thought that a friend was someone who played the games you wanted to play when you wanted to play them. Laura had a difficult problem to deal with. David was a fine healthy child who had moved around a lot in his short life. He had to learn a new way to reach out to people his own age without giving up the considerable charm and intelligence he had already developed. It was important to avoid turning difficulty with approaching other children into a problem that created self-doubts and could have serious psychological ramifications.

I suggested that Laura forget about what had happened in the past and consider that she had a learning problem to deal with that wasn't much different from helping David learn how to ride a bike or eat in a restaurant or dunk his head under the water. In all of these cases and many others, children have to do things they initially find unpleasant, like falling, being somewhat quiet, or getting their eyes and ears wet. In order to achieve more power, children have to learn to discipline themselves and give up certain indulgences. Fortunately in the cases I mentioned, the personal rewards of learning outweigh the inconveniences one has to suffer or the indulgences one has to give up. The same is true with making friends. Considered in this light, one is dealing with a challenge in the present and not a psychological problem of undoing past failures.

Learning to observe and then act for oneself is an important aspect of the development of self-discipline and there is probably no better way to learn how to observe and analyze unfamiliar experiences than to watch natural phenomena—stars, animals, trees, plants, the weather, the soil. Even in a city one can develop this discipline by having and caring for house plants and pets. Our children love to watch seedlings grow, to feed and observe goldfish and algae eaters, to watch insects, to fish off the dock in Berkeley or visit a plant nursery. The slowness with which things grow and change slows down the observer. It's important for children to learn that some changes can't be grasped in a moment and that a great deal can be learned by looking at the same plant a minute a day, or by glancing at the moon every night. There's a bonus to simply observing natural phenomena with your children too. A closeness can grow in that silent sharing that no words or toys could possibly create.

It's important to understand that children like to look at the world for its own sake as well as to master it or understand its relationship to them. Infants and young children love to look, to repeat things, to pick things up and drop them down, to look at and touch animals, to play with water or simply watch it flow. I find that there are a number of components to the way children relate to the world. There is the manipulative component, which involves the child in learning how things in the world can be used. There is the personal component, which involves the child's trying to figure out what things or people will or can do to affect the child's life. And there is the contemplative component—the disinterested observing of the world, the wonder one sees in many children's faces when they see something new or beautiful. There is this experience that does not refer directly to the self, does not involve any immediate mastery of a skill, any push and pull with the world or people. It is a fragile ability because in our society little value is put on acts that do not lead to specific results. Curiosity, exploration, and observation are supposed to have a point if they are to be of value. Otherwise one is wasting time. I learned during the last years of my grandfather's life how deeply this attitude of needing to fill time up with goal-directed activity, of using one's time as a commodity is ingrained in us. He retired as a framer when he was about seventy-seven and spent almost all of his time looking out of the window of his apartment. He sat at the open window watching children play, greeting people, taking in whatever passed his way. I wanted to get him involved in projects, was vaguely annoyed by his doing nothing. One day after I had been bugging him with suggestions about reading books or building bookcases for the house, he told me that he *was* doing something, that he was tired of having to make or build something for someone. He simply wanted to look at the world, he liked to watch children playing, young people talking or running around. He enjoyed seeing the world—he didn't want anything from it or want to do anything to it.

It has taken many years for me to slow down enough to observe the world in that simple way, to watch other people move and work and play without trying to discover what was in it for me. School made me neurotic about grades, and since college I have made great effort to teach myself to be free of worry about being graded or evaluated. By observing, feeling the rhythm of things, one learns unexpectedly—understands without having to quantify or articulate. In a funny way the pure and simple observing I'm trying to describe is learning freed of compulsion, freed of any need to make something of what one has seen or understood.

Helping children learn to observe and listen to others is often a lot easier than learning to observe and listen to our own children. It's hard to listen, for example, when what is said threatens our security and confidence as parents. If a child claims he or she is unhappy at school, this is often taken to mean the child is failing. Immediately a parent sees his or her child as a failure, wonders if remedial class is necessary, is concerned about not providing a rich home setting, and so on. I can just hear the child complaining: "But you haven't listened to me." The child was unhappy, perhaps being treated badly, and it was not an issue of success or failure. Possibly the teacher was brutal or indifferent. Parents have to learn to see the world through eyes other than their own, to see the world without constantly relating it to their ego. To develop even a modest understanding of your child you have to make an effort to see the world as he or she experiences it away from you and your concerns. You have to imagine the world your child lives in and the life he or she leads independent of your own. If you can also respect that life, it is likely that mutual respect will result.

There is another way of not seeing or listening to your child. If you're blinded by the perfection you see in your child, all the pain and confusion your child experiences, as well as all the strategies he or she may develop to manipulate adults, may be filtered out of your perceptions. I know a case of a thirteen-year-old girl whose father and mother saw her as perfect, a genius. They both worked and were involved in many political and social events and so, despite their feelings about their daughter, they didn't see very much of her. As a consequence, she became a master at manipulating them into giving her attention. Her parents were very critical of the institutions in our society, such as schools, hospitals, universities. If their daughter complained about a teacher, they would be on the teacher's back. It was in her interest to complain about teachers she liked because then her parents would jump to her defense and pay some attention to her. Because they perceived her as perfect, they couldn't see what she was doing.

During the first years of desegregation this girl, as well as a small number of other lonely white junior high school students (male and female), hit on an ingenious way to get more attention than they ever had before. All they had to do was complain that the African American students were harassing them. The parents immediately called up images of rape and violence done to their perfect but neglected children. They became vocal about trying to introduce strict discipline in the schools. After a while some of these youngsters felt guilty about what they were doing and admitted that they made up these stories of harassment. These admissions forced some of the parents to look at what they were demanding of their children and how psychic neglect can result from expecting too much.

EXCERPT FROM "ON BEING A FATHER"

I live in a small town in Northern California, and on our infrequent trips to the Bay area, there are dozens of things my wife and I would like to do. Our children, however, usually have four things in mind: to go to a record store, visit a hobby shop, buy clothes, and see a new movie that is not likely to reach our town for a year. On a recent trip I made with Antonia, Erica, and Joshua (who are fourteen, twelve, and ten), they spent an hour or so in Tower Records while I read and had a glass of wine in the pizzeria next door. When they rejoined me, there was something awkward and wicked in their manner. Tonia was holding something substantial behind her back. Her first words were "I know you won't like this, but . . ."

Before Tonia finished, Josh added, "She didn't make us do it. We did it because we wanted to."

Erica agreed, and I told them to stop tantalizing me and tell me what they'd done. Tonia produced a bag containing, as she told me, every David Bowie record ever made. She had spent all her own money and borrowed all of her brother's and sister's money to pay for a dozen records, most of which she hadn't listened to and knew nothing about. She explained this by saying that all her life she had wanted to listen to everything someone had recorded, from beginning to end.

How was I to respond? It was foolish and expensive. She'd never pay her brother and sister back, and I'd probably end up covering her debts. Some of the records were sure to be terrible, and she might be bored by most of them. Yet her design was grand—something I've always loved doing with the books of my favorite authors. Who should I be: righteous, outraged father? Delighted, indulgent father? Practical father? Father with high-brow taste? Or father pretending to love David Bowie? All these possibilities occurred to me as the children waited for my re-sponse to Tonia's escapade.

I tried to appear concerned about the money, but the pleasure I felt about her trying something so ambitious must have showed on my face. She apologized for her extravagance, knowing that we'd be able to find a way to deal with her debt. We managed to acknowledge the practical and give the adventurous its due.

That tension—trying to help my children understand some sensible limits on what's possible, while supporting them when they push those limits and do things that I've never done and that make me revise my sense of limits—has been central to my experience as a father.

When Tonia, my eldest child, was born, fatherhood was pretty much of an abstraction to me. I had been teaching eleven- and twelve-year-olds for five years before Judy and I decided to have a child of our own. The role of a teacher is quite distinct from that of a parent, as my students frequently reminded me when I had to deal with discipline problems. I remember how they would defy me by saying, "You're not my father," or "You're not my mother." The students themselves acknowledged a certain proprietary power that their parents had, one that I've always been reluctant to exercise.

Of course, once a baby is born you achieve instant fatherhood, prepared or not. The helplessness of babies forces parental deci-sions as soon as the baby is home and in your care. What should you do about crying? Should you let other people take care of your child? What are signs of health and growth, and what are in-dications that the baby may be having problems? Facing these new questions, I found I had contradictory tendencies. Let the baby cry herself to sleep. No, pick her up or she'll feel abandoned. The baby fell! We should go to a doctor. No, she's strong and we shouldn't pamper her. Let's take her to a party and let her learn to be around people. No, she should stay home and we should change our social life for her sake. I remember being overwhelmed by choices those first few months.

The choices my wife and I face as parents are much broader than those faced by our parents. We live more than two hundred miles from our nearest blood relatives. My wife is not Jewish, and our lives, though reverent, are not tied to any religious tradition. Since there are no binding traditions and no immediate family pressures, I can choose any fathering role I want. The problem this freedom creates is that many simple situations can become occasions for guilt, inconsistency, and self-doubt.

Having the freedom to choose the kind of father you want to be is not always a blessing. Pressures to adopt one role or another come from many different sources, and many men have a hard time coping with the anxiety created by not having one clear and unambiguous role to play. There are demands made by women who insist upon equal parental roles, by children who will take as much time and attention as they can possibly get, by co-workers or bosses who believe in assertive masculine authority, by experts who sell one form of "parenting" or another, and, of course, by one's own parents, who tend to romanticize the good old days when life was free of conflict and stress. These pressures point to a central dilemma in our society. We have many role choices that are unavailable in more strict and tradition-bound cultures, and, even though some people escape the responsibility of choice by converting to a fundamentalist faith, most of us live with the problems consequent on the luxury of choice.

How do I become a good father? That is the overriding question that seems to face men who accept the freedom our society offers. Over the last eight years I have interviewed a number of men about their experiences as fathers, which they are beginning to examine more consciously as a counterpoint to questions raised by the women's movement. Each man has a strong sense of what sorts of adults he wants his children to become and how he would like his children to relate to him. And each one has learned to modify those ideas in order to maintain a close relationship with his children. The irony is that strong, loving fathers very often have strong, loving children with ideas of their own, and this often leads to intergenerational warfare. Wanting to be a good father is no guarantee that one will become one.

Roger, for example, is a real-estate lawyer who volunteers one night a week to be on call at a legal hotline for poor people in trouble. He was active in the civil rights movement, but since settling into law practice and helping to raise two children, he can only spare one night a week for the progressive political and social causes he still believes in. He feels he has had to make sacrifices in order to become a good father, and feels guilty that he is not doing more to help people outside his family. He is continually surprised that he has to spend so much time working to keep his family happy and cohesive.

Some of the pressure to work at family life came from Roger's wife, Elaine, who, after their second child, decided she had to go back to school and have his help—not only in the large ways of loving and financial support, but in the small ways that affect the quality of daily life.

Bringing up children requires constant attention and decision making. In the course of a morning one has to deal with the rituals of wake-up and breakfast, with decisions about whether to insist that one of the children get up early to finish homework or to let him or her take responsibility for not having done the work. There are no easy answers or formulas for a question as simple as homework. If, for instance, we have friends over, or have a jazz workshop or a film showing, which is more important: homework or sharing our life with our children? We make different decisions at different times.

The morning rituals often involve deciding whether a child feels sick because of a test in school that day, or because another child threatened him, or because he is genuinely ill; whether and how many friends may come over after school; and whether it is better to wear a blue or purple blouse. After school there are further decisions about homework, friends, new clothes, chores around the house. Within this context the dishes must be kept clean, the clothes washed, and somehow one's own work must get done. And then there's bedtime—a whole new series of rituals to be performed just as parents want to return to the adult world. It's difficult, if not impossible, to do all of that alone, and many marriages and relationships break up as much under the burden of making all these little decisions as from lack of love.

Roger saw Elaine becoming demoralized as she devoted herself exclusively to the house and the children. He found it necessary to modify his work schedule in order to accommodate her need to work and have a full life. He chose to cut back on his time with his law firm and learned to deal with his children in small ways: to go shopping with them, to participate in the choice of a nursery school, to attend teacher conferences, read bedtime stories, and help with homework. He enjoys it and he resents it. There is so much else he could be doing for himself and others instead of spending his time watching his daughter try on jeans or his son waste his afternoon building a model rocket.

There are some rewards. He has an easy, intimate relationship with his children that is rare. Still, he often feels that he is making sacrifices for them, and wants them to acknowledge these sacrifices and treat him as if he were someone special. As far as they're concerned, however, he's just doing what good fathers should do—spending time with his children. His occasional pouting or outbursts of anger surprise them, and his sense of sacrifice is something they don't understand.

Roger also wants his children to see that he and his wife are doing something difficult that they feel is counter to major influences in society. He would like his son to be compassionate rather
than macho and his daughter to be a committed feminist, as ways
of justifying his sacrifices. Meanwhile, his son at ten wants to be
an athlete and his daughter, like most of her classmates, likes de-
signer jeans and hopes to be a cheerleader in high school.

Roger's anguish at the prospect of his cheerleader-daughter
cheering for his athlete-son reminds me of the cheerleading crisis
in my own family. Tonia has been an outspoken feminist since
the age of seven, when she first learned that some people felt that
women couldn't do the same things as men. I was delighted at her
insistence on equality and probably bragged about it a lot. Last
year she tried out for the junior-high-school cheerleaders and
made it. The pompoms she brought home were the symbols of my
defeated dreams of a feminist daughter. One day I finally asked
Tonia how she could be a feminist and a cheerleader at the same
time. She looked at me archly and said, "A feminist can be whatever she wants to be."

Roger and I and other men I know suffer from what might be
called the wages of virtue. Because we work hard at child rearing
and maintaining a home, we want to be praised for our efforts.
However, what we do wouldn't seem like sacrifices if money,
power, and obsessive work weren't temptations. Being raised with
one sensibility about what is expected of men and later trying to
change to a more compassionate and less authoritarian way of
functioning can be a struggle. But children can't be expected to
understand the transformation of adult sensibility and the dilemmas that confront us; nor can they be expected to be free of the
temptations that we as adults might reject. Tonia is right, of
course: a feminist—any child for that matter—should be given a
chance to experiment with ways of living, as long as they are not
suicidal or homicidal, and will find a way to do so whether or not
we approve. Best to laugh with your children, and if necessary

learn to tolerate pompoms and music you don't care for. There are worse things, after all. In my experience, the closer one draws the circle around young people, the wilder and more dangerous their experiments are likely to be.

Of course, not every father can arrange his life to accommodate the needs of his wife and children. Ralph, another of the fathers I interviewed, is a factory worker, a shop steward in a large industrial plant. His wife, Ellen, is a paramedical professional in a local clinic. Between them they earn a decent living, but Ralph constantly faces the prospect of being laid off and worries about rumors that his plant will be closed down and its business sent abroad.

Ralph and Ellen have three children, who attend the local public schools. Neither of them feels they spend enough time with their children, but they both have to work to maintain the modest life they have created for themselves. Ralph is a very gentle person, and the children in the neighborhood respect him and seek his advice. His own children tell me that they are proud to be on his teams and feel sad they can't see him more.

Ralph gives his weekends to children instead of to television. That is how he explains the fact that in each different sports season he coaches children's teams instead of watching the pros on TV. He also manages to arrange trips and summer programs for children, and is known for being able to come home from one of his teams' games and wash the dishes while having a beer or two. It is the dishes, not the beer, that make him outstanding.

I asked Ralph why he didn't simply spend what time he had with his own children. It occurred to me that they might resent the fact that they were rarely alone with him. His answer was that he wanted to maintain a sense of community and to teach his children how to be with others comfortably. That was his choice, and he was willing to deal with the tension it occasionally created. His children saw him enough, he felt. From his standpoint there was too much individualism in society, too many families isolated in their own little worlds. He hoped his children would see how important it was to work in mutually beneficial groups. He was distressed by the competitive values expressed on TV and by the pressure his children's friends put on them to accept those values.

The last time I talked to Ralph, he was experiencing conflicts resulting from the kind of father he has chosen to be. Ralph's daughter Rebecca is seventeen. She has been his special child, his eldest and, from what I perceive, his favorite. His dream was that she would go to college and become someone special—perhaps a doctor who would work with the unions, or maybe a lawyer or university professor. Right now he thinks she's nothing but a "hussy." She left high school in her junior year and took off with a friend. They ended up in Southern California and got jobs in a fast-food store—to his disgust, as nonunion labor. Ralph went through a year of misery wondering what he'd done wrong as a father. He even quit coaching Little League for a week; but he couldn't stay away from the field and was persuaded that the kids needed him.

When Ralph last talked to Rebecca, there seemed to be some possibility of a reconciliation. Rebecca said that she had just enrolled in a junior college and was looking for a different type of job. Ralph took that as a sign that he hadn't been all bad as a father. It struck me, as I listened to him, that he was more concerned with his role as a good father than with the quality of Rebecca's life. I mentioned this indirectly. He answered that there were times when he couldn't stand the pressure of trying to be decent and generous and to share his values with his children. He also said something I've heard expressed in similar words from many men of different classes and races: "Maybe I should have been just like my father and kept the kids in their place." Only he and the other men didn't believe it enough to do it. The hardest thing for them to live with has been the time it takes for youngsters to pass from adolescence to adulthood, from testing out their strength to a commitment to lives of their own.

We have to live with our children's experiments, and needn't despair of our attempts to be good fathers. They need our support more when they do things we don't believe in than when they fulfill our desires and expectations. Besides, experimenting with ways of living is not confined to young people. A number of the fathers I interviewed felt that they shifted in and out of different paternal roles, searching for one that suited them and that was nurturing for their children.

John, for example, has children from two marriages. His eldest child is twenty-one, and his youngest is six months old. John was a successful businessman when he first married. He had to travel so much that he hardly saw his children. They had a warm but formal relationship with him, and he feels that it is only over the last few years that he's been getting to know his older son and daughter, both of whom are in college. At the age of thirty-nine John had a mild heart attack; his first marriage fell apart, and he had to force himself out of the business world. He insisted on making it clear to me that he did not drop out, that he is occasionally tempted to jump back into big business, and that it was simply a desire to stay alive that forced him to change his life.

When John was forty-three he married for the second time. His present wife, Joanne, is twenty years his junior, and he expresses admiration, almost awe, of the way she is unimpressed by material success. They run a small publishing company and do quite well, producing quality work. Joanne manages the business and deals with the details of printing and advertising; John works with the authors, most of whom are his friends. He also spends a lot of time at home with their four-year-old son and six-month-old daughter. Being with the children relaxes him, lets him focus on their needs and forget about himself, which is good for his blood pressure.

John told me in one of our talks that he wondered whether his children had a strange idea of him as a father. At times he feels he's very formal, even strict, with the children. At other times he's warm and silly with them. He wants to be open, affectionate, intimate, but feels a bit foolish acting that way. He also worries that if his children are indulged too often, they won't be tough enough to deal with the harsh realities of a competitive society. But then he remembers how he was toughened up as a child and how he became tough in business, and he thinks about his heart and goes soft. He vacillates between toughness and gentleness with his older children as well as with the two young ones. Should he give them everything they ask for? Should they have to go out and earn it the way he did? How much toughness and how much indulgence does love demand?

That is one of the central problems facing not just John, but all parents these days. It is just a way of phrasing the eternal problem of discipline. How much discipline should be enforced within the family, and who should be the disciplinarian?

I have no simple answer to that question, but would like to reflect a bit about discipline within my own family. Judy and I try to share as much as possible in our daily life. She's quite steady, and I tend to be moody. If my writing is going well, or if one of the projects I'm working on is proceeding smoothly, I'm calm, somewhat indulgent, and often playful. If the work is going badly I'm irascible, and until I learned how to control myself, was given to making threats that my children knew I wouldn't carry out. I might tell them they could never go to a movie again if they continued to run around crazy, for instance, when they knew perfectly well that on Friday night they'd be at the movies. Judy is calmer than I am, though not nearly as indulgent as I tend to be. Over the last fourteen years we've worked out a few general principles for disciplining our children.*

First, never use physical punishment. Second, if you find your-

---

* They are now forty-one, forty, and thirty-eight.

self enjoying being the disciplinarian, you may have a personal problem that is causing you to abuse your child. Third, get the whole thing over with as quickly as possible and get back to living harmoniously together as quickly as possible. Don't let punishments linger and breed resentments. And fourth, if you do lose your temper and scream at your children, or hit a young one in frustration (which happens even if you don't believe in physical punishment), remember that if the overall fabric of your family life is coherent and loving, one such moment will quickly be forgotten. No single instant of disciplinary excess can change a decent life.

This reminds me of something I witnessed at John's home. Even though John vacillates over how to discipline his children, a deep love for his family underlies his actions, and I'm sure his children know it. One day while I was visiting, John was feeling particularly nostalgic for the business world and decided that it was time to prepare his four-year-old son, James, for school—a touch of the "real world," as John put it. James was not ready for the real world, and wanted to play with his Lego blocks rather than begin a formal lesson in letters with his father. John got mad at James's resistance, ranted a bit, tried to get harsh but couldn't pull it off, and, grabbing control of himself, asked me to watch James for a second while he went outside and relaxed. As he was leaving the room James turned to me, pointed to John, and said, "That's my daddy. He's nice."

James understood his father's love, and was learning to be patient with his moods even if he didn't understand them. He didn't want me to get the wrong impression of his father.

John is having a difficult time raising two young children, but has recently come to see that his four-year-old needs to be four and not to be treated as if he were twelve or an adult. He has also come to feel easier about the idea that children can be influenced but not molded, and that it is in the nature of growth that unexpected things will happen. John's eldest son told me that he's learning from watching his father with his young stepbrother and stepsister. It may be hard to decide what kind of father to be, as John and his son know, but children will put up with a lot without being damaged if concern for them is authentic.

Robert and Leon, two other fathers I interviewed, have had an impossible time convincing their children that they care for them. Robert is a full-time businessman. He came from a poor family and is determined that his children won't have the same experiences he had growing up. If anything he overcompensates, not permitting his children to see or learn anything about poverty. Leon, on the other hand, is a fulltime activist, a person who has experienced painful discrimination and injustice and is equally determined that his children won't have the same experiences. Both men seem to be cold, obsessed, all work and business. The early part of each of my interviews with them consisted of short, almost hostile answers. However, as we talked and they relaxed, warm, caring people emerged. These two men hardly know their children, yet have devoted their whole lives to making a better place in the world for them. That is the choice they've made as fathers.

I find it interesting that, different as their styles, politics, and appearances are, the way Robert and Leon behave toward their children is nearly identical. They are awkward, slightly embarrassed; they don't know what to do or what to say. It's the little things that cause them problems. The times I've spent with these fathers and their children are usually highly structured; they focus on carrying out some planned activity rather than simply being together. I wonder what these children, who are under ten, think of their fathers, whom they see so little and yet have every reason to respect. They can't have much sense of how their father's work relates to their lives, though as they get older that might become more apparent. Still, there is something missing in their relationship—what I have been calling the "little things" that make up the quality of everyday life. These little things came up in our interviews.

Robert and Leon also wonder what their children think of them, and feel that maybe they've already given up more than they imagined by not sharing time with their children while they're young. It is not merely what the children are missing, but what they as fathers are missing. Attention is often paid to what children get from their parents; parents have to get something from their children, too, and absence cannot build the ease and intimacy that creates that wonderful feeling of pleasure just from being in each other's company. Robert and Leon ask themselves whether the choices they've made in defining a father role for themselves were worth it. My last interview with each of them was tense, curt. They were worried about their children's future and felt that this was not a good time to be growing up. They expressed a confusion I hadn't heard from them before. What was important—kindness or skills? A tough approach or a tender one? To prepare them for bad times, which would be better—fostering inner strength or teaching them to compete even more harshly? Where should you spend your time—with your children, or working to make the world better for them?

The current conservative climate and the romantic plea for a return to family life, piety, and obedience that is a part of it do not negate our need to choose what kinds of fathers we shall become, or to struggle with the more fundamental questions of what makes a good father, parent, and person. If anything, it points up our inability to answer these questions. There *are* answers, tentative certainly, yet guiding us back to humane, caring values, not merely for our own children, but for all children. I've received these answers from children I've worked with over the years.

According to them, a good father is one who loves his children no matter how they mess up; one who's fair to all children; one who tells children what he feels and believes even if they disagree; one who admits he's wrong when he is wrong; and one who can be fun to be with even when there are problems in the family. Children don't expect perfection from their fathers. They know too much about the adult world to expect perfection from anyone. What they want coincides to an amazing degree with what most of the fathers I've spoken to want in their relations with their children—honesty, fun, and the ability to live through conflict without the loss of love.

EXCERPT FROM *PAINTING CHINESE*

My journey into painting Chinese was unanticipated. It began with discovering that I was becoming an old man. About four years ago, my wife, Judy, and I were in a local market buying food for dinner. As usual, I wandered off to the little section where they sold cheap toys and games and chose a bag of small plastic firefighters and policemen billed as a "9/11 Heroes" kit to add to my collection of painted Dungeons & Dragons figurines, nativity scenes, action figures, and other miscellaneous tchotchkes. At the checkout counter, the cashier rang up the food and the figures and asked, in a very pleasant voice, if the playthings were for my grandchildren. I was surprised.

Those days I was feeling young and creative, very much the middle-aged guy who was trying to preserve the child in himself. However, she saw me as a grandfather. I had never seen myself that way, and her casual comment troubled me.

I never experienced anxiety when I passed thirty-five, never had a middle-age crisis in my forties or fifties. I just kept on working on external things: working with children, writing, and advocating for social justice. The work I did was a source of energy and strength, and I always felt I could continue doing it at the same level and with the same intensity as long as I desired. But as I was approaching seventy, there were times when I felt old, tired, and vulnerable. After a twelve-hour day, my hip hurt and I limped. I can trace that back to an auto injury when I was twenty-seven, though I'd been pain-free for over thirty years. It was not just the pain and fatigue that led me to feel old. My wife and I had lost our parents when in our sixties and had witnessed their aging and dying. That witness was painful, and as we inherit the role of family elders, we now both see ourselves moving along the same slow path.

Recently, aging has come closer to center stage as a number of old friends have become very ill, a few have died, and a few are tenuously but stubbornly holding on to life. I see myself in them and on occasion am overwhelmed by the sense of my finitude. Sometimes I find myself surveying my toys and books and plants and wonder what will happen when I'm no longer around to care for them. The possibility that the whole fabric of my life, memories, friendships, and the working environment I have shaped so carefully over the past fifty years can dissolve in a moment is distressing.

My own children joke about my concerns about aging and, I believe, see me as I was when they were younger, just as I still see them as they were as children even though they are in their late thirties and early forties.

For the five years before I turned seventy, I created and directed a teacher education program at the University of San Francisco based on the idea of integrating issues of social justice throughout the curriculum, hoping to bring young idealistic people into public school teaching and to fortify them with the skills and stamina to make their dreams practical realities. I succeeded in recruiting thirty students to the program each year, most of them students of color, and had a wonderful time with them. We created the curriculum together, studied issues of social justice as they applied to the classroom, and experimented with specific ways of teaching and learning through the arts, music, dance, and literature. The program ended bitterly in the fourth year when the university cut it after the funding I had raised ran out. I had put an enormous amount of energy into developing and teaching in the program and during my last year there I felt worn down physically and emotionally, not from the teaching, but from constant harassment by the administration.

During the last year of the program, I took to walking randomly around the neighborhoods near the university: wandering into stores, listening to conversations in restaurants, seeking some new focus or adventure, looking for something to seize my heart and inspire me.

I gravitated toward Clement Street, a predominantly Chinese commercial street in western San Francisco. The Clement neighborhood is home to working- and middle-class people, mostly Mainland and Taiwanese Chinese and Koreans with a mix of Asian Americans and a small number of white people who are moving in as the neighborhood begins to gentrify.

Clement is not a tourist destination, but a vibrant community with Chinese, Japanese, and Korean restaurants; vegetable, fish, poultry, and meat markets; pastry shops; teahouses; kitchenware and hardware stores; and the occasional Middle East market. There are a number of tea and coffee bars where older Chinese men play cards, dominoes, and Chinese chess throughout the day. There's even an Irish pub, a wonderful new- and used-book store, and several rock clubs, as well as the usual commerce of an American street: cell phone and computer stores and small markets (*marquetas*) that sell everything from newspapers and candy to cans of soup and lottery tickets.

I struck up a casual friendship with the owner of one of the *marquetas* I frequented. During one of our brief conversations, a policeman came into the store, looked around, and left. As soon as he was out of sight, the owner said that the cop wasn't "real Chinese." I asked him what was "real Chinese," and he said with pride that it was someone who had come from the Mainland. The others in the neighborhood were just Taiwanese. So much for my image of a peaceful diverse community; old scars had been transported across the Pacific.

I had developed the habit of going to lunch one day at Taiwan Restaurant, and then the next day I went to a restaurant diagonally across the street called China First. I didn't really understand until this conversation that every other day I crossed the Strait of Formosa from China to Taiwan and back.

I loved being a stranger on Clement.

On one of my random walks, I encountered a storefront with

the sign JOSEPH FINE ARTS SCHOOL. There was a poster in the window that stated that classes in painting, drawing, calligraphy, and sculpture were available. Also on display were samples of students' work and small Chinese sculptured stone figures and painted glass bottles that were for sale. I wondered who Joseph Fine was and decided to go in and look around. For years, I had played around with painting when I was bored, in need of some physical form of meditation. My work was a combination of action painting, abstract expressionism, finger painting—all with no training, grace, or talent. Stumbling upon that school on Clement reminded me of the times I'd promised myself to take painting lessons one day. I decided to enroll in a class whatever the school was like and turn casual painting into an integral part of my new life. It would also bind me in a specific way to the Clement world I was beginning to create as a way of providing some transition to my indefinite future. And it was a way to jump into an arena where I could once more encounter the freshness and excitement of learning things I knew nothing about. It would be new, not a renewal, a childlike pleasure. My current journey's goal was not to regain energy to enter the same old frustrating struggles with renewed energy, but to find a new way to grow and be useful without bringing along the old baggage. I was beginning to admit to myself that many of my theories about educating children were neither relevant nor effective anymore.

I walked into the studio and asked to talk to Joseph Fine. A charming, soft-spoken Chinese couple in their mid-forties came out of the back room to talk to me. They were laughing—there was no Joseph Fine, it was the *Joseph* Fine Arts School, and the man introduced himself as Joseph Yan. The studio and school were run by him and his wife, Janny. They said they would be honored to have me as a student.

There was a child went forth every day,
And the first object he look'd upon, that object he became,

And that object became part of him for the day, or a certain
   part of the day,
Or for many years, or stretching cycles of years.
                        —Walt Whitman, *Leaves of Grass*

The Joseph Fine Arts School is located in a storefront squeezed
between a small Chinese market and a Vietnamese restaurant. It
runs from Clement Street all the way through to a backyard sculpture garden and fountain. The front room is for sales of art supplies
and some imported Chinese art. There are three other rooms
along an open corridor leading to the small sculpture garden at
the back. The second room is for intermediate and advanced calligraphy and advanced painting. It is also serves as Janny's working place. The third room is for sketching and beginning painting.
The last room is for sculpture and other forms of clay modeling.
Altogether, about 120 students attend the school during a week.

In the two painting rooms there are tables, some long and
some short. At each of the tables there are painting positions set
up. A painting station consists of an easel pushed toward the
back of the table, an armature to hold brushes, a folded napkin,
several plates and small saucers for mixing colors and for ink, and
a large rectangular piece of flannel placed on the table.

There were no students present when I wandered into the
school, and the setup of the painting positions puzzled me. The
easel was pushed so far away from the chair that it would be difficult to reach. And the flannel and tidily folded napkin made no
sense to me. I was intrigued and decided that this might be the
new and challenging place I was seeking at this stage in my life.

The small ceramic and sculpture studio at the back, leading to
an elaborate concrete fountain sculpted and designed by Joseph,
also has a kiln and several small potting wheels.

In the inner painting room is a corner set up for pencil drawing. There is a stand for an object, a lamp to light it, and a small
easel.

There are Chinese paintings on all of the walls throughout the school. Most of them are Joseph's and Janny's, though some are the works of present and past students.

The entire place is a miracle of packaging. There is no wasted space, yet at the same time it doesn't feel crowded. It was clear to me that someone with a sophisticated spatial sense had designed the school. The source of that aesthetic and spatial intelligence turned out to be Joseph and Janny. They transformed an empty storefront into an elegant, gracious learning environment that projected order, calm, serious work, and playfulness. Usually I enter new places cautiously and with a healthy dose of skepticism probably born out of some of my experiences growing up in the Bronx. But here I immediately felt at home—there was a fairy-tale feeling about my entering Joseph and Janny's world, as if they were waiting for me to take my place in the story. Of course, they weren't, and I wonder what they felt about this older white man walking into their school.

When I showed up for my first lesson, Joseph indicated that I would be in the beginners' class and gave me the tools needed for this new adventure—four animal-hair bamboo brushes, two small, one medium, and one large; rice paper; a bottle of Chinese black ink; and a box of Chinese watercolors, which are made of minerals and organic pigments and don't represent the same color spectrum of Western paintings. There are more earth colors, browns, reds, and vermilions, a yellow, three blues, white, and one green. Each color has its particular application, and I have still not used them all.

I realized at this ceremonial moment that I would be giving up thoughts of oils and canvas. I would not be working directly from nature, like Cézanne, van Gogh, Poussin, and Turner. Instead I would be giving myself to something thoroughly unknown to me—painting Chinese. Having accepted Joseph as a teacher, I was thus obligated to be a willing and voluntary student, to follow wherever he guided me.

After paying for the brushes and other tools for painting, I followed Joseph to the back painting room, where he settled me at a painting station. I unwrapped my brushes and set them in an armature to my right. Then I opened the box of paints and put them on my left with the bottle of ink. Joseph told me to unroll one sheet of rice paper and place it on the flannel that was in front of me on the table. The flannel would absorb any paint or water that bled through the paper. Then Joseph brought me two coffee cups half filled with water and a folded paper napkin and placed them near the brushes. The easel remained empty, and for the first time I realized that the easel was not for painting. I would be working on the flat surface of the table, painting downward rather than in an upright position as I was accustomed to do when I dabbled with painting at home.

This prepainting ritual—unwrapping the brushes, setting up the painting station, getting water, folding a napkin, placing paper on the flannel mat, and preparing to paint—has become second nature to me. I find it calming, a moment when I move from the pressure of the day to the serene and complex world of Chinese landscape painting.

For that first class, I anticipated meeting a number of Chinese people who could teach me how to play Chinese chess (I love games from all over the world) and introduce me to some aspects of Chinese culture in San Francisco that I had no access to. I took the seat Joseph assigned to me. He had carefully thought out the seating arrangement. There were six painting places and six students (some of my subsequent classes were smaller). There were two desks to my left and three across from me at another table that faced toward the sculpture studio.

The other students began to arrive. The first two went right to their places and prepared to work. The other three, who were first-time students like me, waited for Joseph to help them.

The students were all Chinese or Chinese American. Two of them were five years old, two seven, and one six. Four of them were girls. In terms of skill, I was placed in the right class, but it was a shock. When Joseph said "beginning," he meant it. Education is not age specific for him. Two of the children had taken a prior beginners' class, and they were familiar with the rituals and routines of the work. The experienced painters took out their set of brushes and put them into the armature. They opened their boxes of colors and placed them on the table alongside their bottle of ink; each went to the sink and got two cups of water, and then carefully unrolled a sheet of rice paper and placed it on the felt mat, holding down the corners with wooden blocks just as Joseph had shown me.

Once their places were set, the two more experienced students went to a series of cabinets, picked out paintings to copy, and placed them on their easels. There were dozens of these open cabinets throughout the school that contained rows of paintings mounted on cardboard, numbering perhaps in the hundreds, for use as models for student painting. The easels were to hold paintings to be copied, something I had not expected at all. My whole experience with painting was derived from the notion that you painted directly from nature or life or from your imagination. Copying was considered beneath most young artists I knew. And I would never use it in my teaching because I thought it would inhibit my students' creativity.

Nevertheless, sitting among the children thrilled me. I was a child in school again, this time on my own terms. It's funny how sometimes mind, body, and feelings don't match. I was a child in an old guy's body, and when I sat down that day, my body disappeared and the child in me emerged once again. It was like going home when I had no real childhood home to go back to: parents dead, the Bronx three thousand miles and I can't count how many cultures away. Here I was in a Chinese environment with children I knew nothing about and calm and rested, curious and apprehensive, but delighted. I was on the ground again, a sixty-nine-year-old six-year-old. What fun!

For me, learning is an adventure. It's my way of voyaging, and it requires new settings, new people, and a delicate openness on the part of people you choose to learn from and the students you learn with.

Joseph chose paintings for me and the other two new students, and I refocused and looked at the scene he chose for me to paint.

The paintings Joseph chose were simple, traditional paintings of monkeys—monkeys playing, eating fruit, swinging on tree limbs, resting, running. There were monkeys by themselves and monkeys in groups. All of them were rendered simply, though there were variations in the inking and coloring. Though each new student was given monkeys to paint, each of us had a different monkey painting to work from. We could copy the classics, but not from one another. It was intriguing—the method for each student was the same, but the content was different. I took out the writing and teaching notebook I always carry and quickly noted that I should try something like the monkey painting in one of my classes at the university.

Nevertheless, I was very self-conscious. I had to focus on my monkeys and not on my self-doubts or the children sitting next to me. I was more than sixty years older than my classmates and had spent over forty years teaching. In the past, I had taught kindergarten and first grade and was proud of my ability to help even the most reticent pupils learn how to read intelligently and write imaginatively. Guiding young people through their encounters with new ideas, skills, and understanding was, and still is, one of the greatest pleasures I know. I wanted to help Joseph's students, provide advice and resources, and be looked up to by them as a caring expert and mentor. Among children I had developed the habit of being a teacher, engaged in their lives and learning. But here Joseph was the teacher, and it quickly became clear that any advice from me, as a novice and a stranger with no structured relation with the children, was inappropriate. Besides, I knew nothing about painting Chinese and couldn't have provided good advice even if it had been asked for. Painting with the children would clearly be a challenge—how to learn painting and accept the awkward position of being simply a student, but one who clearly stood out in the class. What did the children think of my being there?

The first lesson began with Joseph going to each new student and showing him or her how to hold a brush, lay out a sheet of rice paper on the felt, and pour a little bit of ink onto a saucer. Each student took his or her own path within the structure set for them. They were copying and not copying at the same time. It's difficult to convey this, but they were both within a tradition and encouraged to personalize it. In fact, over all of the time I have been at the school (going on three years now), I have never heard Joseph or Janny comparing students' work.

Joseph began his rounds with me. The students who had been in the class previously had already begun painting panda bears. He explained that the correct use of the bamboo brush was at the heart of Chinese painting and that the first step was to learn how to hold it.

Joseph made it clear that it is crucial, when doing Chinese painting, to forget the way you hold a pen or pencil and think more about how you hold chopsticks (if you know how to use them). He said that the traditional way of holding a Chinese brush has fundamentally to do with painting on a flat surface and not on an easel. The pinky and the ring finger control the brush near the bristles, though the pinky is rarely used. The thumb and the other two fingers control the top of the brush. The brush is held perpendicular to the surface of the rice paper.

In addition to getting the grip right, Joseph informed me that the brush should be held vertically.

He then asked me to study the monkey while he soaked the brushes in water to dissolve the glue that held the hairs together before use. All of these preliminaries may seem tedious, but holding the brush correctly and caring for the brushes are central to the whole process of Chinese painting, where the tool and the product are integral parts of the activity. They express respect for the art form and acknowledge the importance of tradition in contemporary work.

Attention to ritual slows you down. Often I came to class after a day full of pressure and conflict, of juggling a dozen things at a time, and feeling overwhelmed. Before beginning to paint at Joseph's, I brought all of the complexities of work home to Judy. Now, as soon as I entered the storefront for my lesson, they all temporarily disappeared and the rituals took over. They were my transition from one way of pacing life to another.

As I waited for the glue on my brushes to dissolve, Joseph moved on to the other new students. Once all our brushes were soaked and the brushes softened, Joseph came back to me. I asked him to take care of the children first, but he refused, he said, out of respect for my age and to teach the other students the patience required to do Chinese painting. It was the Chinese way, he explained as he poured a little bit of ink on a saucer and put a daub of red paint on the color-mixing pallet at my place.

My painting portrayed a single monkey holding a red peach. The monkey had a red face. The rest of it was outlined in black, though the body was rendered in shades of gray.

Joseph painted the top of the monkey's head and then gave me the brush, told me to continue the painting, and went to the young girl sitting on my left. Fen couldn't have been more than five years old. She was slim and incredibly well dressed—at least compared with the college students I spent my days working with. She was smiling nervously up at Joseph, and her feet were shaking from anticipation or perhaps anxiety. Joseph spoke to her in the same quiet, reassuring tone that he used with me. And he went through the rituals and details in exactly the same way he did with me. We were both students, novices, and he treated us with the same respect and kindness that I have seen him display toward all the students at the school.

Before beginning to paint, Fen looked closely at her two monkeys. I noticed that Joseph was giving the other students more complex paintings than the one he gave me. He assumed, quite correctly, that I would be the student who had the most trouble with the brush and the rhythm and style of Chinese ink painting.

One of Fen's monkeys was chasing the other, and they both looked somewhat maniacal to me. I noticed her giggle at their antics, as did Joseph. Then he took a medium brush and drew the outline of one of the monkeys' heads and told her to continue. There was no pressure involved; he simply set her out on the road, like a parent giving a gentle push to a child who is learning to ride a bicycle.

The other student on our side of the table, Hui Ying, was very intense. She came into the class and immediately raised her hand. She told Joseph she wanted to be first—first to get her monkeys and first to be taught. He smiled, told her to study the monkeys, and went about his business, paying no attention to her anxious demands. When he finally reached her, she had calmed down a bit. The painting on her easel was of three monkeys sitting in a circle. Joseph got her started on the largest of the three. He also looked over to me and indicated I should look to my painting instead of watching him and the children. Clearly I had to get in painting mode and put aside my desire, as a teacher, to see how the children set about working.

I proceeded with my painting cautiously, dipping my brush first in water and then in ink, though I cheated by watching how Fen worked. Instead of teaching her, I was trying to learn from her. I was afraid to make a mistake, but she showed no such fear and was clearly much more confident than I was. She dipped her brush in the water and then dipped the point into the black ink. Joseph had warned us about getting too much water on the brush. He advised us to ink only the brush's point. I worried about what "too much" meant and just how far the point extended down the brush. I was paralyzed, overly analytic, afraid to make a first stroke. The rice paper was so delicate, and I couldn't figure out any way to erase or correct my mistakes.

I did put too much water and ink on the brush, and as Fen's monkey began to emerge, I made my first watery stroke, watching the ink spread out from my line and create a misty aura around what was to be the top of the monkey's head. I wanted to erase the line, but that was impossible without destroying the sensitive rice paper. My other thought was to tear up the paper and try another one, but before I could get around to it, Joseph came up to me and gently took the brush out of my hand.

I was shocked and embarrassed. Was he telling me that I

wasn't capable, that I wasn't ready? I tensed up while he dried off the brush and showed me, slowly, how to do the stroke for the monkey's head by doing it himself. He then inked the brush for me and handed it back without making any judgment, smiled, and encouraged me to go on with the monkey. Later, he added, we could make my stroke into a tree or rock or bamboo. I had just made a stroke, not a mistake. There were no mistakes, just efforts, and, as I later learned, no torn-up papers or restarts in his way of teaching. You just work through what you did no matter what it looks like and use it to teach yourself how to get closer to what you want to achieve in the painting.

Still, I glimpsed Fen's painting with admiration. It was an adorable monkey. She was about to finish up the red around the eyes, nose, and mouth, and I was just beginning to outline the face. She smiled at me and said what I was doing was nice. I didn't agree, but her comment was genuine and supportive. I assume she meant that it was nice that I was trying to paint, and she was right.

Then she turned to her monkey and smiled. She waited for Joseph, who came over and showed her how to dilute the black ink to make a gray to shade its body.

My second attempt was better, and I managed to outline the monkey's head and finish the face in red, though I felt very tense while making my strokes. I noticed how Joseph's strokes flowed and how Fen seemed to paint effortlessly. Their hands, eyes, and minds worked together, while I was worrying about the ink and water, afraid of holding the brush incorrectly, unsure of what pressure to use while making the stroke.

Hui Ying also seemed to be struggling, and I wanted to help her. Joseph sensed my intent and told me, in his quiet voice, that she'd be fine. I checked my impulse to teach and realized that I wouldn't even know how to help her since I was struggling myself. My position was similar to that of experienced teachers who are required to teach subject matter they do not know. The desire to help students is there, the skill and craft of supporting and encouraging students is there, the ability to motivate and help others through new challenges is there. But the substance, the content, the subject matter itself, is a barrier to effective teaching. Trying to teach what you don't yet know is a compromise at best, and even the most talented teachers, when forced into that situation, can at best learn with their students as they work to stay a bit ahead of them. For me at Joseph's, helping the other students was not a possibility. I was truly headed into unknown territory, and it was clear over the course of the semester that the other students, having seen brothers and sisters and friends learn Chinese painting, were better prepared for the experience than I was.

The third new student, Chen, was the youngest of us. He worked quickly and produced a delightful monkey who was throwing a peach. I couldn't see how he worked; he was across the table, hidden by his easel. However, every few minutes he would get up and walk around, looking at everything else that was going on in the room. Joseph had to stare him back to work but was very patient with him. Joseph acted with confidence and trust. He knew everyone would settle into painting and gave us the space and support to do it in our own ways. There was no disorder in the room at all; rather, there was a gentle, almost imperceptible, hum of people doing joyful work.

The other two students, the old-timers, painted confidently. Lynn, the oldest of the children, was serious about her work. I noticed Joseph spent time teaching her more complex techniques than the rest of us were ready for. His technique was simply to demonstrate, on a separate piece of paper or on a napkin, a stroke or way of mixing paints. He did it once and then let her figure out how to integrate it into her work. The fifth child, Pearl, was very playful and voluble. At times, she couldn't resist chatting with other students, but Joseph managed to refocus her whenever she lost concentration and began to socialize. It was clear that Joseph's priority was to nurture our artistic expression.

I already felt like a bad student. I hadn't given myself a chance, but I was pushing too hard, perhaps because of the awkwardness of painting with the children. I didn't know how to be just another student, alongside them. I was one of them as a student, but I certainly wasn't an elementary school child. Usually I am relaxed and willing to take chances when facing a new challenge. Competition doesn't interest me. In my teaching, I'm relaxed with my students and encourage them to push themselves without worrying about competition or the possibility of failure. Yet there I was doing and feeling everything I discouraged in my students.

I even tied my anxiety to age. Maybe I was too old to learn something completely new. For an instant, I thought of giving up. Fortunately, Joseph came over to me during this moment of self-indulgent negativity and said that my monkey's face looked good. I immediately felt that he was putting me on and then checked myself and took another look at the monkey. I had never done anything like this before, and for a first effort I had to admit it wasn't too bad. And in retrospect, I understand that most of this anxiety was imported from the conflicts I was having at the university and had nothing directly to do with the painting or my fellow students.

After a few weeks, I came simply to enjoy painting with the children and left my anxieties at my office. The children's work was charming, and they managed to capture the wicked spirit of the monkeys. They were thinking about the monkeys, not the painting. I was thinking about the painting and not enough about the monkeys.

However, it became clear to me that I could stumble my way through class without worrying about being judged inadequate. As I became comfortable in this new setting, after a few weeks that wicked spirit appeared in my work, too. I still struggled with the brush, but it didn't bother me as much anymore. There was time for mastery and no one rushing me toward goals or objectives. There were no tests, no schedules. All the external threats that often inhibit learning were not there. I was learning to paint Chinese in a supportive and pleasant environment, and that was it.

Part IV

Speculations on Education, Learning, and Politics

The three selections in Part IV are fairly recent and are a response to a number of educational issues that provide difficult challenges to caring teachers today. One of these issues, addressed in the first selection, is what I call creative maladjustment. Many aspects of life in the public schools are oppressive, anti-child and -teacher, and sometimes racist and sexist. There are also structural impediments to learning and to teaching well. Clumsy and negative administrative procedures and textbooks that misrepresent history or insult the culture of one's students are not uncommon. Teachers concerned with equity and social justice and who have pride in their work and respect for their students and the communities they live in often find themselves wanting to oppose authority and agitate for change. That's dangerous if you are an isolated teacher, but there are ways to organize and advocate for reform. That is the topic of the first selection, which consists of excerpts from "Creative Maladjustment and the Struggle for Public Education."

Another current problem is the encroachment of high stakes testing on the content of learning and the accompanying development of "teacher-proof curricula" which turn teachers into automatons. The test obsession denigrates the role of teacher while at the same time putting pressure on teachers to produce narrow performance gains by their students. It also often makes teachers feel stupid for putting up with what they are required to do. This personal and professional dilemma is the subject of the second selection, from the title essay in *Stupidity and Tears*.

Teachers and students often don't speak the same languages. Even when they do, they don't always understand each other's meaning and intent; language barriers that exist within the classroom and the community at large are as often cultural as linguistic. The final selection in this part, chosen from the essay "Topsy-Turvies," discusses these language issues and suggests strategies for turning things on their head, for making them topsy-turvy, as a way of overcoming linguistic and social barriers in the classroom.

CREATIVE MALADJUSTMENT AND THE STRUGGLE FOR PUBLIC EDUCATION

from *"I Won't Learn from You": And Other Thoughts on Creative Maladjustment*

The word "performance" is used in educational circles to indicate test scores and behavior, but for me it is part of an apt and useful theater metaphor. Children are on stage at school, and the teacher is only one of several audiences. Other students, parents, and people in the community are also audiences. Each student faces the simultaneous task of winning the acceptance of each of these audiences while maintaining personal and moral integrity. The construction of a school character is a complex matter with a great deal at stake. Unfortunately schools often simplify the script and divide youngsters into good/bad, normal/abnormal, intelligent/dumb, and high/low potential. This division forces roles on students, ones they only partially play. As a teacher I found it essential to maladjust to dichotomies like these and refuse to allow them to enter into my thoughts or vocabulary. This maladjustment, combined with a *crise de coeur*, inadvertently led me to become involved in the deaf power movement in 1966, four years after I had begun teaching.

I was in graduate school at the time, and it was possible for me to take courses while continuing my work with youngsters in the community where I had previously taught. One of the classes I took, called "Natural Language for the Deaf," advocated a holistic though oralist approach to the education of deaf children. The class was

taught by a wonderful woman, whose life was dedicated to the en-
richment of learning among deaf youngsters and whose educational
philosophy centered around the idea that deaf children will learn to
speak best if they are in an informal, conversational situation in
which reading, writing, and speaking are integrated.

One day toward the middle of the semester an eight- or nine-
year-old girl came to class to demonstrate the effectiveness of this
method. Something in my heart responded to her dignity and intensity. When she began to speak to the class about her school, I
couldn't understand anything she said. She strained and struggled, but what came out was something resembling, but not quite
English. Her face was wracked with tension, and I assumed she
was closely listening to her own voice to be sure what she was
saying was correct. Suddenly, I realized she couldn't hear herself,
couldn't make corrections, and couldn't hear our responses either. Until that moment I had never imagined myself in a world
without sound.

Something was wrong here. This girl was obviously intelligent
and sensitive—her eyes and gestures made that clear. She was in
pain. And she was the best example the school had to show for its
attempts at getting deaf youngsters to speak. Something was
wrong, not with her but with the educational regime she was living under. It was a situation that begged for maladjustment, that
reminded me of the frustration I felt at being told not to speak
Spanish in my classroom.

I decided to visit the school the young girl attended. Even before entering the school it was impossible not to notice that one
was in a sign-language environment. Students getting off the
buses or coming out of the subway station were all signing. Young
children on the playground were signing. Older ones taking a last
puff on their cigarettes or just standing around flirting and gossiping were using sign language. The prohibition on signs began
once youngsters were inside; it obviously did not extend into
their lives outside of school. Before visiting even one class it was

clear that the prohibition of signs in deaf education indicated deep institutional and sociological problems.

This impression was confirmed when I learned that the teachers were all hearing individuals who did not know sign language; that students in this very caring and progressive environment still had to sit on their hands if they inadvertently signed in class; and that the achievement scores of the students at the school were lower than those at schools with a comparable nondeaf middle- and upper-class student body, indicating that some academic connections were not being made. Nevertheless, the staff was very enthusiastic about its work and proud of its success in enabling its students to master spoken English and achieve academically. To me this meant that they had low expectations for their students, accepting barely comprehensible spoken English and below-grade-level scores as excellent work. They had adjusted the school according to coordinates of educational research and philosophy and imposed their grid on the children.

My reading in the literature on the cognitive development of the deaf confirmed my suspicions. Throughout the United States, deaf children were evaluated by researchers who did not sign, were given test instructions in spoken English, and were required to read selections drawn entirely from the nondeaf world. The children were set up for failure and then labeled cognitively deficient. The system stayed in adjustment and the children became abnormalized.

Fortunately, at that time I stumbled upon a reference to William Stokoe's work on a sign-language dictionary in Louie Fant, Jr.'s book on the National Theater of the Deaf. Not one of the "experts" I consulted was familiar with any serious study of the language of signs other than one written about a hundred years before. Stokoe's early works, which he kindly sent me, were done in the fields of anthropology and sociology and not read by educators. They confirmed my suspicions that the language of signs was indeed a language with a syntax and grammar, and that the entire research apparatus dealing with the education of the deaf was culturally biased and intellectually irresponsible.

I believe there were two underlying reasons for this: first, hearing people controlled the education of the deaf and did not bother to learn sign language; and second, this neglect of sign language was reinforced by the predominantly nondeaf parents of deaf children (there had been a rubella epidemic in the late fifties and early sixties that increased the population of school-age deaf children at the time I was writing the paper). The parents did not want their children to sign and become socially identified as deaf. They wanted their children to adjust to the hearing world. They wanted their children to talk, to be "normal," and educators tried to give them what they wanted even though it was impossible. The consequence was lack of communication and often bitter alienation between nondeaf adults and their deaf children.

The most painful thing I discovered during these explorations was that many parents, by neglecting to learn sign language themselves, gave up the possibility of communicating with their children. Instead, often out of anxiety over their children's futures, they chose to turn their children over to educators who promised to get their children to speak. Social norming and linguistic adjustment became a barrier between parents and children, something that often happens to immigrant children today.

I wrote a graduate school paper on the language and education of the deaf, concluding that deaf children should be taught in sign language or bilingually, and that the parents of deaf infants would be best served by learning to sign. A year later the paper was published as the booklet Language and Education of the Deaf. The response was explosive. The Alexander Graham Bell Association for the Deaf, one of the most powerful forces in the area of deaf education, attacked me as an irresponsible outsider who had no right to intrude into the field of deaf education. At the same time, I was invited to Washington, D.C., to speak about the subject at Gallaudet College, the nation's major institution of higher education for deaf people, and to do a summer pro-

gram at Kendall Green, the elementary school on the Gallaudet
campus.

At dinner before the speech, my wife Judy and I had time to
communicate with faculty members from Gallaudet. Powrie Doctor, one of the most respected voices in the deaf community and
a professor at Gallaudet, spoke to us, a rare event. He was profoundly deaf and had been forced to learn oral language at school.
The humiliation of that experience was such that he refused to
use it except in special circumstances such as communicating
with Judy, myself, and other nondeaf friends of the deaf community. He told us at dinner that he could lip-read and speak well
enough to join the hearing world but that he had made the conscious decision, as a deaf adult, to maladjust to the hearing world.
Martin Luther King Jr. and other civil rights activists were heroes of his, and he had visions of a deaf power movement. What
he wanted to do was organize from within the deaf community
and build a movement to agitate for a society in which the deaf
had control over their own education and made their own decisions about how they would relate to the hearing world. The reason the Bell Association was so outraged about my pamphlet, he
informed me, was that once deaf adults understood themselves as
victims of a dysfunctional system and became convinced of the
intelligence they obviously had, the hearing would no longer be
able to control their education and their lives.

Dr. Doctor (that was the way people signed his name) told me
that he went through a painful period of personal and social
struggle during his withdrawal from the world of the hearing. He
had to discover ways of uncovering his strengths while undoing
his internalization of the stigma of being "deaf and dumb," and
healing the injuries caused by being stared at when he was signing and misunderstood when he spoke. He said he decided not to
adjust to being deaf.

Adjusting would have meant fitting into a world managed and
controlled by hearing people—a world where he was considered
damaged goods. Instead he became part of the adult deaf world

where he could live a fuller life while knowing how and choosing when to navigate in the hearing world. He also decided to teach and organize among deaf people and help them learn how to manage the hearing world without being controlled by it.

One of his strategies was to show students how to turn stereotypes of deaf people on their heads—a form of what I've called creative maladjustment. For example, he encouraged his students to take trips on public transportation and observe the gestures and facial expressions of the hearing people around them. Many of these expressions and gestures have meaning in sign language, and Dr. Doctor demonstrated some of the silly, sometimes sexually suggestive or personally embarrassing things hearing people inadvertently sign just by moving their hands or letting an expression pass over their face.

Everyone else at the table cracked up at Dr. Doctor's imitations of hearing people inadvertently signing something silly or embarrassing. I felt excluded from a complex linguistic game. Dr. Doctor, after explaining the jokes, went on to describe the power of such role switching for some of his students. It taught them that they could observe as well as be observed, that stigma was socially constructed, and that they could take a stance toward the hearing world that would not make them feel inferior. Creative maladjustment was one of the tools he used to help his students learn to free themselves from the rage of being under the gaze and control of the hearing world. His goal was to build a community of the deaf that affirmed sign language and was not burdened by the linguistic ignorance and prejudices of the hearing world.

Dr. Doctor was a major inspiration for the deaf power movement, and I'm sure that, over ten years later, when students at Gallaudet walked out of classes, demanded, and won the battle for a deaf president of the college, he must have been laughing in whatever heaven there is for the creatively maladjusted.

The publisher of *Language and Education of the Deaf* received dozens of letters responding in particular to my advocacy of sign language in schools. Some questioned my credentials to write about deaf education. Others called for a deaf power movement. A few were from hearing parents who thanked me for giving them the courage to learn sign language. It opened up a world of communication with their deaf children, they wrote, whereas before there had been only silence and grief.

I like to think I had some small part in the deaf power movement, which has succeeded in changing many of the stereotypes about the intellectual and linguistic capacities of deaf people, and has permanently rid the "dumb" from "deaf and dumb." I have not had much to do with the education of the deaf since 1968, but the idea has stayed with me that the way students behave is as much a consequence of the system in which they are required to learn as anything within themselves, their families, communities, and cultures. The task of helping my students figure out how to creatively maladjust to dysfunctional systems of living and learning has become a significant part of my work as an educator.

In fact, I can imagine classes in creative maladjustment at teacher education institutions, for without teachers who are willing to take the risks on creative maladjustment, public education will continue to fail or be dismantled and privatized.

The ability to break patterns and pose new questions is as important as the ability to answer questions other people set for you. This is as true for teachers who care about their students as it is for the students themselves. It requires the courage to create a bold disruption of routines of thought and practice and implies a healthy love of turning the world upside down—which is very difficult in an academic situation driven by grades.

A central teaching skill consists of detecting and analyzing dysfunctional patterns of obedience and learning, and developing strategies to negate them. It means that teachers have to become sophisticated pattern detectives and sleuth out ways in which the practices they have been taught—or have inherited—inhibit learning.

Unfortunately, the momentum of educational research and the attempt to turn education into a single, predictable, and controllable system with national standards and national tests pulls in the opposite direction. Teaching well is a militant activity that requires a belief in children's strengths and intelligence no matter how poorly they may function under the regimens imposed upon them. It requires understanding student failure as system failure, especially when it encompasses the majority of students in a class, school, or school system. It also means stepping back and seeing oneself as a part of a dysfunctional system and developing the courage to maladjust rather than adjust oneself to much of current educational practice. This means seeing oneself as a worker in a large system run amok and giving up the need to defend the system to yourself or in public. And, in the service of one's students, it might even involve risking one's job and career. There are limits to creative maladjustment within the system, and they sometimes drive one to act, in the service of public education, from outside the system. But it is possible to defend public education without having to defend the public schools as they currently exist.

One powerful way for educators to creatively maladjust is to repudiate all categories and assume responsibility for changing their practice until it works for the children they have previously been unable to serve. Another is to advocate genuine educational choice within the public schools and to demand that teachers, parents, and other groups of educators should have the right to create small schools within the context of large public school systems, with the freedom and resources to operate effectively.

There are risks in becoming creatively maladjusted. You might get fired or find projects you have nurtured into existence destroyed by a threatened bureacracy or conservative school board. You might find yourself under pressure at school and at home to stop making trouble and feel like giving in to the temptation to readjust and become silent. The choice of when, where, how, and whether to maladjust is both moral and strategic, and though it has social and educational consequences, it is fundamentally personal and private.

For those of us who choose to remake the schools and reaffirm the need for equity, decency, creativity, and openness within public education, walking the line between survival and moral action is a constant and often unnerving challenge. We have to think about being part of an opposition within the system and be articulate and explicit in that role. We have to reach out and develop allies and not be afraid to encounter and confront school boards, administrators, and our own unions with clear positions on educational issues backed by first-rate practice. And we must remember and affirm what we often tell our students: that we can become the people we would like to be, that it is necessary to live with hope, and that it is possible to create a decent life and a decent world.

STUPIDITY AND TEARS

From *Stupidity and Tears: Teaching and Learning
in Troubled Times*

Against stupidity the very gods
Themselves contend in vain[1]

> —Friedrich von Schiller,
> *Joan of Arc*, act 3, scene 5

In 1937, Robert Musil, the author of *A Man Without Qualities*,
gave a lecture in Vienna titled "On Stupidity." He began by
asserting

> Anyone who presumes to speak about stupidity today runs the
> risk of coming to grief in a number of ways. It may be inter-
> preted as insolence on his part; it may even be interpreted as
> disturbing the progress of our time. . . . And so a question
> gradually arises that refuses to be put off: Just what is stupidity?

Musil wrote this at a troubling, tragic, and stupid moment in
European history, in the midst of the spread of Nazism. Now,
in the early twenty-first century, we are also in troubling, tragic,
and stupid times, and the issue of stupidity and its relationship
to how people think and react to complex personal, social, and
economic challenges is as important as it was in the late thirties. However, given the scope of the problem, I decided to focus
on a field I know and have worked in for over forty years—
education—and try to understand the ways in which educational
policies and theories about young people, learning, schooling,

and public education are stupid and have the consequence of perpetuating ignorance, keeping poor, defiant, and marginalized youth "in their place." In addition, I want to concentrate on how systems apply pressure on idealistic and creative teachers to make them act stupidly and perform in the classroom in ways that are opposed to their conscience, knowledge, and experience.

I have encountered stupidity in education many times over the years. One particular story stands out. Les Blanc and Maureen Gosling are documentary filmmakers whose works—including *Chulas Fronteras*, *The Blues According to Lightnin' Hopkins*, and *Garlic Is as Good as Ten Mothers*—celebrate music, family, community, and cooking. When my children were in elementary and junior high school in Point Arena, California, Les sent me a copy of one of his films, *Always for Pleasure*. The film takes place in New Orleans before and during Mardi Gras. It's about Louisiana food, the black Indian societies who march in the Mardi Gras parade, and the way in which the run-up to Mardi Gras affects community, family, and culture. The center of the film is the march across New Orleans of the Wild Magnolias and the Wild Chapatulas—two of the black societies—all decked out in flowers and feathers, wearing carnival costumes made to celebrate American Indian tribal dress at its most elegant and elaborate. It culminates in a dance and song contest between the "tribes."

I found the film delightful, an energetic multicultural celebration of life, and convinced the principal of my kids' school to show the film to a student assembly. My children and their friends loved the film, and I went home feeling I had made a small but not insignificant contribution toward bringing multicultural education to the school. After dinner, the phone calls began. One friend called and said she had heard that I had shown a picture at the school that had sexual "exposure" in it. A stranger called accusing me of being immoral, forcing pornographic films on children, and engaging in corruption of the youth. A third caller swore that I would never be able to set foot in the school again after they (who?) got done with me.

The next day I discovered that a group of community members had circulated a petition demanding that I be publicly censured and prevented from ever entering the school, even to pick up my own children. One hundred and fifty-seven people signed it (I still have a copy). It took watching the film two or three times for me to figure out what the problem was. About two thirds of the way through the film, as the tribes are marching toward each other, is a 2.3-second flash of an African American man cutting across the path of the march. Attached to his belt is a five-foot-long purple sock dragging along the ground. That was the exposure.

I thought it would be easy to neutralize the situation by going to the originators of the petition and asking them what they saw in the film and how the whole exposure-fantasy developed. As it turned out, not one person who had signed the petition had seen the film. Worse, they didn't want to see it because they thought it contained pornography. I had come directly against a wall of stupidity. They would not look on what they had not seen, but went ahead with the petition anyway.

Finally I asked Les Blanc to send me a film clip of the offending moment and put it on a loop so I could show it over and over. The night the petition was presented to the school board, I came armed with a projector and the clip and insisted that the board watch it before they acted. Many of the people who had presented the petition left the room in protest before I showed the "obscene" moment. The board members, most of whom were tired after a full day's work, let me show the clip but missed the 2.3 seconds the first time it ran, so I showed the loop over and over until, very slowly, one and then the rest of them started to laugh. The chair said, "Issue closed," and I continued my volunteer work at the school. The fundamentalist Christian community that engineered the petition, though it retreated on this issue, continues almost twenty years later in its efforts to suppress free expression, censor textbooks, and keep biological theory under theological control. Fortunately, in Point Arena, community demographics have changed, and their efforts are not taken too seriously anymore.

This was not the first time I had encountered willful stupidity. Years before, about 1969, when I co-directed an alternative high school in Berkeley, our theater troupe traveled to Claremont, California, to perform at a reading conference. While there, I encountered another example of people making the conscious choice to manipulate ignorance as a way of asserting power and concealing social, political, and personal agendas. Our students and staff were put up at a motel near the college. When we arrived, it was about ninety degrees, and the students decided to take a swim in the motel's pool. We had a meeting with the kids and made it clear that there was to be no naked swimming or guerrilla theater in the pool. Everyone wore a proper swimsuit and was polite to the other guests at the pool. Our staff were deployed about the pool to be sure that the kids were respectful, since some of them were capable of doing crazy things. It was the summer of People's Park in Berkeley, and many of the students used to tease the police by running naked through fire hydrants they had turned on.

Our students went swimming and I was with them, sitting on the edge of the pool, chatting with other guests and explaining how wonderful it was that our students were invited to a college conference. The kids were great, and it was a pleasure to watch them have fun and not be worried, for a short time, about the tension and conflict they were facing in the political climate of Berkeley in 1969.

After about half an hour, the motel manager called me into his office and ordered me to get all of my naked students out of the pool. My students were in the pool, but the only naked person there was a baby unrelated to us in the wading area. I told the manager that we were very careful to be sure that every student was properly dressed and asked him to come out to the pool and see for himself. He refused, stating in a seething and hostile voice, "I will not look upon such obscene nakedness. Get them out of there."

No matter how I tried, he stood his ground and threatened to evict us from the motel. I said his response was stupid and that all he had to do was come out and look at the kids. Finally I gave up and told the kids they had to get out of the pool and begin rehearsing for the evening performance since I couldn't figure out how to deal with being evicted from the motel.

That evening I complained to our hosts about the stupidity of the situation, and the conference director took me aside and said it was stupid but it was also willful. He had received a call from the manager that day complaining that African American students and white students were swimming together in his pool, and that that would chase away his other guests. He was willfully stupid to me in order to mask his naked pragmatic racism. I didn't know whether to scream or cry.

However, the relationship between stupidity and tears is more complex than I imagined then, since I had not thought of myself as stupid or thought about good people who consciously force themselves to become stupid and agonize over the consequences.

I first encountered the idea that stupidity was a form of learned social behavior subject to sociological analysis in an essay by the anthropologist Jules Henry published in 1968 in the *New York Review of Books* entitled "Education for Stupidity." Henry argued that people are not born stupid but can be educated, seduced, forced, or tricked into stupidity. For him, creating stupidity in education has a social purpose. Keeping *some* people stupid is a conscious strategy that prevents them from understanding why they are required to act against their conscience and counter to their intelligence. Stupidity, in Henry's sense, has nothing to do with intelligence. He says he wrote the essay

> to illustrate the development of legitimate social stupidity in elementary and high schools in the United States. There is always a question of how much information the members of any

culture may be permitted to have; and throughout history it has been assumed that most of the population should be kept ignorant. . . . [T]he world is presented to children and adolescents in such a way as to prevent them from getting from school the information necessary to enable them to form an intelligent opinion about the world.[2]

Jules Henry's focus was on students, but what about teachers? Are there ways in which creating stupid teachers perpetuates stupidity in the classroom and keeps stupid systems of education functioning? This question easily can be taken as an insult by teachers, but it is meant in an entirely different spirit. The question is whether making teachers act as if they are stupid serves current public educational systems well: Are teachers who do not question, who do not have educational philosophies or critical perspectives on their work, and who do not have time or tools to think through the nature and consequences of their pedagogy precisely the most desired of employees? And does resistance to stupidity become a form of insurrection or self-destruction?

It is essential to distinguish between stupidity in the context of this essay and some more usual uses of the word "stupid." Stupidity that leads to tears is not a matter of people lacking intelligence, or making clumsy or thoughtless decisions, or acting in ways that make them the butt of jokes. It is not a matter of ignorance. Rather, it is a form of institutional and social coercion that traps people into acting in ways they consider to be stupid and, in the context of teaching, counter to the work they feel they must do to help their students. It can be a form of humiliation similar to that which many students feel in school when they are ridiculed for trying to get the right answer and failing to give the teacher exactly what he or she wants. Or it can be a form of confinement to insane norms of educational programs that restrict creativity and clearly have not worked. Becoming stupid can be demoralizing. But it can also be a call to resistance and the rebirth of teacher militancy.

•   •   •

I first became aware of stupidity and tears when I was in high school. In 1953, I was a delegate from the Bronx High School of Science to the American Legion's Empire Boys State. The four-day retreat was designed as a simulation of a political convention for a national election and included nominating a presidential and vice presidential candidate, choosing candidates for statewide officers, developing a party campaign structure, and drawing up and adopting a party platform. It was supposed to be an exercise in democratic leadership for high school student council leaders.

The first two days were exciting. I was interested in helping draw up the platform and, given that we were in the midst of the McCarthy and HUAC era, I hoped to introduce some statements defending First and Fifth Amendments rights and opposing the intimidation of people because of their political views. At Bronx Science it was impossible to avoid these issues, since many of our teachers were fired for taking the Fifth Amendment or refusing to testify before HUAC. I also wanted to deal with racism in the high schools, which was an issue before the New York City Inter-GO organization, where I was a representative.

However, on the second day of committee meetings I was taken aside by one of our American Legion instructors and told that my proposals, as important as they were, didn't fit the format of the convention, which was supposed to focus on student issues. I maintained that rights and racism were student issues, but all of the other students on the committee fell into line and accepted the argument that high school students didn't know enough to take stands on "adult" issues; the platform ended up dealing with rights to plan dances, control student council budgets, and develop grievance procedures within the school. They accepted being infantilized and neutralized by adult political handlers.

The rest of the retreat unfolded as a wheeling, dealing popularity contest, with Upstate New York united against the City, and well-organized, upper-middle-class students who had arrived at the convention with working political machines outwitting New York City students who had not known one another before and had not been prepped by their local American Legion chapters on how to "take" a convention. (In my community there were union committees and Workingman's Circle committees, but I had never encountered the American Legion or one of the legionnaires.)

As the legion's scenario unfolded, I was accused of not entering the spirit of the game. I wasn't alone, and a small caucus of resisters developed. However, the system had no place for us since the goal was to adopt one platform with one set of candidates and to do it with a minimum of controversy. We were to mime politics and participate in a charade that was no different from the power-and-popularity politics of adult America.

The final event was the actual convention, in which candidates were chosen and platforms approved. American flags, horns, whistles, and confetti were distributed. Cheerleaders were chosen to orchestrate the final event, which was loud with horns blaring, whistles blowing, confetti and streamers flying, and shouting and cheering. There was nothing to choose from, no debate, no contestation of ideas and values. The Upstate crowd won, as it was set up to do. I found myself standing alone, almost crying. I couldn't experience the joy others obviously took from being part of the event. I felt lonely and excluded. The whole thing seemed stupid to me—how could people cheer on command, act engaged, and allow themselves to be manipulated to please the American Legion's sense of democracy as a popularity contest? And yet I wondered about myself. Was I the one who was stupid for not joining in and doing what I enjoyed doing at basketball games? Was I stupid for worrying about issues and ideas when the mock convention was just theater, not meant to change the world?

I remember coming home to the Bronx confused and depressed. Were they stupid, was I stupid? I had no sociological or psychological language to describe my dilemma. When I returned home I told my father that I thought the whole thing was stupid. In his usual way, he said I was the stupid one—stupid not to know that they were stupid or know how to deal with the pressures to act in ways that oppose your beliefs.

This was my first real encounter with an effort to manipulate my will in an obvious and planned manner. Whether I was enthusiastic or not, whether I wanted to cheer and throw confetti or not, I was expected to conform. That was the rule of the game. I felt some guilt at not being willing to play the game but also felt an inner conviction that I couldn't play it. And I was punished for standing outside of the game by being a pariah at the end of the meetings, avoided by all of the "winners." They loved the game and made it difficult for people who resisted the rituals of conformity that had rewarded them. In retrospect I see this as the beginning of a personal awareness of issues of conscience.

Many people throughout the world face similar issues of conscience on a life-threatening level. Whether to act and get into trouble while maintaining self-respect, or conform and feel stupid—this is a major struggle for thinking people.

In the summer of 1998, a year before my father died, he insisted upon referring to himself as stupid. It was his favorite lament at the end of his life. No matter what I would say, he summed up his ninety years as a futile exercise in complicity. Of course he wasn't stupid, just bitter. His attitude toward life was summed up by a Sam Goldwyn quote: "You've got to take the bitter with the sour."

I understand this Yiddish sense of life as a travail to endure and mock. But my father's feelings about his own stupidity remain troubling to me. As we talked during his last three or four months, his philosophy of stupidity emerged and has affected my thinking about how values can be eroded and self-respect compromised, destroyed, or distorted when people succumb to their feelings of vulnerability. He told me he was stupid because of decisions he had made against his own better judgment, because of fear, family pressure, lack of understanding the ways of strangers, and governmental pressure. He also thought he was stupid be-

cause of trusting people too much, of worrying about doing the
right thing and, most of all, abandoning his childhood dreams
and compromising his moral principles.

My father was not stupid in the sense of dumb, thick, dense,
slow, dull, or obtuse. He also did not do stupid things. His words
and troubled reflections embody the original definition of the
word "stupidity," which, according to the etymologist Eric Par-
tridge, comes from the Indo European–Sanskrit *stupere*: to be
knocked stupid or insensible, to be numbed or astonished. The
world he lived and worked in stupefied him, and he had no confidence in his own actions or decisions.

He attended New York City public school and told me how
he'd decided to hide the lunch his mother prepared for him since
it had garlic, kosher salami, and pickles. His teachers and many
of the other kids who were assimilating Jews, Irish, and Italians
laughed at him and several of his teachers told him to clean his
mouth out before he came to class because he reeked of poverty
and garlic, so he decided to bypass lunch. The teachers also kept
calling him to the office and having the nurse examine him for
lice before allowing him to return to class. My father's experiences, which I always believed he exaggerated, became plain
truths when I came upon this quote from a 1939 issue of *Life* mag-
azine praising the baseball player Joe DiMaggio:

> Although he learned Italian first, Joe, now 24, speaks English
> without an accent, and is otherwise adapted to most US
> mores. Instead of olive oil or smelly bear grease he keeps his
> hair slick with water. He never reeks of garlic and prefers
> chicken chow mein to spaghetti.[3]

The idea that chicken chow mein is more American than
spaghetti is just another example of what stupefied my father.
Reflecting upon my father's comments and my own experiences
trying to transform public education, I have concluded that intelligent, painful, and tearful stupidity has four components:

- It implies acting in a way that you consciously understand to be against your principles and that makes you feel foolish to yourself no matter how other people perceive or judge you.
- It means consciously acting stupidly as a form of resistance to being called stupid and has the effect of learning to take control of your own image as stupid, including elements of theater that reveal you are aware of acting against your conscience, and an ironic stance toward one's own life, often expressed through self-deprecating humor.
- It opens you to ridicule and discovery and therefore makes it difficult to trust others.
- Finally, at its most redeeming, it allows you to perceive the stupidity in others and feel part of a silent conspiracy that still honors authenticity, while betraying it.

I know many students and teachers whose feelings about their school lives involve awareness of stupidity and tears. They feel they are forced to act stupidly, which is not the same as being stupid. These are not people who are bitter about life itself or generalize their school experience to an indictment of their whole lives, as my father did. In fact, the things they do outside of school often resist the stupidity of what they felt forced to do during school time.

The cultivated stupidity students manifest is sometimes baroque, adding extemporaneous rap and break-dancing steps to the usual drumming and sleeping. The students face the same cynical forms of schooling and react in the same ways. They are trapped in a system that claims to have their learning and success in mind, though really it is designed and administered as a failure system with high-stakes testing, "teacher-proof" curriculum, unrealizable standards, and punishment for so-called underperforming schools that serve the children of the poor and working class.

And the continual threat of being called a failure from the time they are as young as four or five drives many children to do crazy and stupid things. As one high school student, Reginald, said to me recently, "I'd rather be defiant and stupid in class than let the teacher call me a failure. My friends know I'm not dumb, and we laugh at the teacher together."

Later he elaborated on his frustrations with himself in school. He wanted to learn, couldn't get a handle on what his teachers expected of him, had a few bad years in middle school, and simply could not stand the idea that he wasn't smart enough to make it in school. Since he didn't know how to succeed, he decided he would rather play at being stupid. He would let "them" forget about his mind and pay attention to his behavior. At least, he said, "it kept me from giving up." He did give up trying in school, though, in order to escape from failure, since there was no support for his learning. At the end of the conversation he was as close to tears as such a strong and proud young man allowed himself to be outside of family and intimate friends. Unfortunately, Reginald's behavior ended up hurting him. The tension between willful stupidity and failure leaves no room for the student to win.

The distinction between failing in school and behaving stupidly in order to avoid failing is not often discussed by educators. However, we have to develop strategies for helping students get beyond their terror of failing and of being classified as incapable of learning. This is becoming increasingly difficult as teachers are finding themselves in the same situation as their students. They are being forced to drive the failure system by conforming to regulated and controlled demands from administrators, the state and federal governments, and local politicians. For example, many public school districts these days have adopted a single curriculum tied into an expensive, so-called teacher-proof program such as Open Court or Success for All. These programs come with a script for teachers to follow, lesson-by-lesson and day-by-day. The rationale of these programs is that districts that serve the children of the poor are so badly organized, some form of instructional alignment must be used to achieve uniformity and standards within entire districts that have histories of being dysfunctional. They are intended to ensure that even the worst teachers will be able to deliver adequate learning.

That goal is admirable though foolish, since a terrible teacher will be terrible with whatever he or she is required to do. In addition, there is little evidence that the programs do or even can achieve what they claim. It is an attempt to take the "human factor" out of teaching, when that factor is at the heart of all good teaching. What they do achieve is demoralizing successful teachers and new teachers who come to teaching with a desire to be creative and helpful to students. Teacher-proofing education is an insult to teachers, as it assumes they are stupid and forces them to act as if they were stupid. It denies their will and creativity in the service of putting order into a system that often borders on the chaotic. Certainly the systems need coherence and standards, but it is very unlikely that one can succeed in transforming a system by making the people charged with that transformation into robots who feel stupid and resentful about their work.

Recently I had a student in the teacher-credential program I direct who is an excellent teacher in a difficult school. Roger's students do extremely well in class and are very creative. They also score well on high-stakes tests. He has recently been ordered by supervisors from the central district office to give up his thoughtful, imaginative, and effective practice in order to conform to mandates to follow the script of Open Court. Though he protested that his students were already achieving beyond the district's expectations, he was told he had to fall in line.

What happens when you are ordered to undo good practice and become an automaton? Roger loves his students, and doesn't want to be defiant or lose his job. The only option, he said, was to act stupid and be subversive at the same time. For a while he pretended to comply while preserving the creative and most motivating parts of his curriculum. But the administration was adamant. He had to follow the script, like it or not, and he had to endure what he called the "Open Court police," former district curriculum supervisors assigned to monitor compliance. Going to school every day went from being a joy to being a nightmare. He told me he got through the whole thing by pretending he was on stage, though when holding the script in his hand he saw how to help a child by throwing the script out, he felt like screaming or crying. Eventually he decided that stupidity wasn't worth the sacrifice of his students' learning and he remained subversive for the rest of the academic year. He took a stand against stupidity, but also took a leave of absence for the next year to look into other, more creative, teaching options, and it is open to question whether he'll return to the district or the community whose children he served so well.

Roger and Reginald both acted in ways that were consciously against their principles and beliefs and that made them look foolish to themselves. They didn't act with evil intent, and they knew what they were doing was theater. All three complied and tried to show other people that they were what they were supposed to be—in the case of Roger and Rosa, compliant and stupid teachers, and in the case of Reginald, a stupid kid. None of them, however, learned how to take advantage of their stance toward their school lives; it left them feeling weak, powerless, frustrated, angry, and just about in tears.

Acting stupid or conforming to stupid functioning made all three keenly aware that they were open to ridicule from their friends or peers, and made them a bit paranoid at school. They always had to worry about being discovered to be shams. This made it hard to trust others unless they were co-conspirators and in on the pretense.

Finally, it made them keenly aware of the stupidity of others and of the system in which they were trapped. This consciousness made them, in different ways, feel part of a silent conspiracy to preserve good teaching under pressure. The teachers did not give up their love of teaching and their belief in the capabilities and intelligence of their students. And Reginald is planning to leave high school, get a job, and attend junior college. They did not generalize stupidity into a philosophy of life. They all have rich and interesting lives outside of school. But they all came to consider school to be that part of their lives where being stupid was normal behavior.

Manufacturing stupidity in education has an institutional component. People often get forced into being stupid because there are legal and infrastructural constraints on the systems in which they work that force them to function against their conscience or counter to their experience and knowledge. I remember working with the Chicano Student Union at one of the colleges in the University of California system. Together we planned a summer literacy program utilizing undergraduates, several teachers, and some community activists. We had the support of the local school district and the university and were funded under Title I of the Elementary and Secondary Education Act of 1965.

The act signaled a major commitment by the federal government to provide funds for the education of the poor with an emphasis on African American and other minority children. Title I of the act provided funds specially designated for direct funding to schools for specific children who performed poorly in school and had backgrounds of poverty.

The summer program worked well. Students attended and loved being around the college kids. Community people volunteered to provide resources, and parents came at all hours helping out, working with small groups of children, and learning from the teachers how to help their own children at home. The teachers and college students were excited by their work, and by the end of the summer we had succeeded in raising most of the students' scores to grade level. Everyone agreed that the program should continue during the school year, and we all anticipated that the district would be delighted with our students' test scores. You might say that the program worked in a stupidity-free zone. We acted according to knowledge and conviction, had the freedom to develop the program, and accepted responsibility for the results of our work.

Two weeks before school began, the program coordinators were called into the district office and were told that the program could not be continued during the school year since it no longer qualified for Title I funds. It seemed that federal funding was restricted to programs that served children who were not performing up to grade level. Our success meant defunding. I remember being stupefied by the decision.

The program coordinators were fired, the community volunteers were sent home, the parents were no longer encouraged to volunteer, and the children returned to the system that had failed them in the first place. The bureaucrats, in order to keep Title I money, had to keep the children below grade level. The assistant superintendent told me she felt the whole situation was crazy but that she had no control over it. Stupidity and tears all over again. This time, however, it was not the teachers or the students who were forced to act in stupid and tearful ways. Rather, it was a thoughtless system with built-in failure. It reminds me of current welfare reform programs where people get cut off after five years and are required to work at jobs that can't possibly support their families—stupidity in the legislation leading to tears on the ground. Even the most caring welfare workers are forced to act against their conscience, and frequently feel the pain of the dysfunctional work they are forced to do, which of course is not as substantial as the pain of their clients.

Ironically, the school district we worked in did succeed in retaining Title I funds, since the students' gains during the summer were lost during the school year, and once again they qualified for funding as failures. The next summer the district went to the university and asked it to renew the summer program with some of the same children who had become requalified for Title I during the school year.

This no longer happens. With the recent reauthorization of the Elementary and Secondary Education Act, we now reward successful programs and punish failed programs. In other words, now if you are already a success with poor children, you get money; and if you are struggling, you get money taken away. The failure system plays its stupid games in many forms.

The maintenance of stupidity is based on the ability to make ignorance normal. In many circumstances, making people stupid is a way of making them conform to other agendas that are often not explicit and are neither rational nor reasonable. In education it is easy to see and hard to undo, since resistance to stupidity often implies confrontation with the system it benefits.

There are traditional tales that remind people of what happens when stupidity becomes normalized. In British folklore there is the town of Gotham, where everyone is a fool and stupidity rules. In Yiddish folklore there is a similar town, Chelm, where everyone is a fool and the leaders are the biggest fools of all. Here is a version of an old tale that I adapted to represent some of the stories teachers tell me of their lives in schools these days.

It seems that there was a steep hill in the middle of Chelm, and children were always falling down the hill and hurting themselves. The hill was the only place in town where children could play, yet it was so dangerous that many children broke their arms and legs and even skulls in falls. The people of Chelm couldn't figure out what to do, so they called in the wise men who, after deliberating for several weeks, came up with the following solutions:

1. Proclaim, as town goals, the elimination of all injuries some time in the distant future.
2. Let the town know that their leaders frown upon carelessness and don't tolerate falling.
3. Advise parents to get tough and keep their children indoors.
4. Inform the children that if they got hurt it was due to their own choice, and part of life in a free community.
5. Build a hospital at the bottom of the hill for those injured children whose parents could afford to pay for medical care.

The community accepted these solutions, and the newspapers proclaimed the wisdom of the town's leadership.

Of course the wise men ignored the children's need to play, failed to prevent injuries, and encouraged no community initiatives to transform the environment in the service of the children.

This story came to mind when the following headline appeared on the front page of the *New York Times* (8/23/02):

With New Rules and Higher Pay New York Gets Certified Teachers

The article begins:

> After years of struggling to recruit enough certified teachers to fill even half of its classroom vacancies, New York City has attracted more than 8,000 qualified candidates for the fall, in effect ending what school officials called the most crippling teacher shortages in decades.

So far, so good. Only as one reads on does it become clear that the way eight thousand new "qualified" teacher candidates were identified was simply by lowering the standards for certification. Qualified candidates now include people just entering teacher education programs, Teach for America recruits with no qualifications but special variances from the schools, and other people whose ability to teach poor children is no greater than that of the so-called unqualified teachers of the past. Change the language, build a hospital at the bottom of the hill. As Arthur Levine, president of Teachers College, Columbia University, says in the article:

> It's a disingenuous claim. New York has reclassified what it means to be a certified teacher, and what it means is we will still have large numbers of students this fall whose teachers are unprepared to teach them.[4]

There are strong similarities between the wise men of Chelm's suggestions and many of the current generation of school reform proposals. Reforms under consideration range from proclaiming unattainable national and state education goals to mandating that the United States become number one in education throughout the world without having the slightest idea of what "number one" means or how to achieve this fantasy. Other proposals advocate adopting tough teacher evaluations and offering merit pay to teachers without providing support for teacher improvement or having a vision of what good teaching might look like. Voucher and charter school programs are pushed as solutions to educational problems without considering that they are not immune from the same stupid functioning of the public schools they purport to replace. And perhaps worse is the professionalization of stigmatizing students who are not well served by reforms and designating them as "learning disabled" and "attention-deficit disordered" rather than looking to the institutional causes of their indifference, defiance, and failure. Teachers become designated as "special ed," "hyperactive," and "attention-deficit disordered," as if they have the same bogus disorders as their students. Stupidity becomes institutionalized, and having an MA and credentials in a stupid field means that one's entire livelihood is dependent upon maintaining the stupidity system.

The most common theme repeated in the media by politicians and academics who claim a place in the education-reform movement is that current schooling has or will have a negative influence on our nation's economic competitiveness and standing as a world power. Obsession with national power distorts people's perceptions of the problems youngsters face in schools, and most reform proposals end up by leaving out concern for the quality of children's lives.

The question for many of us educators who live in our own versions of Chelm is what to do to escape this infuriating stupidity. Thinking about the pain of living under regimes of stupidity and particularly about the wonderful young teachers I work with who feel they are compelled to be stupid every day of their working lives reminds me of a quote from Franz Kafka's *The Castle*:

> Dealing directly with the authorities wasn't all that difficult, for no matter how well organized they were, they only had to defend distant and invisible causes on behalf of remote and invisible gentlemen, whereas he, K., was fighting for something vitally close, for himself, and what's more of his own free will . . .[5]

Though we are all familiar with stupidity in our lives, fortunately a certain number of people are always thinking of ways to subvert, oppose, and even eliminate it. Roger, my student, told me a funny story about his reaction to being forced to teach to the scripted program that he knew would undo the work he had already done. He managed to steal some classroom time to keep one of his favorite projects alive. It consisted of telling folktales and fairy tales and then having his students rewrite them as modern stories with contemporary characters and endings. One of the stories he liked to use was "The Emperor's New Clothes." He said the story began to obsess him at faculty meetings and staff training sessions with the "Open Court police." The staff was forced to listen and to comply. They had no input. For him, it was the potential undoing of his own success with his class, and he began to ask the trainers what were to him obvious questions. He wanted to know whether there were statistics to support the new program, or if there was any respect for the children's culture in it. He also asked whether students who failed to go through the program as predicted had other options for learning. The trainers and administrators had no answers, and he told me they were as naked as the emperor, but they had the power. They were not interested in the educational issues or in his particular classroom or work. They wanted alignment above all, no exceptions tolerated. But he knew they had no clothes, and the thought of them as the real fools kept him going for the rest of the academic year. However, the emperor still reigns, so Roger decided he would have to take a year off and reconsider how to continue to serve his students outside of a failure system.

One question that interests me is what became of the child who revealed that the emperor was naked. Did she or he get rewarded and become a national hero? Did his or her action become forgotten as the empire continued to act in naked and brutal ways, and the hustlers and advisers profited from the stupidity system? Did the child give up, internalize the norms of stupidity, and sustain blows to his or her sense of self-worth?

If the child was strong and maintained an open and honest way of confronting stupidity, a rebel might be born. Confronting stupidity when it is sanctioned and so easy to slip into can make for a frustrating life on the margins of self-confidence, employment, and society. It can also lead to major and positive transformations in society, culture, and personal life.

When I was studying philosophy at Harvard in the late 1950s, I remember being intrigued by professors who had fallen under the spell of Ludwig Wittgenstein when they encountered him at Cambridge University. They agonized over traditional philosophical questions, put their hands over their heads, and said, in imitation of their mentor, "God, I am stupid today."

According to many recent accounts, "God, I am stupid today," accompanied by grimaces and expressions of pain, angst, and rage, were characteristics of Wittgenstein's process of addressing with severe honesty and specificity what appeared on the surface to be complex and meaningful philosophical questions. He was a ruthless enemy of stupidity and confusion—and he considered himself to be one of those victimized by stupidity. For me, that was a profound insight into how we are all taken in and end up acting against our better judgment and conscience.

Wittgenstein was seeking to clear away stupidity and sham, to get people to be clear and explicit about what they mean by what they say and do, no matter what pain or questioning it might cause. I think he might have agreed with Oscar Wilde's comment. "There is no sin except stupidity."[6]

Wittgenstein's battle with stupidity and pursuit of insane clarity reminds me of what Jules Henry says at the beginning of his essay "Sham":

> We all live everyday by sham, anyone who fights against it, makes life unbearable.[7]

What was so painful to Roger and Reginald, and to many other teachers and students I talk to, is that by allowing themselves to conform to stupid demands, they become experts at sham. In a recent teacher education class I taught on theater, the students improvised a faculty meeting during which they were being instructed on how to follow a scripted lesson while their students were acting up. The teachers all understood the absurdity of the situation and presented what could be a taxonomy of sham responses that allowed them to conform while at the same time acknowledge the stupidity of the situation and maintain some semblance of dignity.

As Henry concludes:

> . . . sanity is nothing more than the capacity to deal with falseness in a false world; and it can take three forms—to believe sham to be the truth; to see through sham while using it; or to see through sham but fight it . . . we are now in the stage of believing sham to be the truth, while entering the stage of seeing through sham while using it. The third stage is understanding sham and knowing how to fight it. The fourth stage is a world without sham.[8]

I am interested in the third and fourth stages with respect to stupidity: understanding it, knowing how to fight it, and moving toward a world without it. That is where the definition of stupid as "stupefied" comes in. In one of its original meanings, to be stupefied does not mean to be made stupid so much as it means to be astonished, in awe, awakened. It is to experience what the educator and philosopher Maxine Greene has called "wide-awakeness." She describes this state of consciousness as

> . . . the recovery of imagination that lessens the social paralysis we see around us and restores the sense that some thing can be done in the name of what is decent and humane. I am reaching toward an idea of imagination that brings an ethical concern to the fore, a concern that, again, has to do with the community that ought to be in the making and the values that give it color and significance. My attention turns back to the importance of wide-awakeness, of awareness of what it is to be in the world. I am moved to recall the existential experience shared by so many and the associated longing to overcome somnolence and apathy in order to choose, to reach beyond.[9]

One of the most powerful examples I know of moving from the state of stupidity to the state of stupefaction and to the social action implied by wide-awakeness comes from the work of Helen Lewis, a former director of the Highlander Center in New Market, Tennessee, and an adult educator. Helen works in poor Appalachian communities where most of the people are called "hillbillies." The word "hillbilly," according to Longman's Dictionary of the English Language, refers to people who come from "culturally unsophisticated" areas, especially the mountains, hills, and valleys of Appalachia. As anyone who has ever seen Hee-Haw or The Beverly Hillbillies knows, hillbillies are portrayed as ignorant, clumsy, silly, dense—stupid in every way, and an easy butt of jokes and subject to ridicule.

Many of the people Helen works with are sophisticated and fluent in Appalachian culture, which goes back to pre–American Revolutionary times and originates in Scotland, Ireland, and England while having elements of Native American and African

American culture as well. Though the people are materially poor, they are not culturally poor, and the general stereotype of hillbilly culture that equates poverty with ignorance is constructed to allow people in the mountains to be exploited by coal companies, land developers, and corporations that profit from mining and exploiting other local resources while dumping toxic waste and creating land erosion. The premise is that stupid people deserve what they get.

One of Helen's goals, as an educator, is to help the people she works with understand how they are exploited and encourage them to organize and create strategies for community development. A major factor that prevents people from taking power over their own lives is accepting images of themselves that celebrate their stupidity and passivity. The hillbilly image is not merely funny to the rest of America but is paralytic if the people being mocked laugh at their own stupidity. And yet people in the mountains often felt that *The Beverly Hillbillies* and *Hee-Haw* were funny.

Helen's educational strategy was to show videos of these TV programs to people in the mountains who were trying to organize themselves and rebuild economically and socially devastated communities. The first time she showed them to a group, people laughed at the stupidity they portrayed. Showing the same program a second time got people quiet and thoughtful—it didn't seem so funny as they began to see themselves as they were displayed to others. The third time, they moved from laughing at hillbilly stupidity to being stupefied, awakened, to the fact that they had been laughing at themselves. As they discussed this progression they became more wide-awake and began to analyze ways in which they were collaborating with the corporate and political interests that exploited them by accepting the premise that they were stupid and worthy of ridicule. The final stage is to become part of an organized effort to counter exploitation.

Stupefaction and wide-awakeness are steps on the road to undoing passivity and stupidity and moving people toward organizing and resisting the stupid demands made upon them. However, it is important to place educational stupidity in the larger context of the apparent need for teachers to act stupidly and for them to become complicit in making their students stupid. One of the central ideas Jules Henry expressed in his *New York Review of Books* article was that "The world is presented to children and adolescents in such a way as to prevent them from getting from school the information necessary to enable them to form an intelligent opinion about the world."[10] I believe this can be extrapolated and paraphrased: "The field of education is presented to prospective and practicing teachers in such a way as to prevent them from getting the information necessary to enable them to form intelligent opinions about learning, teaching, and educational systems."

One way to overcome this situation is for teachers and other educators to be explicit about their stupefaction and to organize around the wide-awakeness that comes from open reflection on their work. This means confronting the painful fact that the media, educational "authorities," and politicians portray teachers as stupid and incapable of making responsible and informed decisions about educational policies and practices. The teaching profession is not innocent here—often, teachers' organizations are willing to accept stupidity as the price of salary and benefit increases.

The right not to be stupid is a human right, and the cost of remaining stupid and submitting to institutional stupidity is a loss of respect for teaching as a moral vocation centered on respect, dignity, and integrity. One pays for aware and conscious stupidity in tears, as it is hard to live with the sense of betrayal that comes from doing stupid things that are not conducive to learning when children's lives are at stake. And in the end it is the children who suffer from the stupidity of the adults. Complicity with stupid systems is an attack upon the young, and the need for educators at all levels to organize and speak out in the service of wide-awake intelligence is urgent these days, even if it means taking personal risks in economically perilous times. We cannot afford to be cowards. Democracy and decency cannot survive compliant stupidity.

NOTES

1. Friedrich von Schiller, *Joan of Arc*, Act 3, Scene 5.
2. Jules Henry, "Education for Stupidity," *New York Review of Books*, May 9, 1968.
3. "Close Up: Joe DiMaggio," *Life*, May 1, 1939, p. 62.
4. *New York Times*, August 23, 2002, p. 1.
5. Franz Kafka, *The Castle* (New York: Schocken, 1998), pp. 57–58.
6. Oscar Wilde, *The Picture of Dorian Gray* (1891).
7. Jules Henry, *On Sham, Vulnerability and Other Forms of Self-Destruction* (New York: Vintage Books, 1973), p. 120.
8. Ibid.
9. Maxine Greene, *Releasing the Imagination* (San Francisco: Jossey-Bass, 1995), p. 35.
10. Henry, "Education for Stupidity."

TOPSY-TURVIES: TEACHER TALK AND STUDENT TALK

From *Stupidity and Tears: Teaching and Learning in Troubled Times*

Opposition is true friendship.[1]

—William Blake

From things that differ come the fairest attunement.

—Heraclitus

Teacher talk and student talk are essential components that determine the quality of learning in the classroom. When there is dissonance between them, other kinds of strife develop. When I first began teaching, I didn't know how to speak to or with my students. Standing in front of a group of young people is a linguistic challenge. It is not merely a matter of what you say but of how your language is understood and how you understand the language of your students. It is not just a matter of how you present lessons or counsel your students. Language is an every-day, every-minute matter, and nuances of inflection, tone, modulation, and vocabulary are constantly at play in the interaction of students and teachers. There is an unarticulated linguistic sensibility that determines the nature and quality of interaction in the classroom. Teachers are listened to more than they usually think they are, though listening, understanding, and obeying are three different things altogether.

School is a place of anxiety and strife for most students, and achieving the fairest attunement that Heraclitus refers to is a complex matter involving language, patience, visceral perception, intuition, intelligence, and compassion. On a minute-to-minute basis in the classroom, language is central to the development of attunement.

Recently I was asked to sit in on a classroom for a few hours in the hope that I could provide some insights into why the teacher was having trouble with students learning and even paying attention. The teacher was young, highly motivated, and committed, even passionate, about his students' learning. Sitting in the back of a classroom when doing observations often has advantages. The children who'll be closest to you are the ones who either chose to sit in the back or were sent there. They are either the most indifferent or the most defiant. It's the cynical section of the seating arrangement. In the midst of the lesson, one of the back-of-the-roomers turned to another and said, "There he goes again." The other just shrugged and put his head on the desk.

My response was to listen more carefully to how the teacher was talking. He was young and inexperienced, and he had not developed a tone or manner in the classroom that was easy and sincere. He was playing at being a teacher, speaking the way he imagined teachers should talk, looking above the heads of his students, not making eye contact, and pushing on with the lesson, whether the students were understanding what he said or not. It was a function of his insecurity, though unfortunately he saw it as the students' inability to pay attention. He needed what I have come to call a topsy-turvy.

It is easy to create a topsy-turvy. Draw a circle with two parallel arcs in it, as in Figure 1. Then add some circles in the middle, and you have instant eyes and a face. Looked at one way, it is sad. Rotate it 180 degrees and it becomes happy. This is a simple topsy-turvy.

Topsy-turvies are illustrations that, when turned 180 degrees, display two completely different images. For example, a topsy-turvy

Figure 1.   Figure 2.   Figure 3.

might look like a smiling woman from one perspective, but when turned 180 degrees it might look like a nasty and angry pirate. It takes a lot of skill to make a convincing topsy-turvy. I have found that the concept of the topsy-turvy provides a powerful metaphor that helps teachers transform their way of looking at themselves in the classroom. It is a matter of learning how to analyze the presentation of yourself in the classroom and then making a 180-degree shift and attempting to construct how your students see you. This implies an acceptance of opposition, of the idea that what you want as a teacher and what your students want or expect may be dissonant. It also requires the more personal and, in many ways, difficult integration of the idea that how you think you are speaking and how your students interpret what you are saying are not necessarily the same. The hard thing is talking to a whole class when people listen differently. Students interpret, reflect, analyze, and respond to the nuances of language in the classroom, and since most of the permitted language in the classroom is teacher talk, it is to that language that an excessive amount of student emotion and intelligence is committed.

It is essential to realize that this is not a matter of lack of caring or the will to help students. It is more a question of social and linguistic differences in a context where students and teachers are not hearing language in the same way. It is not just teacher talk that is problematic. Student talk has to be interpreted as well. This has nothing to do with language differences. It has everything to do with the way in which language is heard and interpreted, with tone, presentation, attitude, implication, and an understanding of how to convey complex meaning in a way that

is understood by the spoken-to. It is essentially a question of trying to understand what students are saying in a context where
teachers are not accustomed to listening and students are not accustomed to speaking openly and honestly in school.

This places a burden on teachers who are supposed to be the
authorities in the classroom. The exchange of ideas, feelings, social understanding, and conversation in the classroom is fundamentally under the control of teachers unless the classroom is out
of control. This is independent of teaching styles and pedagogical
orientation. Language exists not merely on the level of words, sentences, paragraphs, dialects, accents, and linguistic differences. It
is a social phenomenon that has complex personal implications
relating to how the more formal aspects of reading, writing, and
talking are interpreted on an everyday basis. It has to do with how
things are said, how questions are asked or answered, and how
much teachers and students listen to one another.

New teachers, if they do not come from communities that are
similar to those they teach in, are particularly vulnerable to mis-
communication. The students do not yet know or understand their
teachers' styles of talking. The teachers don't know how they are
being heard. There is a lot of literature about learning style but not
enough about teaching languages and styles. The presentation of
self in the classroom is a major part of the effectiveness of connecting with students and enhancing their learning. If you are
too soft, too hard, too rigid, or too permissive, the students will
become confused and often will feel alienation from the culture
of the classroom. It is a short step from this sense of alienation to
the development of hostility or resistance to learning within the
classroom. Casual remarks can become defining moments in your
relationship with your class.

Over the past few years I have seen teachers tell students how
much they love them and then have found out that some of them
didn't know all of their students' names. Young people are experts
at understanding false pretensions of love and caring. After all,
it's hard to love someone you don't really know. And if you say

you love your students, you can be sure that they will test that protestation of affection.

Recently I visited a classroom where the children were out of control. I found them imaginative and ingenious in their strategies of defiance, but found myself angry at them. I didn't love what they were doing to themselves, and felt they had developed dysfunctional school behavior that would end up hurting them in the future. The teacher, a very caring but inexperienced person, was screaming love at the children, saying how wonderful they were and how much she cared about them. Their response was cynical defiance and mockery. They were in control while they were out of control.

I visited another classroom where the teacher took the opposite tack and applied heavy and punitive discipline. The students' response was the same. There is a fine line between discipline and love that leads to good learning and creative teaching. "Tough love" makes no sense to me. The line I am talking about has to do with creating trust, respect, and a sense of teacherly identity. For, as a teacher, it is essential to be an adult among young people. This may sound trivial or silly, because it is hard to know what it means to be an adult. For me it has to do with passionate and loving authority and knowledge. You have to know what you are teaching, to learn how to understand your students both as individuals and as a group, and to fight against resistance to learning. You are not one of them, and you are being paid; they are required to attend. Teaching is a matter of craft, experience, and art, which makes it a continuing challenge to teach well. A teacher's language and the nature of the conversation in his or her classroom are determining factors in learning.

This implies that teachers should be aware of the major challenge of understanding how they are heard and not merely concentrating on how students speak and respond to teacher speech. Consciousness of the listener is hardly attended to in teacher education. It requires a topsy-turvy, an attempt to pay attention to how you are heard at the same time you are talking. Lovers do this all of the time. They speak to each other and worry about whether they are understood. Politicians do the same thing. They speak in order to win an audience, and if they are not conscious about how they are being understood, they will lose their audience. The same thing is true for actors in live theater, where sensitivity to the audience helps shape the intensity and effectiveness of a performance.

Teaching is performance. It doesn't make a difference whether you are teaching in a structured, full-frontal teaching classroom or in a personalized environment where there is opportunity to work with students individually or in small groups. The way in which a teacher speaks shapes students' attitudes and is a major determinant in the nature and quality of the learning environment.

The all-too-frequent disconnect between students and teachers often hangs on words and inflections. Put one student down or humiliate her or him in front of the other students and a complex ambiance of disrespect has been created.

It is essential, if you are going to teach in a community in which you are a stranger, an "other," not to air your guilt and uncertainty in ways that give children illegitimate authority. This is a complex social, philosophical, and political question. Overt racism simply cannot be tolerated. But white guilt, the anger some African American teachers feel toward African American students who are not performing, cultural confusion, and embarrassment are all part of teaching in America. And it is not just African Americans and whites, but Latinos, Asians, East Europeans, and large-scale immigrations from Ireland, the Middle East, sub-Saharan Africa, Haiti, and the Dominican Republic as well as Native Americans that complicate the picture. Simple assumptions about who students are, what their experiences have been, and what their current conditions and motivations are all require "attunement." Teachers have to develop their listening skills and their talking skills now more than at any time I have personally known in education. How one speaks and how one hears are essential factors in how well one teaches.

Heraclitus said, "From things that differ come the fairest attunement." It is a matter of translation, understanding, and strength. But in a major way it is also a matter of language, communication, and the creative arbitration of differences. Just recently I had to reattune myself. I had a lens-transplant operation; the lens in my right eye was extracted and replaced by a plastic lens. I had to learn to see again and reconstitute a world through new eyes. My organic eye and my plastic eye are learning to work together. It was more a brain problem than a vision problem. The challenge was to reconstruct the visual world and live in it— topsy-turvy in the sense that I had to see the world through new eyes and understand that the world could be turned upside down by something as simple as my eyes. The world didn't change. My vision did. I needed to integrate a changing visual sensibility. It was not a matter of going back to the way I used to see but of adjusting to a world somewhat familiar and thoroughly transformed. Quarters looked like nickels, apples seemed as small as grapes, and the redwoods around our house in Northern California got smaller. Topsy-turvies all the time and attunement all the time—opposites about how the world used to look and the way it looks now, but also the knowledge that it is the same world.

I am not a relativist—my eyes and my brain make my perceptions relative and require new integrations. The issue was how to react to these transformations. As it has turned out, it has been a revelation about the role of sight in the world and the amazing capacity of the brain to adjust to change. My eyes, in a metaphoric sense, were learning to reread the world with a new vocabulary.

The same readjustment applies in education, in particular to teachers who are starting to see and talk from the other side of the desk for the first time. It is a question of keeping one's eyes in focus with the life around us. The way in which children feel they have to display themselves and speak in the classroom is essential to how they choose to perform in school. And the analysis and consciousness of your own language as a teacher is equally essential. How do you sound? How is anger expressed? Who is praised? How is failure expressed in front of the class? How are you exposed when you think you are failing, or perhaps even in despair? How many times a week do you express joy or thanks sincerely felt rather than mechanically administered as a matter of educational policy? Where is your joy in teaching, and how is that conveyed? To me, these are the essential questions teachers must confront, not the questions of test scores or covering the curriculum. Teachers should be as resistant and resilient as their students and learn the fine art of defying ignorant authority intelligently. After all, at its best, teaching is a nurturing and militant vocation and a wonderful thing to be doing in cynical times.

When you see trouble, attune your work and topsy-turvy your practice in the service of your students. Listen when you talk and understand that, as well as talking to your students, you are being listened to. And laugh sometimes at the things you've said under pressure, and share that laughter with your students, and talk, talk, talk about how people speak and listen. We have to become a more literate society, and I think literacy will come not through testing and an obsession with standards, but through patient, intelligent, and sensitive speaking, reading, and listening.

Topsy-turvy thinking is not new. In 1710, Jonathan Swift wrote a short satire entitled "Meditation on a Broomstick" in which he said,

> a broomstick . . . is an emblem of a tree standing on its head; and pray what is man, but a topsyturvy creature, his animal faculties perpetually mounted on his rational, his head where his heels should be, grovelling on the earth! and yet, with all his faults, he sets up to be universal reformer and corrector of abuses, a remover of grievances . . . and raises a mighty dust where there was none before.2

Teaching is a blessedly complex activity which requires complex and continual attunement and in which the upside down of topsy-turvy life in the classroom is one of the great joys and privileges of spending a life with children.

NOTES

1. William Blake, *The Illustrated Poets: William Blake* (New York: Oxford University Press, 1986), p. 86.
2. Jonathan Swift, *A Modest Proposal and Other Works* (New York: Dover, 1996), p. 24.